NATIONAL STUDIES ON INTERNATIONAL ORGANIZATION

MEXICO

AND THE

UNITED NATIONS

by

JORGE CASTANEDA

Prepared for

El COLEGIO de MEXICO

and the

CARNEGIE ENDOWMENT FOR INTERNATIONAL PEACE

Manhattan Publishing Company

New York

1958

VOLUMES PREVIOUSLY PUBLISHED IN THIS SERIES

PRINTED BY BRÜDER ROSENBAUM, VIENNA (AUSTRIA)

Preface

This volume forms part of a series of studies on international organization initiated by the Carnegie Endowment for International Peace and carried out by private institutions and individuals in more than twenty countries around the world. This particular study has been written by Jorge Castañeda, Legal Counsellor of the Mexican Foreign Service, in his personal capacity, with the assistance of a study group brought together by El Colegio de Mexico.

The decision, taken in 1952, to initiate this program reflected both the Endowment's long-standing conviction that international organizations, such as the United Nations, are central to the quest for peace and the assumption that their significance and functioning depend first and foremost upon the attitudes and policies of nations. The fact that the question of Charter review would be on the agenda of the General Assembly in 1955 seemed to afford a unique opportunity for assessing the strengths and weaknesses of the United Nations in terms of national expectations and their fulfilment during the brief but rich testing period of the first ten years. In sponsoring this series of studies the Endowment has sought to encourage an exchange of unofficial national views, with the object of stimulating a closer examination of the past record and future potentialities of the United Nations and of increasing understanding of differences and similarities in national attitudes toward the Organization.

In the pursuit of these objectives, the participants in each country were asked to appraise their national experience in international organizations, especially the United Nations. In doing so they have considered such questions as: What impact has the United Nations had on both the content and the conduct of national policy?

To what extent have the purposes and principles set out in the Charter served as adequate guides to the organs of the United Nations in their operations? Have developments in the practices and the procedures of the United Nations made the organization more or less effective as an agency to achieve the purposes for which it was established? What is, and should be, the relationship of the United Nations to other forms of international organization, including regional systems? Does experience suggest the need for formal revision of the Charter?

These studies have been undertaken on the initiative of the Carnegie Endowment for International Peace. However, they have been carried out independently of that organization and the responsibility for the contents of the individual volumes, therefore, lies with the authors.

In exercising its responsibility for the decision to publish the volumes in this series, the Endowment has been assisted by an advisory review committee, comprising Dr. Alberto Lleras Camargo, former President of Colombia and former Secretary General of the Organization of American States; Sir Ramaswami Mudaliar, Vice-Chancellor of Travancore University, India; and Dr. Bernard H. M. Vlekke, Secretary-General of the Netherlands Institute of International Affairs. Their faithful and wise counsel is most gratefully acknowledged.

The conclusions of the individual studies will be summarized and their significance analyzed in two final volumes prepared independently by Robert MacIver, Lieber Professor Emeritus of Political Philosophy and Sociology at Columbia University; and Maurice Bourquin, Professor of International Public Law at the University of Geneva.

No prefatory note which did not exceed its proper dimensions could possibly acknowledge all the debts which the Endowment owes to scholars and officials in many parts of the world for the help which they have graciously given. To Dr. Alfonso Reyes, President of El Colegio de Mexico, to Señor Daniel Cosío Villegas,

Director of Studies of El Colegio de Mexico, to the members of the study group, and to Señor Castañeda, particular thanks are due for their co-operation in making the present volume possible. The Endowment wishes to record its deep appreciation not only for the scholarship and thought which are reflected in the following pages but also for the patience and unfailing courtesy they have shown in this venture in co-operation over several years.

The Endowment wishes to express its gratitude to the Ford Foundation for providing a grant which, by supplementing funds supplied by the Endowment and the co-operating institutions themselves, made it possible to carry out the project on a broad and comprehensive basis.

February 1958   JOSEPH E. JOHNSON
                                                    President
                        Carnegie Endowment for International Peace

Foreword

The Carnegie Endowment for International Peace and El Colegio de Mexico agreed on a project of study which would reflect the opinion and experience of Mexico with respect to international organization, particularly the United Nations—a project all the more useful because it was intended that its termination would coincide with the tenth anniversary of the United Nations and with the possibility of revision of its Charter.

The study project in Mexico has had to depart somewhat from the standards originally outlined by the Endowment for comparable studies in other countries. The first step was to choose a person who would be entrusted with the principal task of writing the study; an assistant was also designated who was charged with the particular function of studying the reactions of Mexican public opinion and its manifestations in the principal periodicals of the country and in documents which might reflect the attitudes of important segments of the national life, such as large workers' associations, intellectual societies, etc.

As the reader will see, this study deals almost solely with political questions. For various reasons, it was not possible to include separate chapters on social and economic questions, though this had been the desire of El Colegio de Mexico.

When Señor Jorge Castañeda, who had been selected for the main task of research, had progressed far enough in his work, a study group was named whose chief task was to examine his draft, discuss it and propose modifications. This study group comprised:

Dr. Pedro de Alba	Former Mexican representative to the International Labour Organisation and presently Senator of the Republic
Dr. Manuel Sandoval Vallarta	Member of El Colegio Nacional and Under Secretary of Public Education
Dr. Alfonso Noriega, Jr.	Professor in the Faculty of Law of the Mexican National University
Lic. Isidro Fabela	Former Judge of the International Court of Justice and former Acting Minister of Foreign Relations
Dr. Manuel Martínez Báez	Former representative of Mexico to UNESCO and member of El Colegio Nacional
Señor Carlos Péon del Valle	Former Director of International Organizations in the Ministry of Foreign Relations
Señor Eduardo Espinosa Prieto	Deputy Director of Political Affairs in the Ministry of Foreign Relations
Dr. Antonio Martínez Báez	Professor in the Faculty of Law of the Mexican National University and former Minister of Economy

The debates were led by Dr. Alfonso Reyes, President of El Colegio de Mexico, and Señor Daniel Cosío Villegas, Director of Studies.

These individuals were invited, not as representatives of any public or private organization, but in their capacity as private citizens. The study group also adopted the rule that the writer of the study should be solely responsible for it and should, accordingly, remain free to incorporate in his study the observations and suggestions made by the study group.

In a series of meetings, each chapter of Señor Castañeda's study was discussed freely and fully, and the author revised the original text to give it its present form. The manuscript was written in Spanish and later translated into English by Mrs. Marjorie de Urquidi. It was completed in the fall of 1955 and does not cover subsequent events.

December 1957   DANIEL COSIO VILLEGAS
                                          Director of the Project

Contents

chapter one

Introduction

The purpose of this report is to describe and evaluate Mexico's attitude and policy regarding the problem of international organization, with special emphasis on such questions as are raised by the existence and activities of the United Nations. The descriptive part will cover the official point of view of the Mexican government as well as the reaction of public opinion, to the extent that it can be inferred from organs of expression and other means. Mexico's past position on the principal problems of international organization will be examined in the critical and evaluating part of this report, and suggestions and proposals will be made both on the Mexican attitude and on the constitutional or legal changes which may seem desirable in the structure and functioning of the United Nations.

The very statement of the problem raises several questions. In the first place, a point must be chosen from which to focus the survey. The international attitude and policy of a country may be presented in different ways. For some countries this study would fundamentally aim at determining the extent to which the existence and the activities of the United Nations have contributed to the realization of certain specific international goals of the country in question. But it may be asked if in the case of Mexico this would be the most appropriate way to look at the problem. In other words, it is necessary to decide beforehand, in the case of Mexico, whether to study fundamentally Mexican problems of an international character and the possible influence which the activities of the international organizations may have had on them, or, on the contrary, whether to examine *general* problems of international organization, even though these may be approached from a national point of view.

Secondly, the relative extension and importance of the two leading aspects of the report must be determined. The means for expressing public opinion could be especially studied, and the evaluation and conclusions could be related closely to those topics and solutions which seem to prevail in national concerns and views. On the other hand, it would also be possible to develop the evaluation more freely, as a reflection of the personal opinion of those who took part in the present survey, and to present separately, as an appendix, the reaction of public opinion to certain problems.

As is natural, the answer to these questions necessarily has a bearing not only on the nature, scope, general outlines, and conclusions of the study, but even on its external contours.

MEXICO'S FOREIGN POLICY OBJECTIVES

It was felt that no answer could be given to these questions without first forming a judgment, even though tentative, on those objectives of Mexican foreign policy which are in some way related to the existence of international organizations. The following considerations might summarize the conclusion which was reached merely as a working hypothesis, in order to undertake this survey.

Mexico, unlike the great powers, has no major specific interests of a political, territorial, or strategic nature, nor substantial investments, beyond its borders. It does not exert hegemony over other regions nor does it have to protect its own direct interests in those areas which are at present centers of international tension. Moreover, Mexico is one of the few member states which has not been on the "agenda" of the United Nations. Until now, it has not been a party, either active or passive, to any dispute brought before the Organization nor does it have a direct and immediate interest in any situation which might endanger peace. Finally, the birth and the existence of the Mexican state have no relation to United Nations action, as in the case of other small or medium-sized countries like Israel or Indonesia. It can thus be said that Mexico today has fundamentally no *specific* international objectives of a political nature, the fulfillment of which would be dependent on the action of the international organization.

Consequently, unlike what might be a suitable vantage point for a study of a great power and for certain small states, it seems that for Mexico it would be of little value to build a framework around the role played by the international organization in the attainment of certain peculiarly national aspirations. Mexico's interest in the United Nations is of a more general character and the benefits which it expects from the Organization are not particular but are common to a number of countries: the fulfillment of the political, economic, and social aims of the Charter. Its contribution to the work of the United Nations is not directed toward the defense of direct national interests, but toward strengthening the Organization's ability to achieve its general purposes.

As is to be expected, these considerations cannot but influence the nature of the Mexican study. Necessarily, this survey will have a more general and more institutional character than that of other countries. Basically, the contents of the study correspond to the main topics of the United Nations in the order in which they appear in the Charter: purposes, principles, membership, and above all, the different means by which the Organization can achieve its ends.

Of course, the necessity of focussing on general problems from a national viewpoint has not been forgotten. The entire survey pursues precisely that objective. As each of the main topics of international organization is discussed, an attempt will be made to point out what Mexico's position has been and to observe where its permanent interest lies. But, in the early stages of work on the various topics, it was realized that even though frequent differences are found between Mexico's attitude toward certain problems and that of other medium-sized and small countries, their interests, aspirations, and means of action coincide fundamentally. In fact, it would be difficult to find cases in which Mexico has pursued a particular objective in international organizations. Even in dealing with such questions as the raising of living standards, which takes on special characteristics in each country, Mexico's attitude is not found to be essentially different from that of a large number of countries. This purpose of the Organization certainly has more meaning and force in underdeveloped countries than in industrial countries; but, although certain differences exist between Mexico's economic structure and that of other underdeveloped countries which are reflected in the various *domestic* means applied to raise living standards, their viewpoints have basically coincided in the recommendation of certain *international* means of action to attain this common purpose.

Politically, the identity of situations is also evident. The international political problems of Mexico are not at present, by their nature, different from those of many small countries; at least, not those that could be solved through the action of international agencies. On the other hand, with regard to Mexico's ability to contribute to the solution of world political conflicts, the means of action available to Mexico are essentially the same as those available to other countries in a like situation.

All these considerations were borne in mind in order to locate an observation point. Thus, above all an attempt will be made to present the aims, the interests, the means of action, and the achievements of Mexico to the extent that Mexico is representative of a large number of similar states. Moreover, whenever possible, we shall try further to individualize the Mexican viewpoint; as each one of the general problems is examined, the difference, if applicable, between Mexico's position and that of other small and medium-sized countries, especially Latin American countries, will be pointed out.

PUBLIC OPINION

The international situation of Mexico could not fail also to condition the reaction of its public opinion to international problems.

As the evaluating and critical part of this report was begun, an examination of the media of information was initiated in order to present the viewpoints of national opinion concerning some activities and problems of the United Nations. The study yielded such poor results that it was finally decided not to include it as a separate part of the report. In general terms, it might be said that there is practically no opinion in Mexico, at least as evidenced in the normal channels of expression, about any of the structural problems of the United Nations: scope of activities, membership, functions, organs, and so forth. As an example of the lack of public interest in these questions, the "Uniting for Peace" resolution, which implies a new and important concept of collective security as a whole and which might have repercussions in Mexico not altogether different from those which could be derived from a military defense treaty with the United States, is practically unknown outside the Ministry of Foreign Affairs. Since it was adopted, not one monograph or study has been published in Mexico on this serious subject. Even when the United Nations Charter was approved in the Mexican Senate there was no lengthy debate on its importance or implications, nor even a detailed analysis of its provisions. Since then, that is, since

1945, the United Nations Organization has seldom been referred to in the Mexican Senate.

The slight concern of Mexican public opinion for the problems that pertain to the United Nations, and the general ignorance of its structure and functions, cannot fail also to influence this study. As stated above, the reaction of public opinion makes no substantial contribution in Mexico to inspire new or better solutions to the problems of international organization.

Nonetheless, it is felt that although this report could hardly reflect public opinion, it would surely be of some use if it served, on the other hand, to stimulate certain sectors of Mexican opinion and to interest them further in the questions raised by the existence and activities of the United Nations. In other words, this report must be regarded not as the final result of a survey, but rather as a first step toward fostering recognition of the importance which international questions must gradually assume in the national conscience, and toward a better understanding in Mexico of such questions. This partially explains why considerable importance is given to the general statement of the problems and to the description of institutions, which would certainly not be the case if this report were exclusively designed for a foreign professional sector interested only in knowing the particular aspects of a country's position. The need for keeping this circumstance in mind will occasionally require, with respect to certain topics, that greater space be devoted to the general aspect of the report than to the study of the specific position of Mexico.

The reasons for the general lack of interest in international questions might be summed up in a sentence: Mexico is living an epoch of intense nationalism. Since the Mexican Revolution which began in 1910—and which has contributed as have few other factors to the formation of a national conscience—a kind of introspection has been carried on in all aspects of the country's life. Lately, the process of industrialization—as in all countries going through a similar phase of development—has been the cause and effect of a strong economic nationalism. This is in turn reflected, concomitantly, in the appearance of vigorous nationalist signs in all other spheres of national life.

This is not the place to describe and pass judgment on this phenomenon, which is certainly more or less common to all peoples in certain phases of their evolution. The important fact to consider is that nationalism in Mexico and elsewhere has resulted in less concern and even in a relative disregard on the part of public opinion, as well as in governmental spheres, for those international questions which have a more general character and which can be postponed without creating an immediate domestic problem.

Generally speaking, there is still not enough appreciation in Mexico of the possible influence which the promotion of the political, economic, and social objectives of the international organizations may have within the country. Mexico is barely overcoming the purely bilateral concept of international relations. Mexico's foreign policy has been traditionally conceived of as a barrier, as a defense for the protection of domestic development against certain outside influences. The guiding principle of its international relations has been non-intervention, a negative principle.

This circumstance is explained by specific historical causes, but it is no less certain that in our time Mexican foreign policy could also perform a positive function. Increasingly active participation in international organizations would surely be desirable, not only for purposes of protection but in order to procure new resources and instruments, political as well as economic, which could contribute positively to the country's development. Unfortunately, in Mexico and other countries at a like stage of development, this general and long-term aspect of international relations is barely beginning to be properly regarded. As this report will try to show, the broad outlines of Mexico's foreign policy concerning certain general important questions have not always been systematically formulated; among such questions are the new aspects of collective security, colonialism (in spite of the fact that colonial production of similar raw materials under competitive conditions unfavorable to Latin America has caused some concern), the international protection of human rights, domestic jurisdiction of states vis-à-vis international organizations, the relationship between the world organization and the Organization of American States, and above all, the best way to correlate Mexico's position in the two organizations. Even though the absence of systematic formulation has rarely led to serious inconsistencies, it would be desirable if Mexico's reaction to problems of this kind should cease to be empirical and circumstantial.

The reasons mentioned have also influenced the relative consideration and importance granted to international relations within the framework of public administration. Matters concerning international organizations are still considered the exclusive concern of a specific administrative department, so that officials not professionally devoted to international activities apparently are not clearly aware that numerous events which take place in international organizations have serious domestic implications. The share of Mexico's national budget allocated to international activities (approximately one and a half per cent) is one of the lowest even among small countries. Finally, due to the pressure of urgent domestic tasks, few of the country's best men have professionally concerned themselves with international questions.

COMMON GOALS OF THE SMALL POWERS

It was previously stated that it only seemed possible to resolve some of the prior questions raised by this report in terms of a tentative judgment on the international objectives which interest Mexico and on the possibility of attaining them through the action of international organizations. It was also stated that, basically, the international aims of Mexico are not peculiar but are common to a good many of the members of interstate society which are designated as small and medium-sized powers. It is of interest to recall briefly the basic and permanent aspirations of the states belonging to this category, and to point out the ones which, in the author's view, are likely to be fulfilled through the action of international organizations, as well as the specific means of action available to the latter for accomplishing them. The constant consideration of these goals and means of action will serve, in the development of this survey, to fix the position of the small and medium-sized countries on the problems taken up.

The first aim of the small powers is the maintenance of universal peace. This goal is not peculiar to certain countries, but, for the first time in history, small and great powers are equally concerned with its attainment. Countries no longer exist which are geographically or politically distant from conflicts. In any future war, due to its almost unavoidable universalization and its total character, small countries, in spite of their reduced war capacity, will be no less exposed than large ones to all its consequences. On the other hand, while the small powers cannot avail themselves of a specific means of action in international organizations for maintaining peace, certain methods do exist that are specially suitable to their situation. In certain phases of the evolution of a conflict a balance of force is often established between the great powers—this situation occurred more than once in the Korean war—which offers the small powers a favorable opportunity to act decisively to maintain or restore peace. The chapter on collective security will highlight the fact that within a bipolar international society, or at least one characterized by the heavy concentration of political forces, the use of enforcement measures cannot easily operate on a universal basis and is therefore ineffective; that, consequently, the universal and pacifist vocation of the United Nations should preferably be put to work in the strengthening of procedures for the pacific settlement of disputes and conflicts. This is an especially appropriate field for the action of small countries. Due to the large number of votes at their disposal, they could systematically exercise a moderating influence which would be frequently effective and which on occasion could result in a nearly irresistible moral and political pressure in favor of pacific and constructive solutions. The inflexible positions often adopted by the great powers certainly do not facilitate the solution of problems, but at the same time this can represent an opportunity and a stimulus for mediation by small countries.

The second essential goal of the small countries is the preservation of their independence in the face of the external influences which prevent self-determination. The progress of their people depends above all on their own efforts, but the prerequisite of their progress is the absence of external factors which interfere with or delay their development. These factors may vary from foreign aggression or the exaggerated political and economic influence of a great power to the imposition of international standards of economic and social conduct on its domestic order. These standards may have been worked out with the best intentions by the international agencies, but, as happens sometimes, they may be appropriate to more developed communities and thus hinder the development of politically unstable or socially unintegrated countries. Except for this last possibility—which actually has not arisen since the United Nations was created—the international organizations can be an effective tool for preserving and reinforcing the independence of small countries. To that end, small powers can utilize certain principles and means of action appropriate to their situation. A fitting means of strengthening a small country's independence may be the consistent invocation, respect for, and application of the non-intervention principle with regard to other states in the international organizations, in all cases and leaving aside circumstantial political considerations. Likewise, the related principle of safeguarding the domestic jurisdiction of the state against international organizations, in essentially domestic matters (Article 2, paragraph 7 of the Charter), constitutes a defense which contributes to the preservation of the autonomy of small countries.

Finally, the emphasis on the function of law, as a criterion for the solution, as far as possible, of all international questions, also represents an attitude appropriate to small countries. There are many situations in the theory and practice of international organization which allow either a political or a juridical treatment. The differentiation between matters under domestic and those under international jurisdiction, the standard to be followed for the adoption of collective measures (Article 1, paragraph 1 of the Charter), and the determination of what is to be considered aggression, are examples of decisions that can either be made juridically or can be a political function of the United Nations organs. Small countries have an interest in broadening the scope of law in international organizations. "Equal sovereignty" of states means above all the existence of a universal normative order to be objectively and equally applied to large and small states. The political solution, on the other hand, permits, to a greater degree, the play of factors which reflect the inequality existing between states.

The third essential goal of the small powers is to speed up the rate of their economic and social development. The international organizations not only contribute to this by removing the external factors which could delay their natural growth, but also through positive international action which complements their own efforts. The particular means of action of underdeveloped countries in international organizations lies in the creation of international agencies for economic and social development. International financing through existing or future agencies, technical assistance, and the useful activities carried on by specialized agencies and regional economic bodies are examples of the ways in which international organization can contribute widely to the fulfillment of this important goal which is especially characteristic of underdeveloped countries.

chapter two

Nature, Purposes, and Principles of the United Nations

The United Nations is an association of sovereign states bound together by certain common aims. The present world organization is not based on a federal concept, but at most resembles a confederation of states. Its members essentially reserve to themselves that sum of powers traditionally identified with the idea of sovereignty, limiting by multilateral treaty only some aspects of the exercise of those powers. The states retain direct authority over their individual citizens, just as they keep complete control over their finances and armed forces. Correlatively, the international organization lacks resources of its own for achieving its ends. It has no armed forces of its own to enforce its decisions nor can it dispose of the financial resources of its members, nor, finally, can it contact directly or ask obedience of the citizens of its member states, bypassing their respective governments. The accomplishment of the purposes of the Organization, in the same way as with its predecessor the League of Nations, depends basically on voluntary co-operation among the states. In brief, the United Nations is not a superstate authority, but an interstate organization. The Charter of the United Nations sums up the nature and character of the Organization when it states that it "is based on the principle of the sovereign equality of all its Members" (Article 2, paragraph 1).[1]

Many writers on international law as well as a considerable sector of world public opinion are wont to attribute the failure of the League of Nations and the weakness and ineffectiveness of the United Nations to state sovereignty or, to express it better, to the refusal of many states to give up their sovereignty in the degree necessary to endow the international organization with sufficient powers of its own for maintaining universal order. Those who advocate organizing international society along a federal pattern would like the world organization to have real authority in all questions that are international or that have important international implications, not only in respect to an unrestricted power of decision, but also as regards the resources and elements necessary to enforce its decisions. According to this conception, states would not be free to withdraw voluntarily from the Organization; there would be a political-juridical link between the citizens of the various countries and the international organization so that the latter, in those matters broadly falling within its jurisdiction, would exercise direct control and authority over the individual citizens within the federation; its organs would be composed of representatives elected directly by the associated peoples of the federation; many of the functions which at present correspond to those of the state, such as foreign affairs in general, armament, the salient aspects of finance, nationality, migration, etc., would be removed from the national political entities and placed within the scope of the world organization; and finally, the decisions of the latter would be binding and would be

---

[1] By this somewhat unfortunate formula, an attempt was made to express simultaneously the concepts of equality and sovereignty. Actually, states are sovereign and, by that token, equal before international law. *Par in parem non habet imperium.*

adopted by the majority of the representatives. Naturally, between a purely federal conception—a conception really equivalent to world government—and an organization based on the recognition of state sovereignty of its members, there exists a wide range of intermediate possibilities. But all of them generally propose the ideal of reducing the scope of action of the national political entities and the weight of their decision-making power, correspondingly strengthening the international organization.

SOVEREIGNTY AND WORLD GOVERNMENT

Who could doubt the perfection of this ideal? History shows that when social units are broadened in order to include formerly uncontrolled and autonomous powers, and authority is centralized—as happened when the modern national state took shape, breaking with the feudal pattern—social relations are stabilized and finally order and domestic peace are achieved within the new social unit. The frequent and serious international conflicts of recent times—which have paradoxically coincided with a growing feeling of interdependence among peoples—have projected this ideal with new strength on an international scale. On more than one occasion it has been apparent in our times that the unrestricted power of the state, pursuing ends that are incompatible with the welfare of all international society, has been the cause of wars and numerous evils for humanity. International society's lack of effective means to control the arbitrary action of states—a lack which is only the reverse of state sovereignty—represents the greatest weakness of contemporary international order.

But the weakness of a system does not vanish by simply declaring it abolished. Frequently it is suggested that the evils of our times can be remedied by eliminating the idea of sovereignty, as if this were a switch that could be turned on and off at will, forgetting that state sovereignty does not exist *in vacuo* and that the presence of such a notion is an effect and not a cause of the pattern of international relations in this epoch; or, better still, it is a means of preserving the vested interests, material and ideological, domestic and international, of the contemporary state. The interests protected by the state through the affirmation of its sovereignty must be sought in the whole complex of social relations found within the contemporary state, among which, outstanding because of their importance, are relations of production. Since the idea of sovereignty is nothing but the international projection of this picture of social relations, the solution cannot lie in abolishing it, but in creating the necessary conditions, basically internal, so that it can disappear.

What probabilities exist that the immediate future will present conditions permitting the disappearance of the idea of sovereignty?

If there were moments during the last world conflict when it seemed possible that the sacrifice would not be entirely in vain, that self-determination and disarmament would become realities, that the economic and social structure of many countries would be peaceably changed after the war, thereby creating a new order which would preserve the ethical-political content of the liberal and individualistic state but at the same time would establish social justice and economic security, the experience of these last ten years could well force the conclusion that the last war has been the most useless of all. Even in 1945, when the memory of the origins of the last war was still undimmed, the constitutional Charter of the new Organization incorporated practices which represented a clear regression from the League of Nations with regard to the surrender of sovereignty (for example, in the formulation of the principle of domestic jurisdiction of states). Today, in circumstances still more unfavorable than ten years ago, it would be difficult to think of states, especially the great powers, accepting a limitation on their discretion to use their power as they please. Such authors as Bertrand Russell[2] and René de Lacharrière,[3] who have recently written on

---

[2] Bertrand Russell, *New Hopes for a Changing World* (New York: Simon & Schuster, 1951), pp. 72-73.

[3] René de Lacharrière, "L'action des Nations Unies pour la sécurité et pour la paix," *Politique Etrangère*, Vol. XVIII, No. 4 (Sept.-Oct. 1953), p. 308.

this subject, conclude that perhaps only through force, that is, through a new war, or at least through the military supremacy of some nation or group of nations, will suitable conditions be created for bringing humanity closer to world government.

In any case, it would be impractical and fruitless to examine abstractly the problem of what conditions should be present for transcending the stage of international organizations based on the recognition of state sovereignty. The real possibilities of going beyond this phase can only be perceived by specifically examining the crucial problem of international organization, that is, the maintenance of international peace by means of a universal system of collective security. In the relevant chapter, it will be emphasized that collective security can only operate in a universal manner, and thereby be effective, when two requirements or conditions are fulfilled: (1) a relative homogeneity of international society and (2) a sufficient fragmentation of the real factors of power within the society itself. Since our epoch does not present either of these two conditions, the San Francisco Charter could not have organized collective security so that it would operate universally and automatically, without requiring the consent, in each case, and even the voluntary and positive collaboration, of those great powers that have at their disposal the political and military resources for maintaining or restoring peace. That is, precisely in that supreme test of authority, in the use of force to maintain order, the international organization had to resign itself, because of the absence of the two conditions mentioned, to adopting a primitive and undeveloped system, entrusting that maintenance to the members of society themselves. In our time the lack of cohesion and of integration of international society prevents a greater centralization of authority.

THE ORGANIZATION AS AN INSTRUMENT FOR COEXISTENCE IN AN EPOCH OF TRANSITION

The present problem is thus not one of organizing international society according to an ideal pattern which would turn out to be quite impractical, but to reinforce its effectiveness within an inter-state concept, or, as the terms of the Charter state, within the frame-work of the equal sovereignty of its members. If the constitutional charter of a society is to perform its mission adequately, it should recognize and base itself on the reality and present possibilities of that society, setting for itself limited and temporary goals, but at the same time tending to prepare the way for conditions leading that society toward better forms of coexistence. Postwar reality consists in the division of the world, on the one hand, between capitalist and socialist countries and, on the other hand, between a few countries with a high standard of living which are industrialized and have an abundance of technical resources, and a majority of underdeveloped countries, many of which have not even reached political independence. A charter for the postwar international organ-ization had to recognize the heterogeneity of the present international society and to take into account, in the first place, that such a situation endangers peace. The *immediate* goal of the organization could only be that of avoiding an armed conflict among the great hostile coalitions, that is, a Third World War. In other words, its immediate political purpose was to facilitate for the time being pacific coexistence between the capitalist world and the communist world, between the dependent peoples and the colonial powers, between the rich countries and the poor countries. In an inter-national society as heterogeneous as ours, the essential objective of the organization can only be temporary and limited; to serve as an instrument of coexistence in a time of transition.

It is difficult to predict what will be the ultimate result of the ideological and political conflicts that characterize the present world, but it might be said that we live in a transitional period that probably separates two great historical epochs and that will end by dissolving the deep antinomies that divide contemporary states. It is possible that the unity of the world may only be realized through the rule of one great power over the rest and the United Nations does not even represent the embryo of a future world government. But, on the other hand, it is not impossible that a relatively long period free from armed conflicts—to which the existence of the United Nations can contribute—might in itself produce conditions ultimately facilitating a superior synthesis of the various systems and ideologies and prepare humanity for higher forms of coexistence. If we had a broader historical perspective, perhaps the ideological antagonisms which today divide the world would not seem irreconcilable nor their collision inevitable. We live at the dawn of a technical revolution of unprecedented magnitude. The practically unlimited possibilities offered by the pacific utilization of atomic energy may perhaps contribute to a mighty acceleration of the rate of development of poor countries and reduce the gap which separates them from the wealthy. Who can predict the influence which such a phenomenon would have on our ideas on the best way to organize society and on international relations? Perhaps in an economy of abundance produced by a new industrial revolution that includes all countries, the opposition between the great ideological and political systems which today contest world domination would lose significance and importance. Perhaps at that time, when members of international society would be more congenial, states would be inclined to renounce voluntarily a good part of their sovereignty in order to submit to an authentic international authority.

In short, the limitations of the United Nations spring from the society which gave it its origin. Its essential goal is limited and temporary. The Organization does not represent the beginning of a federation of states, but its existence can make an important contribution to the institution of conditions indispensable to its future creation, not only in a negative way, by facilitating at present pacific coexistence among groups of states that pursue different ends, but also by serving as a center for the knowledge, exchange, and eventual synthesis of concepts and programs of social organization; by facilitating a pacific transition from colonialism to independence; by laying the foundation for a future international administration of public services on a superstate basis, through the present and important international functional co-operation which is carried on within the specialized agencies, and above all—perhaps this would be the outstanding objective of the United Nations for backward countries—by serving as a vehicle for transmitting techniques and all kinds of resources to the countries which lack them, thereby speeding up their development.

PURPOSES AND PRINCIPLES OF THE ORGANIZATION

The Principle of the Hierarchy of Aims: The above considerations may act as a guide for approaching the problem of the purposes and principles of the United Nations, as they are stated in the Charter of the United Nations.

Within the Charter's structure there is a natural hierarchy of the different aims of the United Nations. According to Article 1, the United Nations has the following essential purposes which are presented in this order of logical priority: (1) the first aim is to a certain extent negative—it is to prevent the outbreak of war, to preserve peace; (2) if measures for preserving peace fail, and aggression occurs, the second aim is to resist it and to restore peace; (3) the United Nations, through constant economic and social action on a long-term scale and throughout the world, intends to do away with the causes of war and to better mankind's lot; (4) the Organization seeks to encourage friendly relations among nations and to serve as a center for harmonizing their efforts to attain the preceding ends.

When the problem is viewed from a broad historical perspective, perhaps the third of the aims noted, that is, the battle against poverty and ignorance, which are the essential causes of war, appears as predominant. It is possible that the Economic and Social Council may with time become the most important organ of the United Nations because it is the one which tends to attack the causes of war at their root. In some ways, this objective is also a means for achieving the aim of preserving peace, even though raising the standard of living is an end *per se* independently of its con-

tribution to the preservation of peace. But from a practical point
of view, it is evident that maintaining peace is a primary end and
antecedent to the latter, since the prerequisite for raising the standard
of living is to live in an epoch of peace.

Ordinarily, the first two aims enumerated (preservation of peace
and, in turn, restoration of broken peace) are presented as only
one aim: in the terms of Article 1, paragraph 1 of the Charter, the
first purpose of the Organization is "to maintain international peace
and security." As in the League of Nations—although the Covenant
did not so clearly express the hierarchy of aims—the other purposes
of the Organization are considered as ancillary to the first. But as
has already been indicated (and an attempt will be made to illustrate
this in the chapter on collective security) the Organization has little
possibility of directly intervening in the prevention and removal of
threats and breaches of the peace or acts of aggression through the
universal use of a system of collective measures, since this depends
to a very great extent on the voluntary co-operation of the great
powers, a co-operation which must not only be prior and general
but must also exist in each specific case. For that reason, the subsidiary aims of the United Nations, which indirectly contribute to
the achievement of the essential aim, have great importance. In
particular, the Organization's purpose of serving as a center for
harmonizing the actions of nations can be considered, practically
speaking, as the most immediately effective. In a society characterized
by the frequent and basic opposition of its members, it is perhaps
more necessary than in societies of homogeneous membership to
have the structure and functioning of its social organs favor, if not
the harmony, at least the constant contact and exchange of opposing
interests and viewpoints. In the tenseness of the postwar international situation, the Organization's usefulness as a negotiation
center for East and West has not been without merit.

Nonetheless, a great deal remains to be done in this field. Few
efforts would be so worthwhile as those directed toward perfecting
the technique of negotiation and improving the procedures of the

United Nations organs so that their discussions would tend to reconcile positions and not to make them still more extreme and rigid. Small and medium-sized countries could and should collaborate in every way to accomplish this important task.

The Adoption of Collective Measures and the Principles of Justice and International Law: In the San Francisco Conference there was extensive discussion of whether the maintenance of peace and the adoption of effective collective measures should be carried out "in conformity with the principles of justice and international law." The object of a proposal to this effect (presented by Egypt) was to prevent the possibility of "appeasement"—of "another Munich." The great powers which opposed the proposal felt that the functions of the Security Council should resemble those of a police force, which keeps order but does not pass sentence, that is, the Council should initially prevent the use of armed force without investigating which of the parties was morally or legally justified; after carrying out this task, the Council could subsequently promote the pacific settlement of the dispute "in conformity with the principles of justice and international law." Egypt's proposal was rejected in Commission I by 21 votes to 21,[4] and the phrase, as it finally appeared in the Charter, was made applicable only to peaceful settlement. Generally speaking, it might be said that international law and, specifically, the fulfillment of treaty obligations were given a broader and more important function in the League of Nations Covenant than in the United Nations Charter.[5]

It is not possible to say that the omission of the above phrase in reference to the taking of collective measures has had or in practice will have great importance in the work of the United

---

[4] See *Documents of the United Nations Conference on International Organization, San Francisco, 1945* (New York: United Nations Information Organization, 1945), Vol. VI, pp. 229-30 and 453. Hereinafter referred to as *UNCIO Documents.*

[5] The emphasis of the League of Nations Covenant on the fulfillment of treaties was, to a great extent, due to France's insistence. This country attributed great importance to the preservation of the status quo established by the treaties which ended the First World War.

c

Nations, above all if it is considered that the principles of "justice" mentioned in the rejected proposal were kept distinct from the principles of international law; in other words, collective measures might be resorted to either in accordance with justice—an exceptionally vague concept which lends itself to many varied interpretations—or in accordance with international law. Nevertheless, the small powers should insist, as a question of principle, that all the Organization's functions for the maintenance of peace be carried out with due respect for the precepts of international law.

Certainly, situations that have their origin in formally valid international treaties are sometimes unjust in themselves or become inequitable after a period of time. When people suffering such a situation have their legitimate aspirations repressed for long, violence may easily break out; then it is possible that requiring enforcement measures for restoring peace or even measures for a peaceful solution to conform to international law may be an obstacle to a *just*, although perhaps anti-juridical, solution of the situation. For that reason, small powers should see to it that their proposals regarding the necessity for conforming to international law are complemented by a clear and categorical statement in the Charter about the principle of peaceful revision of international treaties.[6]

---

[6] Ordinarily, it is considered that Article 14 of the Charter implicitly authorizes the Assembly to recommend the revision of a treaty, by allowing it to "recommend measures for the peaceful adjustment of any situation, *regardless of origin . . .*" [author's italics], although the San Francisco Conference rejected various proposals to assign it that power expressly. (U.S. Dept. of State, *Report to the President on the Results of the San Francisco Conference by the Chairman of the United States Delegation, the Secretary of State*, Publication 2349, Conference Series 11 [Washington: U.S. Govt. Printing Office, 1945], pp. 58-59.) Article 19 of the League of Nations Covenant stated, on the other hand, that "the Assembly may from time to time advise the reconsideration by Members of the League of treaties which have become inapplicable . . ." In its "Opinion" concerning the Dumbarton Oaks Proposals, the Mexican government proposed an even more categorical formula: "The Assembly shall recommend to the members the revision of those international treaties or agreements which it may not be possible to fulfil, or which may endanger international order or peace among nations. In the case that interested Members, or any one Member, shall not fulfil the recommendations of the Assembly, the latter shall decide upon measures which are to be adopted." (*UNCIO Documents*, Vol. III, pp. 171-72.)

Otherwise, the situation would become intolerable for countries in such situations. If legal channels are blocked, the only door left open is that of violence. As Sir Arnold McNair so well put it, "a system which collectivises the use of force and provides no machinery for the collective revision of the status quo is certain to fail."[7]

As the Rapporteur of Committee I/1 of the San Francisco Conference said, it is difficult to establish a clear difference between matters which should by their nature be part of the Preamble to the Charter, the article on purposes, or the article on principles. In any case, it is of little practical importance whether a certain principle should figure as a purpose or vice versa, although from a technical point of view, objections could be raised to the classification. Thus, for example, it is open to discussion whether the adoption of effective collective measures and the use of pacific means for the settlement of disputes are properly purposes (as stated in Article 1 of the Charter) or whether they are means or principles of action for maintaining international peace and security.

There are other instances in which the Charter is unclear about whether a principle is valid in itself or is merely a means to another end, and a categorical declaration or unconditional statement seems to be needed. For example, Article 1, paragraph 2, of the Charter indicates that a purpose of the Organization is "to develop friendly relations among nations based on respect for the principle of equal rights and self-determination of peoples . . ." The principle of self-determination of peoples should be expressed separately, as an autonomous principle, valid in itself and not merely as a basis for the development of friendly relations among nations. Some nations, particularly the colonial ones, would surely object to the unconditional statement of this principle. But no valid reason exists for not expressly confirming it and for not using it as a guide in all colonial matters; furthermore, the very scope of this precept would be

---

[7] Inaugural Lecture on *Collective Security* given in Cambridge, 1936. Quoted by Georg Schwarzenberger in *Power Politics* (New York: Frederick A. Praeger, 1951), p. 491.

limited by the concrete regulation, present or future, of such measures as the Charter provides for the fulfillment of this aspiration of the peoples (Chapters XI and XII of the Charter on non-self-governing territories and the trusteeship system).

Likewise, the principle of "equal rights" also contained in Article 1, paragraph 2, above cited, should be separately stated and not also related to the Organization's aim of developing friendly relations among nations. This principle is in fact enunciated in Article 2, paragraph 1 ("The Organization is based on the principle of the sovereign equality of all its Members"), but this precept should be expressed so that the concept of equality—which actually means equality under international law—appears as *it is in reality*, that is, as a consequence or derivative of the concept of state sovereignty.

PRINCIPLES OF THE ORGANIZATION
AND RIGHTS AND DUTIES OF STATES

A problem of great importance is that of a declaration of the rights and duties of states. The League of Nations Covenant contained principles addressed to its members as such and it did not actually establish in so many words, at least separately, the guiding principles of the Organization itself. The United Nations Charter, on the other hand, lists in Article 2 both principles for the Organization and for its members. The Charter can be objected to from a technical viewpoint because it indiscriminately sets down guiding principles of the Organization and duties of states in the same article. From another standpoint, the objection is much more serious: on the one hand, the list of duties of states is incomplete, and on the other hand, the Charter makes no reference to the rights of states.

Only three of the seven paragraphs of Article 2 express principles which truly apply to the Organization. They are the following: paragraph 1, the principle of the sovereign equality of all its members;

paragraph 6, the duty of the Organization to ensure that non-member states act in accordance with the principles of the Charter so far as may be necessary for the maintenance of international peace and security (even though the substance of this principle refers to the situation of states not actually members, it deals with a guiding principle of the Organization since the precept establishes the duty of the Organization to "ensure" that non-member states act in a certain way); paragraph 7, the prohibition of intervention by the Organization in the domestic affairs of states.

The other four principles of Article 2 are actually duties assigned to the member states. They are the following: paragraph 2, to fulfil in good faith the duties assumed by them in accordance with the Charter; paragraph 3, to settle their disputes by pacific means; paragraph 4, to refrain from the threat or the use of force; and paragraph 5, to give assistance to the Organization in any action it takes and to refrain from giving assistance to any state against which the Organization is taking preventive or enforcement action.

The first three paragraphs mentioned, which declare the principles of the Organization, should be in a separate article, together with the previously mentioned principle of self-determination of peoples. In turn, the four duties assigned to the member states by the Charter should be included in a separate chapter, dealing exclusively with the rights and duties of states, which should be placed in the Charter after the Chapter on Purposes and Principles. The absence of such a chapter—which, incidentally, is contained in the Charter of the Organization of American States—constitutes one of the greatest gaps in the United Nations Charter. It is difficult to imagine how an international society can be organized without a political decalogue which establishes and defines the relations between its members. The state's international conduct vis-à-vis other states is the fundamental field of action of the Organization. It is especially essential to the small powers that the obligations and, in particular, the prohibitions that are imposed on states be defined. Quite properly, the Mexican government suggested in its "Opinion" on the Dumbarton Oaks Proposals that there be an annex to the Charter called a "Declaration of the Rights and Duties of Nations."[8]

SUGGESTIONS FOR A CHAPTER OF THE CHARTER ON RIGHTS AND DUTIES OF STATES

In view of the importance to the small countries of a chapter in the Charter on the rights and duties of states, it seems desirable to deal fully with this subject and even to present some suggestions on the principles that should appear in such a chapter. The working document used was the Declaration on Rights and Duties of States as drafted by the International Law Commission in 1949 and discussed by the Assembly the same year.[9] This Declaration is a balanced and complete document which might eventually serve as a basis for a chapter of the Charter.[10]

[8] Article 1 of the Mexican proposals for the Charter of the Organization reads as follows: "International Law is recognized as the fundamental basis for the conduct of Governments. In order to determine the essential principles of International Law, the members of the community of nations engage themselves to observe the standards set forth in the "Declaration of Rights and Duties of Nations . . . which are appended to the present Pact . . ." (Mexico did not present a draft declaration, but suggested that one be drawn up by a committee of experts to meet before the Charter was signed.) See *UNCIO Documents*, Vol. VI, p. 60.

[9] For text, see Report of the International Law Commission, General Assembly, Official Records: 4th Sess., Supple. No. 10, pp. 8-9.

[10] In its Resolution 375(IV), 6 Dec. 1949, the Assembly deemed "the draft Declaration a notable and substantial contribution towards the progressive development of international law and its codification and as such commends it to the continuing attention of Member States and of jurists of all nations." The Assembly is waiting for still more comments and observations from the governments before deciding on the exact nature of the action to be taken (a compulsory agreement or merely a declaration). Apart from the advisability of having the declaration of the rights and duties of states appear either as an annex or chapter of the Charter—perhaps the latter would be the better solution at this time—or of having it incorporated in a separate multilateral agreement, it seems obvious that, in any case, it should become something more than just a non-binding declaration, as was proposed by some states. The pertinent document, because of its very substance, should be binding. It would be pointless to have all and each of the articles of the declaration speak of *rights* and *duties*, if they were not actually that because they lacked the essential element of being compulsory. A declaration of rights and duties which is prepared without the sincere purpose of binding those who draw it up would be nothing but a paradoxical contradiction in concept.

Some of the articles of the above-mentioned Declaration will be followed by relevant comments, and if appropriate, by a sketch of the proposed changes, keeping in mind primarily Mexico's interests.

Article 1.

Every State has the right to independence and hence to exercise freely, without dictation by any other State, all its legal powers, including the choice of its own form of government.

It is regrettable that the International Law Commission, in drafting Article 1 of the Declaration which refers to the right of independence, did not preserve the spirit which inspired the corresponding Article 4 of the earlier draft, presented by Panama.[11] The Panamanian draft, although its wording might be criticized, gave real substance to the right of independence: the right of the state to achieve well-being and to develop materially and spiritually. When this substance was removed, Article 1 of the Commission's draft only expressed an empty legal formula, which is actually tautological. In fact, to say that the state has the right to exercise freely all its legal powers is simply to say that the state has the right to exercise its rights.

Article 2.

Every State has the right to exercise jurisdiction over its territory and over all persons and things therein, subject to the immunities recognized by international law.

This article was inspired by Article 7 of the Panamanian draft, but it omitted the second part of the latter which stated that foreigners cannot claim different or greater rights than those enjoyed by nationals. It would be advisable to insert this second paragraph

---

[11] The text of this article in the Panamanian draft is as follows: "Every State has the right to its own independence in the sense that it is free to provide for its own well-being and to develop materially and spiritually without being subjected to the determination of other States, provided always that in so doing it shall not impair or violate the legitimate rights of other States." For complete text, see United Nations Doc. A/19, 29 Jan. 1946.

of Article 7 of the Panamanian draft, which moreover reproduces almost exactly the declaration on the subject made by the 1933 Montevideo Convention on the Rights and Duties of States. It would also be advisable to have this article supplemented by provisions analogous to those of Article 8 of the Panamanian draft, completely omitted by the International Law Commission, which refer to the limits of diplomatic intervention. It is important to small countries that it be clearly provided that states should not have recourse to diplomatic representation to protect their nationals, nor for that purpose initiate a dispute under international jurisdiction, when such nationals have been given access to the competent domestic courts of the respective state.[12]

Article 3.

Every State has the duty to refrain from intervention in the internal or external affairs of any other State.

The general statement of principle does not seem to be sufficient, but should be completed by expressly referring to political and economic intervention. Generally speaking, the text of Article 15 of the Charter of the Organization of American States is better and more complete, with the following provisions:

No State or group of States has the right to intervene, directly or indirectly, for any reason whatever, in the internal or external affairs of any other State. The foregoing principle prohibits not only armed force but also any other form of interference or attempted threat against the personality of the State or against its political, economic and cultural elements.

The clear and categorical statement of this principle, as well as the expansion of its content, is of pre-eminent interest to small powers, above all, in view of the many European ministries of

---

[12] See Article VII of the American Treaty of Pacific Settlement, signed at Bogotá, Colombia, 30 April 1948.

foreign affairs and authors who profess a limited conception of non-intervention.[13]

Article 4.

Every State has the duty to refrain from fomenting civil strife in the territory of another State, and to prevent the organization within its territory of activities calculated to foment such civil strife.

Article 5.

Every State has the right to equality in law with every other State.

Article 6.

Every State has the duty to treat all persons under its jurisdiction with respect for human rights and fundamental freedoms, without distinction as to race, sex, language, or religion.

No amendments are proposed to the three preceding articles.

Article 7.

Every State has the duty to ensure that conditions prevailing in its territory do not menace international peace and order.

It should be stated at the end of the Article that the scope of this duty is limited by what is established in Article 2, paragraph 7 of the Charter, which refers to the prohibition of intervention by the Organization in the domestic affairs of states.

Article 8.

Every State has the duty to settle its disputes with other States by peaceful means in such a manner that international peace and security, and justice, are not endangered.

Article 9.

Every State has the duty to refrain from resorting to war as an instrument of national policy, and to refrain from the

---

[13] See Chapter 3.

threat or use of force against the territorial integrity or independence of another State, or in any other manner inconsistent with international law and order.

Article 10.

Every State has the duty to refrain from giving assistance to any State which is acting in violation of article 9, or against which the United Nations is taking preventive or enforcement action.

The three preceding articles express a little more broadly the principles which were incorporated in paragraphs 3, 4, and 5 of Article 2 of the Charter. If these articles of the Declaration were to be adopted, it would be possible to eliminate the principles already mentioned in Article 2 of the Charter, which, as has been said before, would then be exclusively devoted to the actual principles of the Organization, without including the duties of states.

Article 11.

Every State has the duty to refrain from recognizing any territorial acquisition by another State acting in violation of article 9.

No revision of this article is proposed.

Article 12.

Every State has the right of individual or collective self-defence against armed attack.

It would be advisable to indicate that the right which is confirmed in this article can only be exercised under the conditions established by Article 51 of the Charter.

Article 13.

Every State has the duty to carry out in good faith its obligations arising from treaties and other sources of international law, and it may not invoke provisions in its constitution or its laws as an excuse for failure to perform this duty.

Article 14.

Every State has the duty to conduct its relations with other States in accordance with international law and with the principle that the sovereignty of each State is subject to the supremacy of international law.

Articles 13 and 14 of the Declaration regulate the relations between international law and internal law. Article 13 is acceptable and no amendment is suggested to its text. Article 14 contains two different proposals: the first ("Every state has the duty to conduct its relations with other States in accordance with international law . . .") cannot be objected to, although it only reproduces the principle which was stated more explicitly in the first sentence of Article 13, since conducting its relations with other states in accordance with international law simply means carrying out the obligations arising from the sources of international law; on the other hand, the second proposal of Article 14 ("the principle that the sovereignty of each State is subject to the supremacy of international law") is difficult to accept.

The validity of this principle is one of the most discussed problems of international law, and it may be questioned if the enormous difficulties arising from its interpretation and application make its adoption advisable, at least at the present stage of vagueness in the fundamental concepts of international law. In the first place, the article does not make clear whether sovereignty should only be subject to conventional international law—a more acceptable proposition—or if it should also be subject to international law derived from other sources which are only a "subsidiary means for the determination of rules of law," such as doctrine (Article 38 of the Statute of the International Court of Justice).

Secondly, the concept of sovereignty is the least defined and most discussed concept of political science, and thirdly, the very principle of sovereignty's subordination to international law permits very diverse interpretations, no one of which has basically more than a very doubtful theoretical value. According to various authors, the concept of sovereignty is open to all manner of content. Some feel that it should be carefully distinguished from the concept of power, and others find that both are one and the same notion. For some, sovereignty can be limited and for others, a limited sovereignty would be a *contradictio in adjecto*, since sovereignty is essentially absolute, something all-comprehensive and unrestricted, a *suprema potestas*. Some authors ask themselves if sovereignty is an essential characteristic of the state, while others prefer to substitute for it the concept of independence, and still others speak of domestic and foreign sovereignty.[14]

Before such a diversity of concepts, it might first be asked in what sense Article 14 uses this term, and secondly, what value should be placed on the meaning to be given it, especially when some authors like Jean Spiropoulos, a member of the International Law Commission that worked out the draft Declaration, have maintained that the concept of sovereignty is really the problem of the premises which the observer arbitrarily may wish to choose so as to determine the content of the idea,[15] all of which means that its content will have only a relative value.

Furthermore, this article has the even greater theoretical defect of suggesting that part be taken in a practically insoluble theoretical-doctrinal discussion: The discussion between the "dualists" who consider domestic and international law to be two independent and distinct spheres or dominions, and the "monists" who maintain the

---

[14] Moreover, the "solidarist" line of thought completely denies the existence of collective sovereignty. According to this group, sovereignty is an idea which cannot be reconciled with even the existence of international law. If sovereignty should exist, it could only belong to the *civitas maxima*, that is, a universal society provided with a complete political organization. See Georges Scelle, *Précis de Droit des Gens: Principes et Systématique* (Librairie du Recueil Sirey, 1932), Vol. I, pp. 13-14.

[15] Jean Spiropoulos, *Théorie Générale du Droit International* (Paris: Librairie Générale de Droit et de Jurisprudence, 1930), p. 128.

essential unity of all law. Within this monist school, the position of the Declaration supports that one of its two branches which considers domestic law as subordinate to international law, as a "delegation" of the latter (known as the "supremacy" theory of international law). In fact, if sovereignty represents an order which is not independent but is "subordinate" to the supremacy of international law, it can only be considered that the latter is the basis of the state's legal order and that this in turn is only a delegation of international law.

This is not the place to discuss the merits of both theses, but in order to demonstrate the very relative value of each one, the conclusion arrived at after their analysis by the jurist Spiropoulos himself may be quoted:

> On examining it [the monist theory which advocates the supremacy of *jus gentium*] more closely, one is bound to admit that its postulates—assuming that their scientific formulation, as such, were logically possible—have only a relative value and that, from a purely theoretical viewpoint, it has a no more solid basis than the dualist concept.[16]

On the other hand, and outside the bounds of international law doctrines, it should be asked if the spirit behind Article 14 of the Declaration reflects adequately the conditions required by the present political structure of the world, or if it represents an ideal which will only be fulfilled in a more or less distant future.

In the first place, it has to be considered that only that phase of "sovereignty" which affects the external affairs of states would be subject to international law. Article 2, paragraph 7 of the United Nations Charter prohibits the intervention of the United Nations in matters which are essentially within the domestic jurisdiction of states, except, naturally, in cases of the application of enforcement measures under Chapter VII of the Charter. Now, if in practice it was possible in the past to distinguish between foreign and domestic

---

16 *Ibid.*, p. 77. Author's translation.

affairs, it is very difficult to do so at present, because of the interdependence of states and the complexity of international life. Due
to the practical impossibility in many cases of clearly drawing the
line between those two spheres of action, the principle of subordination of sovereignty can open the way to unjustified interference in the domestic affairs of states.

But even limiting the formula of Article 14 of the Declaration
to such matters as are essentially and obviously foreign, the question may still be raised if that principle is not contrary to the facts
of present political reality. In the last analysis, the tendency to
subordinate state sovereignty to international law represents an
exaltation of the values and aims of international society over those
of state community, a very laudable tendency insofar as it signifies
a rein on the uncontrolled arbitrariness of the state, but unacceptable
if it goes beyond that and if it tries to forget—as would appear
to be the case among adversaries *à outrance* of the idea of sovereignty—that the basis of political organization in our times continues to be the national state, the only instrument known to our
epoch by which people can attain certain goals. It is true that in
recent times we have seen how many matters which formerly came
within domestic jurisdiction are now regulated by international law.
One of the clearest cases of this is that of the international rivers
which today are subject to international rule. However, this only
means that at a given moment it seemed advisable to take this
problem out of the national sphere and subject it to international
rule. It could not be assumed that that was due to a necessary and
irresistible principle that governs the development of international
law, as if the latter had a sphere peculiar to it, which it always
should have had and which it would have completely achieved
except for the intransigent sovereignty of the states.

Basically, it is not a question of a logical-juridical and natural
subordination of an order with hierarchically inferior aims, vis-à-vis
the supremacy of another order. In reality we face a problem of
two historical spheres, of two orders created by man to reach

different ends, orders that mutually limit, broaden, or diminish each other. The coexistence of both orders is perfectly possible: the law of the international community limits the sovereignty of the state, but in turn international law is limited by national legal orders in the sense that it is only applicable to that realm which has been previously granted by the state to the international community. The problem is not one of subordination and supremacy, but of limits, of spheres varying in content for historical and contingent reasons.[17] No natural law exists which operates for a necessary and constant increase of international jurisdiction and which can be called on for help in case of doubt.

To accept in principle the general subordination of sovereignty to international law would signify the disappearance of the sum of powers which is implicit in the idea of sovereignty *per se*. Then, says Politis, one of the most representative internationalists of the school which opposes the idea of sovereignty: "When freedom of action is vindicated [the state's freedom of action in international matters], it is necessary to prove that it is granted by the law to which it is subject."[18] But, in reality, as has previously been affirmed, the state's freedom of action is not subject to international law, but is limited by it. Since sovereign states are historically prior to, and are the creators of, international law, they preserve a freedom of action—which by its pre-existence does not originate in the former— in all those spheres which they have not yielded to international law itself, or in other words, where international law still has not placed a prohibition, a limitation.

---

[17] To speak of separate spheres, of spheres of interests and different ends, does not mean the acceptance of the "dualist" position. This tendency, and its opposite, pose the strictly legal problem of the essential unity of law or of its division into two different legal provinces, while the interests, ends, and tasks discussed here have historically belonged to one or the other of two political spheres, a fact which can be demonstrated empirically and which does not prejudge the problem of whether the law which governs those spheres is unitary or not.

[18] N. Politis, "Les Limitations de la Souveraineté," *Recueil des Cours, Académie de Droit International*, Vol. 6 (1925, I), p. 21. Author's translation.

For the above reasons, it would have been preferable to keep to the formula of the Panamanian draft,[19] a formula which reflected the real situation on this point, that is, the *limitation* of sovereignty by international law, without discussing subordination and supremacy which are very debatable concepts on doctrinal grounds and contrary to the requirements of present political reality. The formula of the Panamanian draft made it possible to reconcile the affirmation of the principle of sovereignty with international law. The principle *pacta sunt servanda* is not at odds with the affirmation of sovereignty. Once a treaty is signed, the parties are naturally obliged to fulfil it and, since the treaty is a source of international law, it prevails over the liberty of action of the states. But sovereignty is the basis itself for the conclusion of the treaties, or, in other words, states are free to conclude a commitment or not to the extent that there is no limitation by international law.

---

[19] Article 13: "The sovereignty of the State is subject to the limitations of international law, and it is the duty of every State to adjust its conduct to international law in its relations with other States and with the community of States." *Op. cit.*, p. 37.

chapter three

The Question of Jurisdiction

To determine the sphere of competence of the United Nations is one of the most important and most difficult problems presented in the theory and practice of international organization. The solution to this problem—which at first glance might seem to be a mere procedural one—involves, in the last analysis, passing judgment on the present situation of the state vis-à-vis the international community and taking a position on the present nature and future character of the Organization. To establish the competence or, in other words, to indicate the boundaries of the action of the United Nations means to determine, on the one hand, the categories of matters or questions that can be acted upon by the Organization, and, on the other, the matters which are reserved to the state. That is to say, it is the same as determining the limits of sovereignty for the contemporary state. Therefore, few questions have stirred up as much controversy in the United Nations as this.

d

Traditionally, domestic activities and foreign or international activities of states have been differentiated, though until the creation of permanent international organizations it was of slight importance to determine precisely which questions might relate to domestic or foreign spheres, since in both, the sovereign will of the state was the rule for all important questions. Only very slowly and gradually, from the beginnings of the modern state, has the law of the international community been broadening its sphere over the international activities of states. The right to make war—the most significant international activity—has been removed from the state by positive law practically only in our time.

The problem of defining which powers the states have renounced and which they have reserved arises only when the state limits itself in foreign affairs by participating in international organizations, that is, by giving up certain important international activities in favor of the international community.

The League of Nations Covenant as well as the United Nations Charter deal with the problem and solve it in principle. Leaving aside certain important differences that will be studied further on, both organizations are competent, in principle, to deal with the international activity of states, and are not competent, also in principle, to intervene in the domestic affairs of their members. But neither of the two constitutional charters indicates which matters belong respectively to one or the other realm, nor do their texts clearly reveal a rule for solving that question. In addition, as we shall see later, in spite of the incidence this question has had in numerous political disputes which have been examined, above all in the United Nations, it seems difficult to deduce from the practice of international organizations in almost thirty years of activities, a solid and more or less uniform criterion for solving the question legally or even politically in the future.

The difficulty of the problem is obvious. The structure of the modern state does not allow a clear-cut division between domestic and foreign activities. Given the increasing economic interdependence of states, measures adopted by a country in matters traditionally considered within domestic jurisdiction may have a decisive influence on the life of other peoples. Even for the maintenance of peace and security, which is an international question *par excellence*, the boundaries between the two realms tend to disappear. The incidents leading up to the most recent war highlighted the fact that wars are not dependent on specifically "international" causes, but that they develop from the internal conditions of states. It cannot be denied that the internal structure of the Nazi state, above all to the extent that it was reflected in the systematic persecution of racial and political minorities, was an important harbinger of the last war; then how is it possible, even though international law did not control this aspect, not to consider it international?

Lastly, another factor must be mentioned that tends to complicate the distinction between what pertains to the international community and what pertains to the state. In the contemporary world, it is undeniable that there exist horizontal currents of human solidarity which cut across national frontiers. Independently of class solidarity —which in spite of the postwar resurgence of nationalism, still has considerable influence on even essentially political international questions—the postwar world has created favorable conditions for the vigorous emergence of another form of ethnic and cultural solidarity which knows no national barriers. This phenomenon has been especially notable among the African and Asiatic states which recently achieved their independence; the tenor and character taken on by the anti-colonial struggle in the United Nations show that those peoples feel directly affected by the vicissitudes of the dependent populations to which they are ethnically and culturally linked. The new Islamic countries feel deeply that they are part of a particular culture and world. This is a sociological reality of great force which cannot but exert an influence in shaping the concepts of domestic and international jurisdiction.

THE PROBLEM IN THE LEAGUE OF NATIONS

The defense of the domestic jurisdiction of the state in the League of Nations Covenant was of American inspiration. President Wilson, concerned over the isolationist tendency prevailing in the United States at the end of the First World War, insisted that the Organization be expressly prohibited from intervening in the domestic regulation of matters about which American public opinion was touchy, such as tariffs, the racial question, the immigration problem, etc. His suggestion was incorporated into Article 15, paragraph 8 of the League Covenant, which declared that the Council should make no recommendations as to the settlement of disputes that arose out of matters which by international law were solely within the domestic jurisdiction of a state.

The claim of the exclusive competence of states was not conceived of as a general principle which could prevent all action by the organs of the League, but only as a technical and legal formula which would prevent the Council of the League from making a recommendation on the substance of a dispute without the consent of the parties. It was only in connection with the settlement of disputes that the claim of incompetence could be raised against the action of the Organization. Moreover, the decision regarding competence had to be unanimously voted by the Council members.

Another of the major obstacles to the League's declaring itself not competent was the requirement that the matter in question belong "solely" to domestic jurisdiction, under international law. Many matters which are domestic in principle might not be "solely" domestic due to their international repercussions. In its celebrated advisory opinion in 1923 on the nationality decrees in Tunis and Morocco, the Permanent Court of International Justice recognized that matters such as nationality which are fundamentally domestic in themselves and are not governed by general international law could nevertheless be subject to the intervention of international organs when the state that challenged the competence of the international organ had made special agreements on the matter with another state. Since the number of international treaties on this type of matter increased constantly, there were fewer and fewer cases in which the exclusive competence of the state could be invoked. Therefore, for the above reason and because of the practical difficulties, the application of the League Covenant, instead of protecting the autonomy of domestic order, as its authors wished, tended in practice to broaden the range of action of international organs.

The claim of the exclusive competence of the state was honored to an extraordinarily limited degree by the League. It was invoked in very few cases and always with negative results, that is, in no case was the claim of exclusive competence admitted.[1] The principle was not applied partly because the League's functions in the economic and social fields were very limited, especially in comparison with the functions later assumed by the United Nations, and the number of controversies arising out of these functions were few.

DOMINANT TENDENCIES IN THE POSTWAR WORLD

At the end of the Second World War a number of opposing tendencies existed with respect to each one of the essential principles supposed to sustain the new Organization. As will be remembered, at that time there appeared an abundant political literature mainly characterized by its emphatic internationalism. Plans for federations and world governments were rampant, and naturally they had little place for state sovereignty and for the idea of the exclusive competence of the state. Nonetheless, the opposite tendency also had great force. It was essentially apparent on a governmental scale, with various shades and degrees according to the countries. One of the most notable results of the war, in spite of the many signs to the contrary in the public opinion of that time, was the revival of nationalism attended by a strengthening of state sovereignty. The

---

[1] Lazare Kopelmanas, *L'Organisation des Nations Unies* (Paris: Librairie du Recueil Sirey, 1947), Vol. I, p. 215n.

great protagonists of the approaching ideological battle were not inclined to accept excessive interference in their social and economic life by the future Organization, an interference which many sectors of public opinion felt to be identified with the philosophy of "the other side." The same uncertainty about the possible future arrangement of forces and influences in the Organization, an uncertainty which was an important factor in the acceptance of the veto, likewise worked in favor of the domestic jurisdiction of states. Furthermore, the new states, which had just achieved their independence or were about to achieve it, saw in the idea of sovereignty a symbol and guarantee of their new freedom and, at the same time, an instrument for national integration. Only in some European states (France, Belgium, and Norway, among others), as well as in countries of the American continent like Uruguay, with a certain internationalist tradition, did conceptions prevail in official circles that indicated less preoccupation with the defense of state sovereignty.

The various tendencies noted were already clearly reflected in the proposals of Dumbarton Oaks, drawn up by the governments of the United States, Great Britain, China, and the Soviet Union, as well as in the comments of many states on these proposals. Some governments, when referring to this problem, went so far as to suggest the complete elimination of the principle of domestic jurisdiction. Others favored its preservation but limited the application of the principle to the pacific settlement of disputes, while still others sought not only to broaden its scope against any intervention of the Organization, but to codify the matters which should be considered subject to domestic jurisdiction. Nevertheless, since in this first stage the specific proposals on the matter were introduced within the general concept held by every state about the new Organization, it was not until the San Francisco Conference, at a time when those different general concepts were merged into certain basic principles, that the governments had an opportunity to elaborate their viewpoints on the problem of state jurisdiction. As we shall see, the evolution of the Mexican position from the comments on the Dumbarton Oaks Proposals to the final phase of the San Francisco debates can be clearly followed.

MEXICO'S COMMENTS ON THE DUMBARTON OAKS PROPOSALS

The antagonistic tendencies mentioned and the uncertainty of the times about the future course of the Organization were reflected in the evolution of Mexico's position during the successive phases of the setting up of the new Organization. The Inter-American Conference on Problems of War and Peace took place in Mexico City scarcely two months before the San Francisco Conference. In its Resolution XXX on the establishment of a general international organization, the American republics made known their viewpoints on the proposed Organization. Generally speaking, that resolution reflected the desire of the Latin American countries to increase and intensify the participation of small powers in the new Organization: in the first place, by making it more democratic through broadening the powers of an Assembly that would be fully representative; and, secondly, by enhancing the role of law over solely political considerations in the solution of conflicts, even proposing the extension of the jurisdiction and competence of the International Court of Justice.

Mexico's position in that Conference can be unreservedly described as advanced. In the Mexican government's comments on the proposals of Dumbarton Oaks, comments which were also presented to the Inter-American Conference, a number of amendments were introduced to those proposals which gave a marked international cast to the whole Mexican stand.

Besides suggesting that the Assembly be granted "the powers that ought to correspond to it in a democratic system" and establishing respect for human rights as one of the pillars of the Organization, proposing that there be drawn up a declaration for that purpose as an annex to the Charter and suggesting an international organ to ensure its observance, Mexico proposed, along the same line of thought, two very important changes directly related to the problem of the Organization's competence. The first amendment was "to include [in] the Constitution of the General International Organization the pledge of all the States for the incorporation of international law into their respective national laws."[2] The second was to suggest the elimination of any restriction on the Organization's competence in cases of international controversies.

The second amendment is directly related to our question. Mexico proposed the elimination of all restrictions on the competence of the United Nations in cases of international controversies, so that it would always be possible to apply one of the procedures for pacific settlement provided for by the Charter.[3] There would no longer be a "domestic jurisdiction" of the state in which the Organization should not intervene, from the moment that any matter, even though domestic, constituted or created a "situation which may lead to international friction."

In the comments of the Mexican government on the Dumbarton Oaks Proposals, the reasons for Mexico's position are clarified. The four-power authors of the Proposals had initially preserved, in substance, the corresponding Article 15, paragraph 8, of the League Covenant. They provided for a limitation of the powers of the Council and Assembly to intervene in the pacific settlement of disputes: they were not to intervene in "situations or disputes arising out of matters which by international law are solely within the domestic jurisdiction of the state concerned." This provision appears in the Dumbarton Oaks Proposals as Article 7 of Section A (Pacific

---

[2] *Documents of the United Nations Conference on International Organization, San Francisco, 1945* (New York: United Nations Information Organization, 1945), Vol. III, pp. 160-61. For the complete text of the "Opinion of the Department of Foreign Relations of Mexico Concerning the Dumbarton Oaks Proposals," see pp. 54-188. These volumes are hereinafter referred to as *UNCIO Documents.*

[3] *Ibid.*, p. 162.

Settlement of Disputes) of Chapter VIII. Mexico proposed, instead of amendments to this article, its elimination:

> Article 7 should be eliminated, since in the new organization of the Community of States the questions specified in Article 1 —"any dispute, or any situation which may lead to international friction or give rise to a dispute"— . . . could never be considered as being solely "within the domestic jurisdiction of the State concerned", but, by their very essence and taking into account the purposes of the general international organization, would necessarily have to be within the jurisdiction of the latter or of the Permanent Court of International Justice.[4]

It may be said without exaggeration that in its comments on the Dumbarton Oaks Proposals, Mexico took the most radical position possible, going beyond even such states as Belgium and Uruguay which have always been noted for their tendency to seek the broadest possible sphere of action for the international community with the correlative narrowing of state jurisdiction. Mexico's position on this point is partly explained, nevertheless, because it was one aspect of an organic whole: the sum of the Mexican proposals for the new international organization. In Mexico's proposals, the veto practically disappeared, the General Assembly had broader powers, the international protection of human rights was guaranteed in the Charter, the rights and duties of states were to be defined in an annex to the Charter and international law was to be automatically incorporated into the national laws of the members. Within such a concept it was only logical that the competence of the new organization should not be limited by any restriction or exception in case of international disputes. It was also natural that when the basic proposals of Mexico were not accepted in San Francisco its viewpoint on the problem of domestic jurisdiction of the state as regards the international organization would have to be changed.

---

[4] *Ibid.*, p. 133-34.

THE PROBLEM AT SAN FRANCISCO

At the beginning of the San Francisco Conference, the four sponsoring governments jointly presented an amendment which radically modified the Dumbarton Oaks Proposals and thus changed the setting in which discussions on this question would take place.[5] The amendment was designed to reinforce considerably the domestic jurisdiction of states. According to the explanations of Mr. John Foster Dulles, spokesman of the four powers on this question, the amendment was necessary because the comments of the governments and the debates in San Francisco had emphasized the general desire to change the character of the Organization:

> The scope of the Organization was now broadened to include functions which would enable the Organization to eradicate the underlying causes of war as well as deal with crises leading to war. Under the Social and Economic Council the Organization would deal with economic and social problems. This broadening of the scope of the Organization constituted a great advance, but it also engendered special problems.
>
> For instance, the question had been raised as to what would be the basic relation of the Organization to member states: Would the Organization deal with the governments of the member states, or would the Organization penetrate directly into the domestic life and social economy of the member states? As provided in the amendment of the sponsoring governments . . . the Organization [would] deal with the [member] governments.[6]

This shift in the general structure of the Charter necessarily had to be accompanied by a new solution to the problem of competence. In the League Covenant and in the Dumbarton Oaks Proposals, the clause on domestic jurisdiction was only a technical and legal formula to prevent the organs from intervening in the pacific settlement of dangerous international situations or disputes, when these

---

[5] See *ibid.*, p. 623.
[6] *Ibid.*, Vol. VI, pp. 507-08.

arose from a domestic issue. Now the clause was thought of as a general principle, as a brake on *all* activity of the Organization. "Nothing contained in this Charter shall authorize the Organization to intervene in matters which are essentially within the domestic jurisdiction of any State . . ."—stated the joint amendment. But, in addition, the concept of the clause as a particular exception to the Organization's competence in the pacific solution of disputes was also expressly preserved. The joint amendment continued as follows: "or shall require the members to submit such matters to settlement under this Charter."

Due to the different concept introduced by the joint amendment of the four powers, the new draft differed in various ways from the formula of the League and of Dumbarton Oaks. First, the scope of the provision was broadened by passing it from Chapter VIII (Arrangements for the Maintenance of International Peace and Security) to Chapter II (Principles). Secondly, the clause no longer spoke of questions that are "solely" within domestic competence, but of questions that are "essentially" within domestic jurisdiction: that is, the independence of domestic order is protected against the Organization's interventions in such matters as immigration, tariffs, nationality laws, etc., which even though not "solely" domestic, because of their possible repercussions in other countries, are nevertheless "essentially" domestic; "essentially," as used in the joint amendment, means "essential to the sovereignty of the State."[7] Thirdly, the old standard that, in order to restrain the Organization, the affair must be domestic "in accordance with international law" was eliminated.

The three changes noted tended to strengthen the domestic order. Nevertheless, this question could not fail to be influenced also by recognition of the fact that the maintenance of peace is the primary and supreme aim of the United Nations, that it dominates all the

---

[7] See Hans Kelsen, *The Law of the United Nations* (New York: Frederick A. Praeger, 1950), p. 779; and Australian statement in *UNCIO Documents*, Vol. VI, pp. 511-12.

rest, and that the Organization is built around it. In contrast to the League, there is in the United Nations no obstacle, not even domestic jurisdiction, to prevent the Security Council from taking effective action *when peace is threatened.*[8] The final phrase of the joint amendment reads thus: "but this principle shall not prejudice the application of Chapter VIII, Section B" (now Chapter VII of the Charter). This Chapter refers to the determination of the existence of threats to the peace, breaches of the peace, or acts of aggression and the measures which the Organization may take, including the use of armed force.[9] In other words, on the one hand the sphere of international jurisdiction is diminished, by restricting the matters falling within it, but on the other hand, when the peace is threatened, the claim of domestic jurisdiction cannot be an impediment to the Organization's taking adequate measures to maintain or restore international peace and security.

Finally, like the corresponding provision of the League Covenant, neither the joint amendment nor later the Charter indicates a specific pattern or a procedure for determining the domestic or international nature of questions.

The clause which was finally approved and incorporated into Article 2, paragraph 7 of the United Nations Charter as one of the basic "principles" of the Organization was drafted thus:

---

[8] In the League system the claim of exclusive competence could hinder the application of the sanctions provided in Article 16 of the Covenant. See Kopelmanas, *op. cit.*, p. 209.

[9] An Australian amendment which was finally approved in San Francisco tended to protect still more the domestic jurisdiction of the state. In accordance with the original provisions of Chapter VIII, Section B, the Security Council could either make recommendations to the parties or apply enforcement measures in case of threats to the peace or acts of aggression. According to the joint amendment of the four sponsoring governments, the claim of domestic jurisdiction would not prevent either Council action. But according to the approved Australian amendment, only when the Security Council decided on *enforcement measures* under Articles 41 and 42 of the Charter would the affected state be prevented from blocking the action of the Council by means of the claim of incompetence. The Council is not empowered to make *recommendations* on matters "essentially" within domestic jurisdiction even if a threat to the peace exists. See below, p. 74 and *UNCIO Documents*, Vol. VI, pp. 436-40.

Nothing contained in the present Charter shall authorize the United Nations to intervene in matters which are essentially within the domestic jurisdiction of any state or shall require the Members to submit such matters to settlement under the present Charter; but this principle shall not prejudice the application of enforcement measures under Chapter VII.[10]

POSITION OF MEXICO AT SAN FRANCISCO

As we have seen, the initial reaction of Mexico (in the "Opinion of the Ministry of Foreign Relations of Mexico concerning the Dumbarton Oaks Proposals . . .") was to oppose a clause on domestic

---

[10] What meaning does the term "intervention" have in Article 2, paragraph 7? According to Hersh Lauterpacht (*International Law and Human Rights* [New York: Frederick A. Praeger, 1950], p. 167) "intervention" is used in a technical sense in Article 2, paragraph 7; that is, "it implies a peremptory demand for positive conduct or abstention—a demand which, if not complied with, involves a threat of or recourse to compulsion, thought not necessarily physical compulsion . . ." In other words, intervention signifies dictatorial interference sustained by force or the threat of force in the affairs of a state. Under this interpretation suggested by Lauterpacht, a recommendation could not mean an intervention in the sense of Article 2(7). Since the Assembly only has the power to "recommend," this organ could not "intervene" in the domestic affairs of its members.

The English author Georg Schwarzenberger (*Power Politics* [New York: Frederick A. Praeger, 1951], p. 448) offers the three criticisms that follow, and which seem to us to be pertinent to the Lauterpacht theory:

First, in principle, all intervention in the technical sense is illegal. Thus, to interpret intervention in this clause in the technical sense would mean to say that the United Nations, which may be presumed to act in conformity with the principles of justice and international law, should refrain from committing an illegal act, which is absurd.

Second, the organs of the United Nations, under the constitutional provisions which establish its functions, have no competence to "intervene" in the technical sense in the affairs of their members. The interpretation of Lauterpacht would make Article 2, paragraph 7, of the Charter meaningless, a result of juridical interpretation which should be avoided.

Third, this interpretation is contrary to the antecedents. The San Francisco Conference refused to accept international law as the yardstick by reference to which it would be determined whether a matter was essentially within the domestic jurisdiction of a state. It would be somewhat artificial to hold that the most important words of the sentence should be interpreted in an entirely pragmatic way and that one word in the same sentence should be construed in a highly technical sense.

jurisdiction.[11] Later, in its draft amendments to the Proposals, Mexico accepted the principle but suggested that the Court should decide in case of doubt whether or not a matter pertained to domestic jurisdiction; in other words, Mexico proposed to give an important role to law in the settlement of questions of domestic jurisdiction. When the four powers presented their joint amendment, which reinforced and broadened the scope of the domestic jurisdiction of states and which rested the settlement of such cases more on political than juridical considerations, it was to be expected that Mexico would be opposed. Nevertheless, this was not the case. The Mexican delegate on the drafting committee for the Preamble, Purposes, and Principles of the Charter at the San Francisco Conference

> recalled to the Committee that *non-intervention* [author's italics] was one of the essential principles of the inter-American system; and that, after extensive discussion, at the recent Conference of Chapultepec, the principle had been formally endorsed. That was not to say that at some future date the International Organization might not have so much authority and prestige that it could be permitted to intervene, even in matters which were normally within the domestic jurisdiction of the state. [The Delegate of Mexico] therefore, wished to express himself in support of the sponsoring government's text . . .[12]

Mexico's change of attitude is partly explained, as has been pointed out, by the rejection, as a whole, of the basic proposals which it presented and which formed an adequate framework for proposing the elimination of the domestic jurisdiction clause. Nonetheless, an additional influence in this issue was the close bond between two notions which at that time were not clearly disassociated.

Mexico has always been noted for its attachment to the principle of non-intervention, in the sense of the interference of one or several states in the affairs of another. This tradition is so strong and

---

[11] See above, p. 44.
[12] *UNCIO Documents*, Vol. VI, p. 495.

the principle so precisely corresponds to the situation of Mexico that when the closely related question of domestic jurisdiction was brought forward à propos of the creation of the international organization, it would have been difficult not to have associated the two. The tie between the two principles is clear, but the differences are also, especially when precise legal norms are sought. In spite of this, the declaration of the Mexican representative fundamentally invoked the principle of non-intervention.

Likewise, the two problems also appear to have been closely linked in a work published in Mexico at that time. Referring to Article 2, paragraph 7 of the Charter, which consecrates the principle of domestic jurisdiction, the author states: "This is one of the most transcendent principles and it surely will give rise to conflicts in interpretation and application, because with one exception it proclaims the principle of non-intervention . . ." Further on, the author cites the important Non-Intervention Protocol subscribed to in Buenos Aires in 1936, by which the High Contracting Parties "declare inadmissible the intervention of any one of them, directly or indirectly, and for whatever reason, in the internal or external affairs of any other of the Parties." The author's comment is as follows: "Nevertheless, the United Nations Charter emasculates that Protocol and, with reservations, only leaves validity to Non-Intervention in domestic affairs (Article 2, paragraph 7)."[13] As may be noted, neither in the above-mentioned statement of the Mexican representative in San Francisco nor in the work just quoted is there a distinction made between the principle of non-intervention and the principle of the reserved domain of states vis-à-vis the international organization.

But the best proof of the confusion which existed between these two concepts is furnished by the Mexican government itself in its official report on the results obtained by the Mexican delegation to the San Francisco Conference. Upon examination of the initiative

---

[13] Raúl Noriega, *La Carta Mundial* (Mexico: Editorial Superación, no date), pp. 40 and 42-43. Translated from Spanish.

taken by Mexico "to eliminate all restrictions on the competence
of the Organization in cases of international controversies, in order
that it may always be possible to apply some one of the procedures
of pacific settlement provided for in the Pact," the document states
the following: "As had been proposed by the Ministry of Foreign
Relations, paragraph 7, of Section A of Chapter VIII of the Dumbarton Oaks Proposals was eliminated. On the other hand, the principle of Non-Intervention in the domestic affairs of the States, which
was vigorously defended by the Mexican Delegation, was maintained."[14]

The declaration that Mexico achieved success in eliminating paragraph 7, Section A, of Chapter VIII, which contained the domestic
jurisdiction clause, cannot but be surprising. The clause referred to
of paragraph 7 was certainly omitted from Section A, which dealt
with "Pacific Settlement of Disputes," but not because it had been
eliminated, but because, as has been stated before, it was passed
from Chapter VIII to Chapter I on "Purposes and Principles." It
was thereby broadened in scope and finally stated even more forcibly than it had been in the original clause which Mexico asked
to have eliminated.

As for the second question considered a triumph for the Mexican
Delegation, the maintenance of the principle of non-intervention in
the domestic affairs of states, the government's opinion is also unrealistic. Article 2, paragraph 7, of the Charter does not deal with
the principle of non-intervention, in the sense used by all the authors
of textbooks on international law and always understood by Mexico,
that is, the illegal intervention of a country in the affairs of others.
This Article prohibits the intervention of the *United Nations*, "this
term meaning 'the Organisation,' not the individual Members."[15]
The report of the rapporteur of the drafting committee to the rele-

---

[14] Government of Mexico, *Memoria de la Secretaria de Relaciones Exteriores*
(Annual Report of the Ministry of Foreign Relations), septiembre de 1944-
agosto de 1945, Vol. II, p. 199. Translated from Spanish.

[15] Kelsen, *op. cit.*, p. 770.

vant Commission of the San Francisco Conference states: "It is evident that the subject we are dealing with is not the intervention of one state in matters which fall within the domestic jurisdiction of another, but that we are dealing with the relations of the Organization and its members . . ."[16] If Mexico could make any complaint about the results of the San Francisco Conference it would be precisely because the principle of non-intervention was not clearly expressed in the Charter. Mexico proposed in its amendments that the Charter include the following principle: "No State has a right to intervene, directly or indirectly . . . in the domestic or foreign affairs of another."[17] Mexico's suggestion was not accepted, basically due to the fact that the non-intervention principle does not have the same meaning and scope for European countries as it has for the inter-American system.[18] It was unlikely then that a formula as absolute and radical as that proposed by Mexico would be accepted. The fact is that "the obligation of the Members to refrain from intervention in domestic matters of other states is not expressly stipulated by the Charter,"[19] but simply implied in the duty established in Article 2, paragraph 4.

The last phase in the evolution of the Mexican attitude may be seen in Mexico's reply to the celebrated note sent by Dr. Rodríguez Larreta, then Foreign Minister of Uruguay, to the American re-

---

[16] *UNCIO Documents*, Vol. VI, p. 486.

[17] *Ibid.*, p. 66.

[18] Some European authors differentiate between legal and illegal interventions, the former including "humane intervention," the intervention and financial control of the insolvent debtor states (England, Germany, and Italy against Venezuela in 1902; United States against Haiti in 1915, etc.) and even intervention in the interest of balance of power. Cf. Charles Rousseau, *Droit International Public* (Paris: Librairie du Recueil Sirey, 1953), p. 329; Pierre Mamopoulos "Le Déclin de la Souveraineté," *Revue Hellénique de Droit International* Vol. I (1948), pp. 31-40; and L. Oppenheim, *International Law: A Treatise* ([7th Rev. Ed. by H. Lauterpacht] London: Longmans, Green, and Co., 1948), Vol. I, p. 278.

[19] Kelsen, *op. cit.*, p. 770. The Secretary-General of the Mexican delegation to San Francisco, Dr. Alfonso García Robles, recognized that the non-intervention principle is not adequately formulated in the Charter. See his book, *El Mundo de la Postguerra* (Mexico: Secretaria de Educacion Publica, 1946), Vol. I, p. 116.

e

publics scarcely five months after the San Francisco Conference. The Uruguayan Foreign Minister raised an extremely important issue: he proposed collective action by the hemisphere republics whenever democracy or fundamental human rights were endangered in any of them.[20] The idea did not prosper because most of the American states opposed it; for Mexico, this note served the purpose of clarifying concepts and sharply defining its position on the problem of the reserved domain of states vis-à-vis international action; Mexico's answer clearly distinguishes between domestic jurisdiction as a limitation on the activity of the international organizations and nonintervention as a principle to restrain other states. Mexico completely rejected the Uruguayan Foreign Minister's suggestion on the grounds that Article 2, paragraph 7 of the Charter, which Mexico had wanted eliminated in its original form, was one of the guiding principles of the Organization; and that that provision reserved to the domestic domain of states the form of internal government and the protection of human rights.

THE PRACTICE OF THE UNITED NATIONS: GENERAL REMARKS

How has the domestic jurisdiction clause been interpreted and to what extent has it influenced the activities of the United Nations?

The scope of the future functions of the Organization is dependent upon the way in which this clause is interpreted. Its authors thought that by reinforcing the principle the Organization would be restrained from intervening directly in the lives of the peoples and from imposing standards in social and economic fields which would be unacceptable to governments. But the formula finally approved was general and flexible enough to permit the Organization to broaden its range of action in the future, as far as international conditions made this advisable. Mr. John Foster Dulles made a com-

---

[20] U.S. Dept. of State *Bulletin*, Vol. XIII, No. 335 (25 Nov. 1945), pp. 864-66.

parison of the situation existing between the Organization and the member states and that existing between the United States federal government and the states of the Union; in both cases, he said, the evolution of institutions was to be expected: "Today, the Federal Government of the United States exercised an authority undreamed of when the Constitution was formed, and the people of the United States were grateful for the simple conceptions contained in their Constitution."[21]

Unfortunately, the vision of the future did not facilitate the solution of the present problem, at least as regards the criterion for interpreting which matters were to come under domestic jurisdiction and which under international jurisdiction. The comparison with what happens between a federal government and its states can hardly serve us as a model. In the Mexican Constitution there exists a method for clearly determining whether a function or activity belongs to the federation or to the states: the "residual" method. If a power is not expressly assigned to the federation, it belongs to the states. In the case of the Organization and the member states, there is no like criterion. In deference to the views of the great powers, even the phrase to the effect that the claim of incompetence could only operate when the matter was domestic "according to international law," was rejected. Apart from the question whether there would have been real value in having that phrase included— since no decision could be made without determining whether or not the matter was regulated by international law—the fact that it was not approved (the vote was 18 in favor to 14 opposed, thereby falling short of the required two-thirds majority) clearly indicates the desire to turn away from international law as the source of the decisions to be made in each case. This hypothesis is strengthened by the opposition of at least two of the four sponsoring governments at San Francisco (the United States and the Soviet Union) to having the International Court of Justice decide on the question

---

[21] *UNCIO Documents*, Vol. VI, p. 508.

should it be brought up (this proposal was also rejected, by 17 votes in favor to 14 against).[22]

In reality, the broad and vague terms of the provision that was finally approved, together with the frustration in San Francisco of all efforts toward determining juridically questions of domestic jurisdiction that would arise, left the solution of such cases to basically political considerations in the practice of the Organization. Fundamentally, the domestic jurisdiction clause has become a political principle rather than a juridical limitation; it has been accepted that the interpretation to be given in each case is a political function of the organ to which the claim is submitted; in spite of having been proposed on several occasions, there has been no case until now in which a solution of the question by the International Court of Justice according to positive law has been sought.

APPLICATION OF THE PRINCIPLE
IN CERTAIN SPECIFIC CASES

The Security Council as well as the General Assembly dealt with the case of Spain. It was deemed by a Security Council sub-committee in 1946 that the Franco government was a potential threat to international peace and security and a cause of international friction.[23] The Security Council did not, however, take any action, because of a Soviet veto, but later in the year a resolution adopted by the General Assembly undoubtedly assumed that the Organization was competent. The approved resolution recommended that Spain be debarred from membership in the Specialized Agencies, that members of the United Nations withdraw their Ambassadors and Ministers Plenipotentiary in Madrid,[24] and that the Security Council consider taking measures to remedy the situation if a demo-

---

[22] *Ibid.*, pp. 509-12.
[23] Security Council, Official Records: 1st Yr., 1st Series, Sp. Suppl. (Rev. ed.), Report of the Subcommittee on the Spanish Question, June 1946.
[24] General Assembly Resolution 39(I), 12 Dec. 1946.

cratic Spanish government were not established within a reasonable time.

In 1948 the Security Council dealt with the problem of the change in the political regime in Czechoslovakia. Argentina, a member of the Council, submitted a resolution drafted by Chile, a non-member, to appoint a sub-committee to investigate the way in which the change was brought about, clearly implying the interference of the Soviet Union;[25] the proposal won a majority, but was vetoed by the Soviet Union, which considered that the question of a change in the political structure of a state was within domestic jurisdiction. The resolution was, therefore, not approved.

In 1949 and 1950 the General Assembly studied the accusations against Hungary, Bulgaria, and Romania of violation of human rights and fundamental liberties. The accusations were made as a result of the trial of Cardinal Mindszenty in Hungary, the imprisonment of several ministers in Bulgaria and, generally, the suppression of political liberties and freedom of belief and expression in those countries. There was an international element in the question due to the fact that the peace treaties which ended the Second World War with those states established their obligation to respect human rights, and provided as well for the appointment of tripartite commissions to settle disputes relative to violations of the treaties. When the accusation was submitted, the three defeated states refused to appoint their respective representatives to the commissions. The International Court of Justice, which was requested by the Assembly to interpret the treaties, declared that the defeated states had the obligation to appoint their representatives, but that if they refused to do so, the Secretary-General of the United Nations could not appoint the third member of the commissions as provided in the treaties. Thus, the way to settling the disputes within the framework of the treaties was blocked. In 1950, the question was whether, in view of the impossibility of using legal procedure, the Assembly

---

[25] For text of proposal, see Security Council, Official Records: 3rd Yr., No. 56, 281st Mtg., 12 April 1948, p. 2.

was empowered to pronounce judgment on the "respect for human rights and fundamental liberties" in those states. The General Assembly adopted a resolution to the effect that the refusal of the three governments to appoint their representatives indicated that they were perfectly well aware of the violations they were committing, and member states were invited to submit evidence of the violations to the Secretary-General.[26]

In the case of Indonesia, the Security Council refused to act in 1946 when the Ukrainian SSR charged that military action against the local population by British and Japanese troops threatened international peace and security. More than a year later, in August 1947, when large-scale hostilities had broken out, the Netherlands had reoccupied two-thirds of Java, and certain negotiations had already taken place which implied, as judged by the Council, a *de facto* recognition by the Netherlands of the Indonesian Republic, the Security Council decided to intervene with relative energy, in spite of the Netherlands' insistence that the large-scale hostilities were a "police action" and that, moreover, the question was within its domestic jurisdiction.

The problem of the treatment given to persons of Indian origin in the Union of South Africa has been on the agenda of every Assembly session except one since 1946. The policy of discrimination followed by this country affects huge Indian and Pakistani communities. Although the Union of South Africa and certain colonial and other powers feel that the matter is within South Africa's domestic jurisdiction, the Assembly has intervened in the question to the extent of appointing committees of inquiry and recommending round tables of the interested countries. Little has been accomplished toward the solution of this matter because of the refusal of the Union of South Africa to co-operate.

Another situation relative to the Union of South Africa which has concerned the Assembly for some years is the so-called *apartheid*,

---

[26] See General Assembly Resolution 385(V), 3 Nov. 1950.

that is, the policy of racial segregation practiced by the Union. The Group Areas Act, which establishes a systematic racial discrimination in every imaginable field (marriage, property, business, housing, community locations, agriculture, etc.), completely stratifying society and keeping the non-European population almost in slavery, has been widely discussed and condemned in the General Assembly. The Union of South Africa and a number of other countries have unsuccessfully tried to block the action of the Organization by maintaining that social legislation comes essentially within domestic jurisdiction.

The questions of Tunisia and Morocco were brought before the Security Council and the Assembly between 1951 and 1955. The various complaints were presented by as many as fourteen Asian and African states. Although with certain minor differences in each case, domestic autonomy was requested for the Tunisian and Moroccan populations. The problem had an international element in that both Tunisia and Morocco, although French protectorates, did not cease being subjects of international law, as was recognized (in the case of Morocco) by the International Court of Justice, and their relations with France originated in their respective international treaties: the Bardo Treaty and the Fez Treaty.

The Security Council refused to take up either case. In 1951 the Assembly postponed consideration of the Moroccan case "for the time being,"[27] but in 1952, despite the opposition of France and certain colonial and other powers, although with the discreet tolerance of the United States, the Assembly adopted resolutions for each, though these merely expressed the hope that the unequal negotiations between France and the representatives of the Bey and the Sultan should succeed.[28] In 1953—after the French deposed the Moroccan Sultan, the two protectorates were shaken with internal agitation, and all civil and political liberties were suppressed—the

---

[27] General Assembly, Official Records (G.A.O.R.): 6th Sess., 354th Plenary Mtg., 13 Dec. 1951, p. 269.
[28] See General Assembly Resolutions 611 and 612(VII), 17 and 19 Dec. 1952.

Asian-African group recommended that martial law and other "exceptional measures" be terminated, that negotiations be resumed between the two parties in each case, that free elections be held, that the Tunisian people be permitted to exercise their "legitimate rights to full sovereignty"[29] and that the Moroccan protectorate's "full sovereignty and independence"[30] be ensured within a period of five years. At that time the closeness of the political and military ties between the Atlantic powers led the United States to change its position. The pertinent draft resolutions, although obtaining a simple majority of votes, did not win the two-thirds necessary for approval;[31] one of the main changes in the composition of the votes was the different position of various Latin American countries. The rejection of the resolutions was equivalent to a denial of the competence of the Assembly, since the argument for domestic jurisdiction was the basis of the negative attitude of many states.

Finally, the Assembly considered in 1946 the question of creating an *ad hoc* committee to receive and examine information transmitted by the colonial powers, in accordance with Chapter XI of the Charter, on the progress of dependent populations under their control. The committee was set up in spite of the opposition of several colonial and other powers, which considered it a violation of the principle of domestic jurisdiction; later, Soviet proposals requesting information about the dependent peoples' participation in local administrations, about immigration policy, and about periodic visits to those territories were rejected. Domestic jurisdiction was the argument upon which the rejection was based.

In the majority of cases studied, the raising of the principle of domestic jurisdiction has not seriously hampered the Organization's action. The challenge to the competence of United Nations organs has only occasionally succeeded in preventing the adoption of a

---

[29] G.A.O.R., 8th Sess., Annexes: Agenda item 56, p. 3.
[30] *Ibid.*, Agenda item 57, p. 4.
[31] See *ibid.*, 455th and 457th Plenary Mtgs., 3 and 11 Nov. 1953, pp. 265-67 and 293.

proposal when three of the great powers have concurred, as in the cases of Tunisia and Morocco, or when the matter has been presented before the Security Council and a great power in the minority could use the veto to restrain the Organization.

Until now, the question of domestic jurisdiction has been brought up in the United Nations primarily in connection with political disputes between two or more states. Such disputes may have been related to an economic or a social question; but the problem has almost always arisen in reference to the Organization's power to intervene in the settlement of a situation or controversy between states. The formula to be applied has been the second phrase of Article 2, paragraph 7 of the Charter:"or shall require the Members to submit such matters to settlement under the present Charter."

On the other hand, what had appeared the greatest danger in San Francisco—the direct intervention of the United Nations in economic and social matters—has not materialized. It was clearly accepted from the beginning that the Organization's powers to propose concrete economic and social measures for specific states could only arise at the request of those states. The increase in the economic and social functions of the United Nations has not given rise to a tendency to intervene directly in the life of the peoples in those fields. The Organization's functions have been limited to making studies and general recommendations on international co-operation and coordination. The mechanism used for applying the international standards formulated in the United Nations to the different countries has fundamentally followed the classic canons: the drawing up of treaties freely subscribed to by the members. Certainly, a number of multilateral conventions have been discussed and approved in the United Nations, but this is only the first step in their formation. The dissident minorities are sufficiently protected since the convention only becomes binding by signature and ratification; moreover, it is always possible to insert reservations. Thus, international norms in economic and social matters are adopted by the states only insofar as they voluntarily accept them.

THE INTERESTS OF UNDERDEVELOPED COUNTRIES: THE SITUATION OF MEXICO

What has been Mexico's policy on this issue and what solution is most to its interest?

Except for a factor peculiar to Mexico—the existence of large groups of Mexican population who live abroad—the situation and interests of Mexico are not generally different from those of other small and medium-sized powers in this respect.

Of course, it is evident that the small powers are in greater danger than the great powers of being subjected to undue intervention by the international organization. Apart from the fact that the great powers can block the action of the Organization by veto in almost any situation or dispute, even within the General Assembly the combined will of three great powers prevails in really important questions. But, in addition, although there have been occasions, such as the treament of Indians in South Africa or the cases of Tunisia and Morocco, when small powers have taken the initiative to demand intervention for quite weighty reasons, it is obvious that, in most cases, any movement to persuade the United Nations to intervene will most probably originate with the great powers, which have political, military, or economic influence on other countries. It would therefore have seemed natural that in most cases the small powers would have determinedly maintained the principle of domestic jurisdiction against the great powers.

Nonetheless, that theoretical pattern does not conform to the practice of the United Nations. The main reason for this is the struggle against colonialism, which is actually the desire to change the political status quo of certain regions and which requires the intervention of the Organization if it is to be carried out pacifically. In this field, the interventionist movement of the small powers has come up against the interests of the Western European countries (and, on occasion, of the United States) which enjoy the benefits of that status quo. The second important reason is that small countries are sometimes forced by the exigencies of the political and ideological conflict dividing the world to indulge in frequent inconsistencies which often do not sufficiently take into account the precedents established. Perhaps the clearest example of this inconsistency would be the case of some Latin American countries which had scruples about upholding the Organization's competence in the cases of Tunisia and Morocco, despite their anti-colonial tradition and the fact that the independence of whole populations whose dependent status had originated in international treaties was at stake; while these same countries had no trouble supporting the Organization's intervention in the case of the change of government in Czechoslovakia although the precedent thus set could easily be turned against them because of the political instability of many Latin American countries. Last of all, an explanation of why the theory has not worked out in practice should likewise take into account that until now not enough cases have been dealt with in the United Nations to establish a definite pattern.

In any event, in proposing a future line of conduct for Mexico in this respect, it is hardly possible to think of a policy which would not be to defend consistently the principle of the reserved domain of states vis-à-vis the international organization.

Certainly, the danger foreseen in San Francisco has never arisen: the Organization has not tried to bypass governments and directly impose international norms of an economic and social character. But the state's exercise of its economic and social functions can create international situations and controversies. A country like Mexico, in full economic development, socially unintegrated to a certain extent and scarcely institutionalized politically, may easily affect foreign vested interests. Fortunately, Mexico has left behind in history the period of internal political convulsions which, in the past, gave rise to countless international claims against the country; but this is only one of the first phases in the life of an independent state. In order to achieve its economic independence and reach the level of social unity necessary for building an integrated and organic nation, Mexico will still need highly favorable conditions for many years to come. Naturally, the first of those conditions is to keep itself free of such interference as might impede its natural development, be it from other countries or from international agencies. Economically, the Mexican state will require the liberty of action necessary to claim its natural resources for the nation's benefit and to screen future foreign investments so as to have a balanced economic development. Socially, Mexico will have to continue to establish standards of conduct in such matters as religion, labor relations, land holding, culture, and others which, although they are based on historical experiences and circumstances peculiar to the country, might not conform to certain international patterns appropriate to socially more developed communities. It is difficult to think that Mexico, over a fairly long period, will actually abandon the principle of the reserved domain of states as regards international agencies: likewise, it will have to go on basing its nationalist position on certain doctrinal developments which are corollary to or connected with the same principle, such as non-intervention, equal treatment for foreigners and nationals, the Drago Doctrine, the Calvo Doctrine, etc.

DOMESTIC JURISDICTION: THE COLONIAL PROBLEM AND UNDERDEVELOPED COUNTRIES

On the other hand, the position of the small countries on the problem of domestic jurisdiction cannot be dissociated from another factor, peculiar to the contemporary world, but which has arisen with special force in the postwar world: the colonial peoples' demands for independence. Even though the San Francisco Organization fell short of establishing adequate legal bases for directing dependent populations toward independence, more than twenty nations have succeeded in emancipating themselves since the war from the political tutelage of colonial powers, by armed force, by the enlightened interest of some European states, or, partly, by the intervention of the United Nations. To meet those demands, the structure of the Charter allows some margin between liberation by armed force and the maintenance of a status quo which fundamentally favors colonial powers. Thanks to the exertions of many small states, it has been possible to direct the Organization's activity, although weakly, toward greater intervention and vigilance in the administration of trust territories, as well as toward aid to peoples without a government of their own that wish to achieve total independence or a higher degree of domestic autonomy. At the core of this question is the problem of domestic jurisdiction. How long a time it will take dependent peoples to emerge from the various forms of colonialism will depend in part on the attitude of many small powers on this matter. Probably in coming years the Organization will continue studying the already familiar colonial questions; but, in addition, it is not unlikely that in the near future the United Nations will become the outlet for the whole vast colonial problem of Africa.

The problem for the Latin American countries is not merely to put into practice a tradition of independence or to express their natural sympathy for a noble cause. Lately, our governments have come to realize that the independence of the colonial peoples is already an important economic problem which will become more acute in the future. United Nations discussions have already reflected anxiety over the fact that the inhuman working conditions in the colonies, the preferential tariffs of the colonial powers, and generally, the integrated economic planning of huge regions of Africa from an imperialist standpoint, are beginning to affect the Latin American economy. Therefore, there are two opposing interests. In its future participation in the United Nations, Mexico should couple its interest in the safeguarding of domestic jurisdiction with the need to aid in the liberation of dependent peoples. But this requires that a criterion be worked out and maintained for distinguishing between the different cases.

The San Francisco antecedents do not clearly demonstrate the thesis that the treatment given within a country to national groups or racial minorities does not come under the domestic jurisdiction of the state. Opinions about this are contradictory and the rapporteurs' reports do not seem to be conclusive. Norway, one of the few countries which made written statements on this matter in San Francisco, felt that it was natural to accept the fact that "under the Charter some matters, such as the treatment of racial elements, have been removed from the sphere of domestic jurisdiction."[32] On the other hand, Australia, in explanation of the previously studied amendment which tended to reinforce domestic jurisdiction, said the following:

> If the members of the Organisation really desire to give the Organisation the power to protect minorities, their proper course is either to declare that they recognise the protection of minorities as a matter of legitimate 'international,' and not merely of 'domestic' concern, or to make a formal international convention providing for the proper treatment of minorities.[33]

France was one of the few other countries that also made a declaration about this matter, although its opinion on the scope of the formula finally adopted is not clearly shown in the San Francisco proceedings. According to Lazare Kopelmanas,[34] the drafting of Article 2, paragraph 7, of the Charter exactly follows the wishes of the French government to the effect that the Organization is permitted to intervene in a state's internal affairs when very serious violations of fundamental liberties might in themselves threaten peace.

So much for antecedents. In practice, as we have seen, the Organization has oriented its interpretation of the Charter in many cases toward the protection of national and racial minorities and, to a lesser extent, it has encouraged non-self-governing populations to make some progress in their struggle for independence.

These favorable precedents, together with the Charter's lack of clear provisions and the contradictory nature of the San Francisco

---

[32] *UNCIO Documents*, Vol. VI, p. 431.
[33] *Ibid.*, p. 439.
[34] *Op. cit.*, p. 227n.

antecedents, permit Mexico to base its interpretation of the Charter and its policy on this matter on its general conception of the aims and principles of the Organization. Self-determination of peoples is one of the essential principles of the United Nations, second only, in Mexico's opinion, to the purpose of maintaining peace and international security. It is sufficient to recognize the importance of this principle to decide in favor of the Organization's competence in a situation or dispute which involves the fate of large national or racial groups that seek independence in foreign affairs, domestic autonomy, or decent living conditions within another community. Such a position would not be contrary to the Charter, it would be to Mexico's permanent and immediate interests, and it would be founded upon its tradition.

If Mexico should adopt that position systematically as a line of action,[35] an adequate juridical basis would be indispensable in order to avoid inconsistencies and setting precedents which might affect Mexico in the future. Of course, care would have to be taken not to base that position on the Organization's power to promote respect for human rights (Article 55 of the Charter). It was clearly established in San Francisco that nothing contained in the corresponding chapter of the Charter "can be construed as giving authority to the Organization to intervene in the domestic affairs of member states."[36] The proposed policy would only apply to the systematic and severe persecution of large population groups, with special reference to nationality, race, or religion—that is, situations similar to that found in Germany before the Second World War or

---

[35] In a statement made by the Mexican delegate when the General Assembly was considering the treatment of people of Indian origin in the Union of South Africa, considerations similar to the present ones were used to maintain that: "The case before us does not concern one or two people, nor even thousands of people; it is a problem of races, of vast human groups. The contemporary positive law created in the birth and development of the United Nations is giving rise to a new legal concept concerning the fate of human groups, or groups of men and women." G.A.O.R., 8th Sess., *Ad Hoc* Pol. Ctte., 19th Mtg., 26 Oct. 1953, p. 91.

[36] *UNCIO Documents*, Vol. X, p. 272.

in the present-day South Africa—or to the situation of entire peoples who seek to free themselves from the yoke of colonialism, situations that are explosive in themselves and can endanger peace or create serious international friction. To base the Organization's intervention on respect for human rights would serve as a precedent for undue interference precisely in those cases in which intervention was prohibited by Article 2, paragraph 7 of the Charter.

In other words, it would be necessary to limit this policy to really serious cases. Ultimately, its main basis would be that the primary aim of the Organization is to maintain international peace and security and that situations like those mentioned always present a potential danger. Moreover, it would be necessary to prove that the cases in question really involved the self-determination of peoples. Finally, when dealing with racial groups that evidently did not aspire to independence or self-government, but only sought decent living conditions within another community, it would have to be ascertained whether it was actually a question of different elements in the population, in other words that they were subjected to really discriminatory treatment and systematic segregation, or whether their living conditions, low as they were, did not compare unfavorably with the living conditions of most of the population.[37]

THE PRACTICE OF THE UNITED NATIONS FROM MEXICO'S POINT OF VIEW

Of the cases dealt with in the United Nations in which the principle of domestic jurisdiction[38] was a major issue, Mexico voted for

[37] Nevertheless, it must be granted that the criterion proposed for purposes of differentiating is neither clear nor precise and that the juridical basis for this idea in the Charter is not much more solidly supported than the opposing thesis of the colonial powers. Beyond this question, however, it is a legitimate political position, clearly consistent with the spirit of the Charter, which is not contrary to its letter nor to the legislative antecedents and which satisfies the interests and aspirations of many small countries.

[38] Mexico did not take part in consideration of the case of Czechoslovakia nor in the second phase of the Indonesian case, which were presented to the Security Council when Mexico was not a member.

proposals that implied the Organization's competence in the case of the treatment given the Indians in South Africa and *apartheid*, that is, in cases where the fate of segregated population groups was at stake. Mexico took the same position with respect to the cases of both Tunisia and Morocco. In 1950 Mexico voted against the fundamental paragraphs of a resolution on the observance of human rights in Hungary, Bulgaria, and Romania, on the ground that they violated the domestic jurisdiction of those countries, and Mexico abstained from the resolution as a whole, thus becoming the only Latin American country not to vote affirmatively.

From the Mexican viewpoint, the usefulness of Article 2, paragraph 7, is measured in two opposite directions: on the one hand, it must be asked if the United Nations has been allowed to act in those matters where it was to Mexico's interest that the Organization intervene, that is, in the different aspects of the colonial question and related questions; on the other hand, if the United Nations has been restrained from intervention in the rest of the cases.

As for the first aspect, it must be recognized that the formula has turned out to be broad and flexible enough to authorize in practice an interpretation to protect dependent populations; Article 2, paragraph 7 of the Charter has not paralyzed, although it has sometimes partially hindered, the struggle for independence by the colonial peoples or by those subject to a restricted sovereignty. Mexico's permanent interests have been satisfied to the extent that the Organization has considered itself competent. Undoubtedly, the intervention of the United Nations has been weak and not completely effective; but, in the first place, the Organization's action in these matters is not only limited by the general construction of Article 2, paragraph 7, but also by the Declaration Regarding Non-Self-Governing Territories and by the international trusteeship system of Chapters XI and XII of the Charter. Moreover, in cases not affected by these Chapters, a more energetic intervention by the Organization, in the present international situation, would perhaps have been dangerous. The best guarantee against a conflict over some decisive action of

f

the Organization is the agreement of the great powers. When the five permanent members reached an agreement, even though partial, to decide on the Organization's intervention in the Indonesian case, the matter was finally settled without the outbreak of more widespread hostilities. In the cases of Tunisia and Morocco, when the five great powers did not reach an agreement on the legal possibility and the necessity for intervention, the executive organ, namely, the Security Council, ignored the affair. The Assembly, where unanimous agreement among the great powers is not required, could not take decisive action, which might have endangered peace, because the Charter permits it only to draw up recommendations; in the Assembly, constitutional limitations work in the same way as the veto, that is, they prevent the adoption of serious measures that could endanger peace. In any event, the limited intervention of the Assembly, through recommendations which carry the moral pressure of the international community, has influenced the solution of the cases mentioned.

As for the second aspect of interest to Mexico, Article 2, paragraph 7, has filled partially and in general terms its function of protecting domestic jurisdiction in the other cases presented. Undoubtedly, the principle has not always been respected, but the cases when the Organization has intervened in the internal affairs of its members have not been frequent or serious. In order to gauge its importance, it must be remembered that the formula of domestic jurisdiction does not operate alone, but in relation to the constitutional limitations of the organs empowered to intervene. Thus, the additional guarantee for the state implied in such limitations has either paralyzed the Organization's intervention, or the interference has been reduced to a recommendation.[39] Finally, it is fair to ask whether the viola-

---

[39] According to the Belgian author Joseph Nisot, domestic jurisdiction is protected for still another reason: the United Nations has no absolute power to decide if a matter comes under Article 2, paragraph 7, of the Charter, and the decision of the United Nations may be challenged by a state (this would not have been the case if the words "in the judgment of the Organization" had been inserted in Article 2, paragraph 7, as was proposed at San Francisco

tions of the principle of domestic jurisdiction of the states have been due to the attitude of the member states or to an inadequate construction of Article 2, paragraph 7.

CONCLUSIONS

Mexico's possibilities for proposing changes in the Charter on this subject are limited. In the first place, it might be suggested that law should have more influence in the determination of those questions which should be considered subject to domestic jurisdiction. This possibility is in accord with the general tendency favored by small powers to broaden and strengthen the function of law in the life of the United Nations. But there are few possibilities of eliminating political considerations in this matter; when the intervention of the United Nations is based on the decision that there exists a threat to the peace (latter part of Article 2, paragraph 7 of the Charter), the fundamental consideration to be borne in mind is not the domestic or international character of the matter, a question where law might be relevant, since the Organization would intervene in any event, independently of the character of the matter. When a threat to the peace is invoked as the basis for the intervention, the fundamental question is how to determine whether such a threat really exists; and that can only be done through the Organization weighing

---

by Belgium in an amendment that was defeated). See "Art. 2, Par. 7, of the United Nations Charter as Compared with Art. 15, Par. 8, of the League of Nations Covenant," *The American Journal of International Law*, Vol. 43, No. 4 (Oct. 1949), pp. 776-78.

Mr. Nisot's opinion is not supported; it is not demonstrated that the members voted against the Belgian amendment because they planned to keep for themselves the right to decide which matters came under domestic jurisdiction; on the contrary, it is more likely that many countries voted against the Belgian amendment because they considered it useless, since, obviously, the decision would have to be made "in the judgment of the Organization." It is clear from the San Francisco proceedings that the power to decide on the interpretation of a provision of the Charter, in the case under study and in all others, belongs, in principle, to the organ authorized to apply it. See Lauterpacht, *op. cit.*, pp. 180-83.

actual situations politically; in such cases, the application of law is almost excluded.[40]

In cases when the basis for intervention is not a threat to or a breach of the peace or an act of aggression, legal criteria might be used to determine whether the dispute grew out of an international or domestic matter, but it is not certain that the use of the only methods suitable for such a determination would necessarily result in the strengthening of the reserved domain of states, which small powers desire. In fact, the legal determination of the international or domestic character of a matter might be arrived at in two ways: the first is the codifying of subject matters, and the second is leaving the decision to the International Court of Justice.

As for the first solution, apart from its advantages or disadvantages for Mexico, it is evident that the present moment is not favorable for codifying international law: this is proved by the General Assembly's inability to adopt a single draft drawn up by the International Law Commission. We live in changing times when the validity and force of many of the basic principles of international law are being questioned. It is difficult to think, especially when dealing with a question that is related to all aspects of the idea of sovereignty, that a substantial majority of states would accept the codifying of subject matters; in such conditions, its value would be very limited. But even supposing that it were feasible to accomplish this with some success, probably the very nature of the situation would make it necessary to adopt a criterion for drawing up a systematic classification of domestic and international questions. This criterion would have to be based on whether or not the matter had been regulated by a treaty, either multilateral or bilateral. Since the number of matters regulated by treaties is on the increase, it is probable that the list of matters subject to the competence of the state would be a very reduced one. The adoption of the hypothetical

---

[40] The same thing would happen, *a fortiori*, in the other two situations hypothesized by Article 39—breaches of the peace and acts of aggression—although there would always exist the debatable possibility of defining aggression.

but probable criterion referred to might be a psychological impediment to having the organs responsible for solving this question take into account another important factor,[41] namely, in accordance with what was said at the San Francisco Conference, the fact that a matter may be regulated by a treaty does not necessarily mean that the matter is no longer "essentially"—as distinguished from "solely"—within domestic jurisdiction. Actually, it would not be sufficient to base the competence of the Organization exclusively on whether or not the matter is regulated by a treaty; certainly it is not easy to appreciate the difference between the terms "essentially" and "solely" from a juridical standpoint. A matter is or is not regulated by international law, with no need for further qualifications; but, in view of the evident intention of the authors of the approved formula, and in order not to leave without meaning or application a term like "essentially" that was given so much importance, it must be concluded that this term was meant to introduce not a strictly judicial but rather a political element, which has some psychological value in the solution of specific cases. The incorporation of that element tends to operate in a "conservative" way, safeguarding, as was intended, the reserved domain of states against the international organization. Thus, if only regulation by a treaty is used as the criterion for determining the domestic or international character of a matter—and it is difficult to imagine a different criterion—there will be the risk of considering matters not "essentially" international to be under international jurisdiction, which is not in the interests of small countries.

Decisions on this problem in every case by the International Court of Justice would have the lesser disadvantage of not permanently "freezing" the classification of subject matters in a way that probably would not favor the interests of the small powers. Certainly, the decisions of the Court set important precedents, especially for the Court itself, but since every case is different and since, under Ar-

---

[41] See discussion of the Belgian amendments, *UNCIO Documents*, Vol. VI, pp. 511-12.

ticle 59 of the Statute, the decisions of the Court have no binding force except between the parties and in respect to that particular case, the judicial solution would not have as serious disadvantages as the codification. But in the last analysis the fundamental objection raised above with regard to codification would hold just as true with regard to decision by the Court. The latter would be inclined to consider, according to a strictly juridical criterion, that a matter comes within international jurisdiction when it is in some way regulated by a treaty, and it would probably pay little attention to the political and psychological element found in the spirit of Article 2, paragraph 7, where the term "essentially" is meant to protect domestic jurisdiction and can be appreciated better by a political organ than by the Court.

Another aspect of the application of Article 2, paragraph 7, which might warrant a change in the Charter, is the scope of the Security Council's intervention in cases of threats to the peace, breaches of the peace, or acts of aggression. If the Council decides that there has been a threat to or breach of the peace or an act of aggression, it can intervene under the latter part of Article 2, paragraph 7, even if the situation has arisen from a matter unquestionably within the domestic jurisdiction of a state. But the Council's intervention is limited; it cannot make a declaration concerning the very essence of a dispute or situation which pertains to an internal question, nor can it make recommendations about its solution; it can only take measures to maintain or restore peace. It has been said with reason that this situation is incongruous. The Council cannot maintain or restore peace *in vacuo:* that is, it is impossible to correct a situation without examining and attacking its causes. The inability of the United Nations to propose solutions from the beginning on the essence of the matter may result in latent situations developing into greater conflicts.

The experience of recent years could shed some light on the solution of this problem. On the other hand, its solution also depends on how the purposes of the Organization are understood. If the primary, overriding aim of the United Nations is the unqualified maintenance of peace—a peace characterized solely by the absence of armed conflicts; if only a vague reference to "justice" and "international law" guides the United Nations in making recommendations on the substance of a dispute; if the terms "justice" and "international law" are interpreted and applied by many states more on the basis of political leanings than the merits of the case; if the Organization has frequently had some success in checking hostilities, but has seldom been able to impose a solution to the substance of a dispute; and, finally, if the reserved domain of the state, which after all deserves some protection, is at stake, perhaps it should be concluded that, in the last analysis, it is preferable to limit the functions of the Security Council to the initial phase of maintaining and restoring peace, and to let the restraining force of the Council, imposed *manu militari*, act as a pressure on the parties to find a settlement on the substance by themselves. Nonetheless, an intermediate solution might be possible; the purpose of the present Charter system is to protect domestic jurisdiction against the almost irresistible pressure of the decisions or recommendations of the Security Council. But, undoubtedly, the state's vital interests would not be affected if the Security Council could, as Norway proposed in San Francisco, suggest that the substance of the dispute be submitted to conciliation even though the matter threatening peace should be domestic. This situation was anticipated in Article 11 of the League Covenant and it was applied in 1937 and 1938 (at least with respect to an inquiry) at the Spanish government's request in relation to the Franco rebellion and the German and Italian intervention.[42]

---

[42] See *UNCIO Documents*, Vol. VI, pp. 430-32.

chapter four

The Principle of Universality and the Admission of New Members

The problem of the universality of the United Nations can only be understood in relation to other factors. As Georg Schwarzenberger correctly states, "universality *in vacuo* is meaningless."[1] The number and character of the members of a society are necessarily dependent on the purposes or tasks that they set for themselves and the means of action that they have available. Ultimately no society, including the United Nations, can avoid the following minimum standard: the extent to which the admission of a member can contribute to the attainment of the aims of the society.

This century's experience shows that wars tend to become universal. It would appear natural that an international society to preserve peace would therefore be organized on a universal basis. If all peoples can suffer the effects of war, it would be logical to

---

[1] *Power Politics*, 2nd rev. ed. (New York: Frederick A. Praeger, 1951), p. 430.

suppose that all should help contribute toward avoiding it. It has been rightly said that peace is indivisible. The first impression is therefore favorable to the universality of the Organization. Nevertheless, to recognize that the maintenance of peace is a desire common to all peoples does not suffice to reach a conclusion in favor of the universality of the United Nations. Each state's contribution to the attainment of a common end, and, consequently, the membership of the United Nations, depends not only on the purposes but also on the means of action available to the Organization.

As previously stated, the United Nations has at its disposal three basic means of action to achieve the goal of maintaining peace: first, the establishment of an armed system of collective security to discourage and, if necessary, to eliminate aggression; second, the establishment of adequate mechanisms and procedures for applying the methods of peaceful solution and for setting up a forum to air disputes; and third, the promotion of international co-operation in economic, social, cultural, and humanitarian fields, that is, acting directly, although over a long period, on the causes of war. None of the three means of action, considered separately, is more important than the others; their lesser or greater importance and their respective possible effectiveness depend on the special circumstances of each case in which they act; it is a matter of concurrent means of action. In order to form an opinion on the most desirable membership of the United Nations, one must study the problem in relation to each one of the three means of action discussed.

The effectiveness of a system of collective security greatly depends on the forces available for checking aggression. If collective security is organized within the framework of the United Nations, it would seem natural that the more members contained in the Organization, the more effective the system of collective security would be. Nevertheless, this first sketchy view of the problem does not completely reflect reality. So that this theory would operate in practice, first, the combined forces of all the members of the international community would have to be far superior to those which any one member of the community could mobilize; and, second, the interests of all the members would almost automatically have to coincide for repressing any aggression. Such a situation may have occurred in history and perhaps it will again occur in the future, but it is not the situation which basically prevails at present. The political reality with which the contemporary political and juridical instruments for repressing aggression have to conform consists fundamentally of two blocs of states, with their respective members closely united among themselves, and with military power that, for all practical purposes, will tend to balance out in time, or, at least, reach a point of saturation above which supremacy will no longer matter. If the interests of one of the two greatest powers is vitally affected—independently of whether it is the victim or the author of the aggression—it can only rely for the defense of itself and its group on the manpower and resources of the states with which it is politically associated; this will be true even assuming that the collective security system of the United Nations works in its favor. The "almost bipolar distribution of power centers"[2] which characterizes our world makes it extremely difficult, if not impossible, to marshal overwhelming forces in support of the victim of an aggression, and so to build a universal system of collective security. In the present circumstances, the universality of the United Nations does not necessarily result in the most effective collective security system.

The difficulty of creating an effective system of collective security can at present suggest two opposite conclusions, and it has actually done so. The first, unfavorable to the universality of the United Nations, might be expressed in this way: the possibility of successfully repelling an attack largely depends on the plans and measures previously adopted. If the state which is expected to attack is a member of the international organs charged with planning the col-

---

[2] Alexander W. Rudzinski, "Admission of New Members," *International Conciliation*, No. 480 (April 1952), p. 190.

lective action, its knowledge of the preparations, the procedural obstacles to which it can resort to hamper the collective action, and the fears and doubts that it can sow among the loyal members, would be an obvious disadvantage for organizing collective security. Therefore, the idea of forming a smaller and more homogeneous organization, excluding the Soviet Union and its satellites, has the support of a certain sector of American public opinion. In accordance with this opinion, universality would be a hindrance to and not an advantage for adequately building up collective security and, therefore, for securing peace.

This viewpoint does not sufficiently take into account various decisive factors. In the first place, the organization thus created would only be a military alliance which would necessarily encourage the creation of another rival alliance; in the second place, such an organization would wreck the possibility of utilizing the second means of action of the United Nations which has been appreciably effective, namely, negotiation and mediation within an organism embracing both camps. Moreover, as regards the lesser conflicts, there would be a smaller possibility of resolving them fairly and in the interest of the affected populations; the relative balance of power within the United Nations is a partial guarantee that local conflicts will not be solved to the exclusive interest of any one of the great powers. Finally, the possible moral authority and psychological impact on the rulers of the USSR of decisions taken by an organization representing most nations would be lost.

But the difficulty of creating in these times a universal system of collective security can likewise suggest another conclusion. Mexico has made a special effort to demonstrate its merits during recent years. It is to reinforce and perfect the most feasible means of action of the United Nations at present: the pacific settlement of disputes. Since San Francisco many countries have persisted in emphasizing the possibility of perfecting the techniques of negotiation, conciliation, and mediation. Certainly, the scope of this means of action is limited. If a great power decides to take measures which necessarily lead to war, the procedures for a pacific settlement will fail; but, in the same way, collective security will fail, at least in the form in which it was foreseen, that is, as a universal means of action which basically tends to prevent war, and the reason for the United Nations' existence would disappear. Outside of the above-mentioned possibility, and even in some cases where the interest of a great power is involved, the procedures for pacific settlement, if pursued by the United Nations with more energy and effectiveness, could contribute substantially to the maintenance of peace.

If the problem of United Nations membership is looked at from the point of view of pacific settlement of disputes, undoubtedly the conclusion points to the universality of the Organization. First, all conditions being equal, the United Nations can exert more pressure on those states which, on entering, voluntarily committed themselves to settle their disputes amicably by pacific means than it can exert on those outside the Organization; secondly, new members can offer new points of view and solutions to settle pending disputes, turning the Organization away from courses which appear futile and, at any rate, they can surely become eventually a new factor of equilibrium and mediation in the United Nations.

The third means of action available to the United Nations for maintaining peace, namely, international co-operation in economic, social, cultural, and humanitarian fields, would also be reinforced by the universality of the Organization. New members do not just contribute new and valuable experience and resources, but their entrance permits the United Nations to exert on them a more direct influence in those fields. It facilitates international coordination of important activities and it helps strengthen an international spirit.

The study of the aims and means of action of the United Nations suggests the conclusion that the Organization should incline toward universality. The provisions of the Charter, the practice of the Organization, and the suggestions to be proposed will be examined in the light of this consideration.

MEXICO'S ATTITUDE AT SAN FRANCISCO

The provisions of the League of Nations Covenant set stricter formal requirements for admission than the United Nations Charter in that the former established as a condition that the candidate give "effective guaranties of its sincere intention to observe its international obligations, and . . . accept such regulations as may be prescribed by the League in regard to its military, naval and air forces and armaments." Nevertheless, the course of events favored in practice a liberal interpretation of the Covenant. The need to balance the increasing power of the fascist states was an influence in facilitating the admission of new members.

At the San Francisco Conference, several Latin American states, especially Mexico and Uruguay, maintained that the Organization being created should be universal from the beginning. The Dumbarton Oaks Proposals, which in turn reproduced the Moscow Declaration of 30 October 1943, restricted admission to "peace-loving states." Before the Conference, in the "Opinion of the Department of Foreign Relations of Mexico concerning the Dumbarton Oaks Proposals,"[3] Mexico had criticized the provisions of the proposals, stating that the selective entrance system placed extremely grave obstacles in the way of the achievement of the aims of the new Organization. In place of the restricted admission and voluntary withdrawal system, Mexico proposed an Organization with unrestricted admission in which "all States, Dominions and Colonies having a free government" would participate without meeting prior conditions.[4] This phrase (which was similar to the one used in the League Covenant describing the legal status of eligible applicants) was not an especially apt one in view of the contradiction between

---

[3] *Documents of the United Nations Conference on International Organization, San Francisco, 1945* (New York: United Nations Information Organization, 1945), Vol. III, pp. 54-174. Hereinafter referred to as *UNCIO Documents*.

[4] *UNCIO Documents*, Vol. III, pp. 60-61.

colonial status and "free government";[5] but, on the other hand, it had the advantage of proposing an authentically universal Organization. Mexico held that the Organization should at all times include all existing states, and that therefore the Charter should not establish provisions for the exclusion or voluntary withdrawal of any state. Likewise, a list of the states existing at the time of the setting up of the Organization was to be appended to the Charter. For the purpose of reinforcing the principle of universality, it was also proposed that Chapter XII of the proposals concerning the relations between the victorious powers and the enemy states during the Second World War should appear in a separate protocol, so that the Charter, even in its transitory provisions, would not give the impression of discriminating against any state. For the same reason, the name "Permanent Union of Nations" was proposed for the Organization, or a similar one which would not imply discrimination against any state, since the name United Nations had become identified with the victorious powers during the war. The only exception made to the obligation of being a member of the Organization was for those states of such small area that they could not assume the responsibilities stipulated in the Charter (for example, San Marino, Monaco, Liechtenstein, and Andorra).

But in its later "Amendments to the Dumbarton Oaks Proposals," Mexico accepted the limitation that only "peace-loving" states (instead of "all States") should have the *opportunity* of becoming members (instead of the *obligation*), although it added that "the tendency should be to make the Organization, in due course, include all the Members of the Community of Nations, without any State being lawfully entitled to remain outside the Organization."[6] At San Francisco, the principle of unrestricted universality was defended most stubbornly and consistently by Uruguay.

---

[5] During the League's existence, not a single colony presented an application for membership.

[6] *UNCIO Documents*, Vol. III, p. 180.

Article 4 of the Charter finally established the following conditions for admitting an applicant to the United Nations: "an applicant must (1) be a State; (2) be peace-loving; (3) accept the obligations of the Charter; (4) be able to carry out these obligations; and (5) be willing to do so."[7] The admission of applicants is effected by a decision of the General Assembly upon the recommendation of the Security Council. In addition, Articles 5 and 6 of the Charter provide for the suspension of the rights and privileges inherent in membership and definite expulsion. The Charter does not include any passage on voluntary withdrawal; nonetheless, an interpretative commentary on the Charter, which was approved at San Francisco, provides that "If, however, a Member because of exceptional circumstances feels constrained to withdraw, and leave the burden of maintaining international peace and security on the other Members, it is not the purpose of the Organization to compel that Member to continue its cooperation in the Organization"; the following non-exhaustive "exceptional circumstances" are mentioned: inability of the Organization to maintain peace and Charter amendments which the state finds itself unable to accept.[8] Finally, the Charter did not establish the specific factors to be taken into account in determining whether or not a state requesting admission to the organization is peace-loving.[9]

The Potsdam Declaration of 2 August 1945, although *res inter alios acta* with regard to the states that did not sign it, contains

[7] Interpretation of Article 4 of the Charter given by the International Court of Justice in its Advisory Opinion of 28 May 1948. See I.C.J., *Reports of Judgments, Advisory Opinions and Orders, 1947-1948*, p. 62.

[8] *UNCIO Documents*, Vol. VII, pp. 266-67.

[9] In connection with this, the report of the Rapporteur of the Committee concerned with provisions on membership (Committee 1/2) states: "The Committee did not feel it should recommend the enumeration of the elements which were to be taken into consideration. It considered the difficulties which would arise in evaluating the political institutions of States and feared that the mention in the Charter of a study of [the admission procedure] would be a breach of the principle of non-intervention, or if preferred, of non-interference. This does not imply, however, that in passing upon the admission of a new member, considerations of all kinds cannot be brought into account." (*UNCIO Documents*, Vol. VII, p. 326.)

important qualifications for the admission of new members which obligate, at least morally, the governments of the United States, the Soviet Union, and Great Britain. The three governments asserted that Franco Spain should not be admitted; they offered to support the applications of states that were neutral during the war and to favor the admission of ex-enemy states (Bulgaria, Finland, Hungary, Romania, and Italy), once peace treaties with "recognized democratic governments" in those states were signed.[10]

ANALYSIS OF THE MEMBERSHIP REQUIREMENTS

In the first place, what is meant by "peace-loving state"? Naturally, it is an extremely subjective concept which permits all kinds of interpretations. Peoples are normally peace-loving but governments, although they generally do not want war, sometimes use means of action that can give rise to conflicts. Only fascist governments in the recent past have used and defended war as a national political instrument. Probably many representatives at San Francisco mentally associated the "non-peace-loving" state with the then recent and painful memories of fascist barbarism.[11] It must be remembered that the United Nations were originally a military coalition against the fascist states. Undoubtedly, the term "peace-loving state" is largely due to the political climate that prevailed when the Charter was drawn up.

---

[10] In San Francisco, Mexico proposed an interpretative commentary on the chapter relative to the admission of new members, which, although drafted in general terms, referred to the exclusion of Franco Spain from the United Nations. The text of the interpretative commentary is as follows: "It is the understanding of the delegation of Mexico that paragraph 2 of Chapter III [Article 4, Chapter II of the Charter] cannot be applied to the states whose regimes have been established with the help of military forces belonging to the countries which have waged war against the United Nations, as long as those regimes are in power." This commentary was unanimously approved by the San Francisco Conference. *UNCIO Documents*, Vol. I, pp. 615-16.

[11] John MacLaurin, *The United Nations and Power Politics* (New York: Harper & Bros., 1951), p. 114.

Other meanings have also been given to the term "peace-loving state." For example, the peace-loving state has been identified with the democratic state. When the League was created, there was a marked tendency among the statesmen of that time to identify the two concepts. In San Francisco the problem presented new facts. Should "democratic" only be understood to mean the individualistic democratic-bourgeois liberal state, that is, only that category known in political science as the *"Etat de Droit,"* with all its historical characteristics, such as the division of powers, the multi-party system, the emphasis on individual rights, the universal political representation based on the individual "citizen," etc.?[12] Or should it also include the new types of functional, economic, and "popular" democracy? In any case, the need to build the Organization on the participation of all the great powers, including the USSR, made it useless to bring up the problem. Moreover, if only "democratic" states were accepted, it would also be necessary to exclude many states, among others, a good many Latin American states.

It might also be thought that the term "peace-loving state" referred to those states that respect human rights. Undoubtedly, the domestic regime of a state, and especially the way fundamental liberties are respected, can influence its international conduct. Nonetheless, for the purposes of Article 4 of the Charter, lack of respect for human rights can only be relevant if it poses a real and immediate danger to international peace; otherwise, respect for human rights would become an independent and distinct requirement for the admission of new members, which would be contrary to Article 4 of the Charter.

Actually, it is impossible to give a precise or single meaning to the term used in the Charter. At San Francisco it was recognized—and it could not have been otherwise—that the Security Council and

---

[12] According to G. Schwarzenberger (*Power Politics, op. cit.,* p. 439), whoever maintains that democratic communities have a monopoly on being peace-loving would have to overlook the aggressiveness of the great North American democracy and French Jacobinism in the nineteenth century.

g

the General Assembly would have wide latitude for judging which specific factors should be taken into account for the admission of new members. The Advisory Opinion of the International Court of Justice on 28 May 1948[13] did not go far toward a solution of the problem. Of course, the Court recognized that states could not decide this question by invoking factors different from those contained in the exhaustive list of limiting factors set forth in Article 4 of the Charter, and, especially, by making their consent dependent on the entrance of other states. But this does not help (nor could it have done so) in solving the problem of how to interpret those requirements which the Charter *does* establish, such as the quality of being a peace-loving state.[14]

---

[13] The request for an Advisory Opinion was due to the Soviet Union's refusal to give its consent to the admission of several states, unless the Western members of the Council would not, in turn, oppose the admission of the Communist applicants. In the case of Italy, the Soviet Union clearly stated this motive before the Council. The General Assembly put these two questions to the Court: "Is a Member . . . juridically entitled to make its consent to the admission dependent on conditions not expressly provided by paragraph 1 of the said Article [4]? In particular, can such a Member, while it recognizes the conditions set forth in that provision to be fulfilled by the State concerned, subject its affirmative vote to the additional condition that other States be admitted to membership in the United Nations together with that State?" General Assembly Resolution 113(II)B, 17 Nov. 1947. The Court, by nine votes to six, answered both questions negatively.

[14] Actually, the possibility of interpreting the membership requirements in the broadest fashion amounts to authorizing a state "to make its consent dependent" on conditions not provided for in Article 4 of the Charter, when it pronounces itself on the admission of an applicant. The judges who delivered a Dissenting Opinion (French, Polish, British, and Canadian) gave an affirmative answer to the Assembly's questions, stating that: "A Member . . . called upon to pronounce itself by its vote . . . on the admission of a State . . . is participating in a political decision and is therefore legally entitled to make its consent to the admission dependent on any political considerations which seem to it to be relevant." I.C.J., *Reports of Judgments, Advisory Opinions and Orders, 1947-1948*, p. 92.
The majority opinion of the Court to the effect that a state cannot make its consent dependent on considerations other than those specified in the Charter inevitably leads to this conclusion: a member can act as it pleases if it is careful not to state its motives. It must be inferred from the Dissenting Opinion that the motives of a state for opposing the admission of an applicant are not to be expressed "juridically" in the statements and arguments which are set forth, but in the vote.

Under these circumstances, in view of the enormous latitude of judgment permitted by Article 4 and of the particularly political character of the problem, it might be held that, for purposes of admission of new members, a peace-loving state is one which is designated as such at the discretion of both the Security Council and the General Assembly, in accordance with their respective voting procedures. In any event, the lack of juridical directives to determine this objectively amounts to the same thing.

The problem could also be viewed from the standpoint of which considerations *should* be borne in mind by the members called upon to make a decision on this matter: To look at the problem from this angle is to ask oneself how the aims of the Organization are best achieved. We have previously discussed the problem of universality in relation to the purposes and the means of action available to the United Nations for achieving its essential aim of maintaining peace. In this regard, there can be no doubt as to the advisability of having a large number of countries participate in the tasks of the Organization. For that reason, it would be desirable to have the members, when deciding on this question, interpret as liberally and generously as possible the requirements of Article 4 for the admission of new members. The most practical way to accomplish this, since it would largely avoid political considerations, would be to use entirely formal criteria. Thus, a peace-loving state might be one that had had no decisions rendered against it by any competent organ of the United Nations, declaring it an aggressor or guilty of a breach of the peace, or one that was not at war with any member state.

As for other requirements established in Article 4, namely, that the applicant accept the obligations of the Charter and be willing to carry them out in practice (the two requirements are one), the problem presents no difficulty. By their very nature, these requirements are fulfilled through a formal declaration to that effect as prescribed by the Charter. The last condition, that the applicant be able to carry out the obligations of the Charter, if interpreted in the same spirit of promoting universality, could be solved by using the following criteria: states considered unable to carry out the obligations of the Charter would be those that could not do so because of their small size (Monaco, San Marino, and Liechtenstein),[15] or because, like Switzerland, they are prevented by their status of permanent neutrality from assuming the obligation imposed by the Charter to lend military co-operation against the aggressor.[16] Likewise, it might be stated that the extreme domestic instability of a regime makes it unable to fulfil the obligations of the Charter; thus, it could be maintained that the applications of those states that are in a state of civil war are premature.

THE PRACTICE OF THE UNITED NATIONS

The lack of a solution to the problem of admission of new members was for many years one of the greatest failures of the Organization. Even though it did not represent a danger to peace, it created an

---

[15] Smallness of area in itself is not an obstacle to the fulfilment of the obligations of the Charter, but the extreme dependence of these small states on their larger neighbors prevents their participation as sovereign states at least in the political activities of the international agencies. The League of Nations examined the applications of the three "states of small area": Monaco, San Marino, and Liechtenstein. The applications of the first two were withdrawn before the Assembly came to a decision. The third application was rejected in the Assembly by a vote of 28 votes to 1. The Assembly deemed that Liechtenstein, although a "sovereign State," had delegated some aspects of its sovereignty to other powers and apparently could not fulfil the international obligations derived from the Covenant. League of Nations, Records of the 1st Assembly, 28th Plenary Mtg., 17 Dec. 1920, pp. 652 and 667-68.

[16] In spite of its status of permanent neutrality, Switzerland was admitted to the League of Nations. The Council, "while affirming that the conception of neutrality of the Members of the League is incompatible with the principle that all Members will be obliged to co-operate in enforcing respect for their engagements, recognise[d] that Switzerland is in a unique situation, based on a tradition of several centuries which has been explicitly incorporated in the Law of Nations . . ." agreed that Switzerland would "not be obliged to take part in any military action or to allow the passage of foreign troops or the preparation of military operations within her territory." League of Nations, *Official Journal*, No. 2, March 1920, pp. 57-58. A similar solution would hardly be consistent with the more severe enforcement system of the United Nations Charter.

impasse which contributed to international friction and hindered the efficient work of the United Nations.

Between 1946 and 1955, more than thirty states applied for membership. Of these, only nine had attained membership by 1955, and they were mainly recently created states and some that were neutral during the last war; that is, states that appeared as not unconditionally committed to either of the two great coalitions when they were admitted. They were the following: Afghanistan, Iceland, Thailand (once its pending dispute with France was settled), Sweden, Yemen, Pakistan, Union of Burma, Israel, and Indonesia. Up to 1955, the United Nations had not approved the applications of the following States: People's Republic of Albania, Austria, Bulgaria, Cambodia, Ceylon, Finland, Hungary, Ireland, Italy, Japan, The Hashemite Kingdom of Jordan, Democratic People's Republic of Korea (North Korea), Republic of Korea (South Korea), Laos, Libya, Mongolian People's Republic, Nepal, Portugal, Romania, Spain, Vietnam, and the Democratic Republic of Vietnam.

Most of the applicants were considered by the Security Council between 1946 and 1947, and again in the summer of 1949. The result was always the same: the applicants sponsored by Western countries were vetoed by the Soviet Union; the applicants sponsored by the Soviet Union did not win enough votes, because most of the Western states voted against them or abstained (since the resolutions of the Security Council require seven affirmative votes, abstention in these cases amounts to a negative vote). In that way, the admission of the two groups was blocked.

To solve the difficulty, the United States proposed in 1946 that all the applicants for membership be admitted *en bloc*.[17] The Report by the President of the United States to Congress on the participation of the United States in the United Nations in 1946, states that, "in an effort to promote universality of membership in the United Nations to every extent consistent with the Charter, the United

---

[17] Security Council, Official Records (S.C.O.R.): 1st Yr., 2nd Series, 53rd Mtg., 16 Aug. 1946, pp. 42-43.

States, waiving certain doubts entertained with respect to whether Albania and the Mongolian People's Republic met the requisite qualifications, proposed that all eight applicants be admitted *en bloc*."[18] Mexico, then a member of the Security Council, warmly supported the idea of simultaneous admission of all the candidates.[19] The proposal was likewise supported by the Secretary-General and by five countries in addition to the United States and Mexico; on the other hand, the Soviet Union strongly opposed it.[20] In view of the Soviet opposition, the United States withdrew its proposal; nevertheless, since it had had substantial support, Mexico resubmitted the proposal a little later on its own account, although it had to withdraw it for the same reason.

During the year that it was a member of the Security Council, Mexico showed itself to be decidedly in favor of universality. It maintained that the Council was not competent to impose criteria different from those specifically set forth in the Charter. Likewise, it proposed that instead of asking for proof that a state was peace-loving, a state would have to be demonstrated not to be, thus turning the burden of proof in the applicant's favor. Mexico, moreover, voted for the admission of every one of the applicants, including Albania and the Mongolian People's Republic.

It was not long before the situation changed radically. Two years later, the USSR proposed to the Security Council that all the candidates be admitted simultaneously, *en bloc*, the solution which

---

[18] U.S. Dept. of State, *Report by the President to the Congress for the Year 1946 on the United States and the United Nations*, Publication 2735 (Washington: Govt. Printing Office, 1947), pp. 39-40.

[19] See statement by the Mexican delegate, S.C.O.R., 1st Yr., 2nd Series, 53rd Mtg., 16 Aug. 1946, pp. 45-46.

[20] The representative of the USSR (Mr. Gromyko) said in this connection: "I cannot agree that we should adopt resolutions for the wholesale admission to the Organization of all countries who have applied for membership. Countries cannot be regarded as things and dealt with in accordance with a standard measure. When we discuss the question of admission to the Organization, we are bound to discuss each concrete application separately, taking into consideration all the facts and circumstances relating to the application in question." *Ibid.*, 28 Aug. 1946, p. 47.

had been previously suggested by the United States and rejected by the USSR.[21] This proposal was rejected by the representatives of the United States and Great Britain, who called it "horse trading" and maintained that every application should be considered on its own merits. A short while later, at the fourth session of the Assembly, the USSR made another proposal aiming at simultaneous admission, *en bloc*, of all the pending states.[22] Mexico, together with other countries, supported the Soviet proposal, deeming it a suitable way to achieve universality since it permitted the admission of all candidates.

Since the Charter's provisions do not facilitate the admission of new members and since, in practice, the antagonism between the great powers blocked the desirable entrance of all the candidates, there was clearly no other solution but simultaneous admission. In the beginning, the United States understood the nature of the problem and tried to give it a suitable solution. Its rejection by the Soviet Union at that time prevented the only feasible solution, although as has already been noted, it later was in turn to present the same solution. The refusal of the United States to accept a political compromise in this matter and the persistent search of some Latin American countries for a solution by means obviously contrary to the Charter[23] prevented the participation of many can-

---

[21] The Soviet delegate said the following: "The USSR delegation deems it essential that the question of the admission of new Members should be solved forthwith. To facilitate the solution of this question, the Government of the Soviet Union is submitting a proposal for the simultaneous admission to membership in the United Nations of all the twelve States whose applications have been repeatedly examined. Though there are serious grounds for objecting to the admission to membership in the United Nations of some of the above-mentioned countries, the Soviet Union is prepared to withdraw its objections to their admission in order to facilitate the solution of the question of the admission of new Members, provided that no discrimination will take place in respect of Albania, the Mongolian People's Republic, Bulgaria, Romania and Hungary . . . as they comply with all the requirements for admission set forth in the Charter." S.C.O.R., 4th Yr., No. 31, 428th Mtg., 21 June 1949, pp. 11-12.

[22] General Assembly, Official Records (G.A.O.R.): 4th Sess., *Ad Hoc* Pol. Ctte., Annex, Vol. I, p. 8.

[23] See below, pp. 92-93.

didates in the activity of the Organization for a number of years. The two great powers placed the responsibility on each other.

The American point of view could, apparently, have more moral justification. Certainly, the admission of the Western candidates was prevented by the vote of a single state, while the Soviet candidates lacked the required majority in the Council. Nevertheless, the numerical disproportion was misleading. The usual membership of the Security Council is not truly "representative." A proof of this is that the idea of simultaneous admission always received a higher proportion of votes in the Assembly than in the Security Council.[24] As was so well expressed by the Philippines and Egypt in an explanatory Memorandum on the matter,[25] in practice an equation has been reached which reflects the political and juridical reality of the Security Council and which can be formulated: one veto equals four abstentions. The veto has become the great "equalizer."

In the General Assembly, the treatment of the problem followed different lines from those of the Security Council. A fundamentally Latin American trend of thought favored an interpretation of the Charter (contrary to the terms specified in Article 4) according to which the General Assembly could pronounce itself finally and definitely on the admission of a candidate even without the favorable recommendation of the Security Council, whether because the applicant had been vetoed or because it had not obtained the required majority. This tendency ended in a new request for an Advisory Opinion of the International Court of Justice. On 3 March 1950, by 12 votes to 2, the Court decided that the Assembly could not decide on the admission of a state without the prior *positive* recommendation of the Security Council.[26] Probably in view of this

---

[24] See the General Assembly vote referred to on p. 93.
[25] Report of the Special Committee on Admission of New Members. See G.A.O.R., 8th Sess., Annexes: Agenda item 22, p. 19.
[26] I.C.J., *Reports of Judgments, Advisory Opinions and Orders, 1950*, p. 10.

failure, the draft resolution proposing that the Assembly recommend reconsideration of all the applications to the Council received a surprising number of votes in the sixth session of the Assembly in 1951 (22 against 21, with 16 abstentions), although it did not obtain the two-thirds majority necessary for adoption.

Again, in 1952, several Latin American countries continued insisting on solving the problem by means of an unorthodox interpretation of Article 4 of the Charter. A Special Committee on Admission of New Members was established to study the problem as a whole, although actually it occupied itself almost exclusively with the different proposals presented by Peru, the Central American states, and Argentina. The solutions proposed by the Latin American countries were to consider the question of the admission of new members as a procedural question and not as a substantive one in the Security Council, making the veto inapplicable; or to maintain that the Assembly could take a final decision, even without a favorable recommendation by the Security Council. Certainly to the surprise of the Latin American countries sponsoring this resolution and, in any event, to their great disillusionment, the four permanent members of the Council which formed part of the Committee (the Soviet Union was not represented), held a different opinion, that is they considered that the question was substantive, that the veto was therefore applicable, and that the Assembly could not decide on the admission of new states without the prior and favorable recommendation of the Council.[27]

The establishment of this Committee represented the maximum effort made to solve the problem outside the Charter, as was proposed by some Latin American countries. The negative conclusions of the Committee were perhaps the greatest stimulus to solving this matter through the only feasible channel, that is, through negotiation among the permanent members of the Security Council.

---

[27] G.A.O.R., 8th Sess., Annexes: Agenda item 22, p. 16.

CONCLUSIONS

After eight years of failure, universality, applied almost un-
restrictedly, was the only solution possible, as Mexico maintained
at San Francisco. The Secretary of State of the United States himself came to recognize this. In 1950, before he assumed his present
office, John Foster Dulles wrote the following:

> I have now come to believe that the United Nations will best
> serve the cause of peace if its Assembly is representative of
> what the world actually is, and not merely representative of
> the parts which we like. Therefore, we ought to be willing
> that all the nations should be members without attempting
> to appraise closely those which are "good" and those which
> are "bad". . . .
>
> Some of the present member nations, and others that might
> become members, have governments that are not representa-
> tive of the people. But if in fact they are "governments"—that
> is, if they "govern"—then they have a power which should be
> represented in any organization that purports to mirror world
> reality. . . .
>
> If the United Nations membership were made substantially
> universal, that might end a preponderant voting superiority
> of the United States and its friends which, while pleasant, is
> somewhat fictitious.
>
> Communist governments today dominate more than 30 per
> cent of the population of the world. We may not like that
> fact; indeed, we do not like it at all. But if we want to have
> a *world* organization, then it should be representative of the
> world as it is.[28]

Within the present system of the Charter and from a practical
viewpoint, the ideas of Mr. Dulles might be translated, as we have
previously suggested, into a restrictive and formal interpretation of
Article 4 of the Charter; that is, only formal criteria should be
used (as opposed to substantive criteria of a political nature) in the

---

[28] *War or Peace* (New York: Macmillan, 1950), p. 190.

application of the requirements specified by the Charter for admission. Thus, a "peace-loving" state might be understood as a state which has never had a competent organ of the United Nations declare it aggressor or guilty of a breach of the peace. To satisfy the requirement that a state be willing to carry out the obligations of the Charter, it would be sufficient to have its application for membership contain its categorical and avowed offer to fulfil the purposes and principles of the Organization. As regards the requirement that the applicant be able to carry out the obligations of the Charter, only certain objective situations should be taken into account, such as those states that would be unable to do so because of their small size, or those with a permanent neutrality status, like Switzerland, which would prevent them from giving the cooperation demanded by the Charter for the application of enforcement measures.

As for the possibility of amendments to the Charter, Mexico should propose, when the eventual review conference is held, that the United Nations be organized in the future on the basis of universality, requiring only that the applicant have the characteristic institutions and other conditions specified by international law for an independent state. The studies which the Assembly has been making on the colonial problem and the "factors" which distinguish and characterize different political groups might serve as guides for this purpose. In order to make a judgment on the most suitable way to propose the drafting of the corresponding article of the Charter on the admission of new members, it might be necessary to know the final result of those studies and to observe the incidence of those "factors" in the solution of the problem of dependent peoples. Also a complementary solution might be provided for in doubtful cases, namely, a request that the International Court of Justice pronounce itself on whether or not an applicant was a "state."

chapter five

Collective Security

ASSUMPTIONS OF COLLECTIVE SECURITY

Collective security—the maintenance of international peace by collective action—rests on several assumptions, some of which are no different from those permitting the preservation of public order and peace within states. Common to both spheres are: the existence of standards which regulate the relations of the members of the group; the common belief that respect for these standards and, fundamentally, for the state of things which they reflect, is beneficial to each individual and to the group; the anticipation that at any moment a member might violate the standards and harm others or all of the group; and finally, the prior acceptance of the consequences and sacrifices implied in the necessity for anticipating and applying sanctions against violations of the standards. On the other hand, the situation is different as to the authority which maintains or restores order. Within states, an authority over and above the members—one in which they do not *directly* participate—enforces its decisions by means of the use of its *own* resources and without necessarily requiring the voluntary co-operation of each individual. In the international order there is nothing similar. There is no superstate authority over the members of the group, having an autonomous will of its own which may be different from the sum of the wills of the states. The states participate directly in each decision and their collaboration is necessary for applying the decisions on each occasion, since the international authority lacks its own means of action. In brief, on an international plane, government and governed are confused. International authority is only the union of those countries which at the same time dictate and are the object of their own decisions.

Naturally, the present difficulty of creating a real international "authority,"[1] that is, of establishing a federation of states, is the greatest obstacle to the complete effectiveness of an international system of collective security. Supporters of world government base their criticism of the United Nations on the evident fact that the Organization lacks the powers which they deem necessary, and they propose an obvious solution: the abandonment of state sovereignty to the extent necessary to give sufficient powers to a superstate authority so that it can maintain international order by itself. Those who try not to confuse a wish with reality and agree that at present, however desirable it might be, the states are not willing to give up a larger measure of their sovereignty are obliged to pose the problem of collective security in more limited and difficult terms.

It is not impossible in itself, even outside a federal organization, to establish a sufficiently effective system of collective security if two other factors are present which normally appear in the domestic sphere, but only occasionally in the international sphere: first, a relative homogeneity of the members of the group, and second, a broad enough dispersal of the real factors of power to prevent any

[1] See Chapter 2.

individual member from blocking or defeating the concerted action of the others.[2] Normally, within sufficiently integrated national communities, there do not exist opposing interests of ways of life and ideals which might imperil the very existence of important sectors of the population; the similarities are greater than the differences between social groups; the minorities accept the majority decisions because the latter, if they are to be applied to the entire population, must necessarily take into account to a great extent certain elements common to all the group. A society which is deeply divided on vital questions could not survive as a unit. As for the second assumption, generally, in the modern state no individual forces exist powerful enough to oppose the entire state community. When one of these assumptions is absent, inevitably there is a break in the state order.

What happens in the international sphere is not fundamentally different. The classic Wilsonian conception of collective security is based on the above assumptions, although only now, with certain historical perspective and new terms of comparison (the second postwar period), is it possible to understand this fully and judge the importance that such assumptions had in their time. The membership of the Genevan society was relatively homogeneous; almost all the members of the League lived under the aegis of capitalist democracy. The entrance of the Soviet Union signified the late appearance of a heterogeneous element, but not powerful enough (due to its isolation and lack of the necessary force to proclaim violently its new philosophy beyond its frontiers) to destroy the fundamental unity of the group. In 1920, moreover, the world's forces were more or less distributed. The international oligarchy included no less than six great powers, with relatively differentiated political interests. Under those conditions, it was possible to hope that the collective security system of the Covenant would function almost automatically because of the very nature of things. If a state

---

[2] René de Lacharrière, "L'action des Nations Unies pour la Sécurité et pour la Paix," *Politique Etrangère*, Vol. XVIII, No. 4 (Sept.-Oct. 1953), pp. 317 ff. Some of the viewpoints presented in this chapter are inspired by de Lacharrière's original and intelligent study.

committed an aggression, it was foreseeable that it would be to the interest of all the members, due to the absence of closely knit blocs, to join in repressing it. Concerted aid would be given almost spontaneously to the victim. And the resultant coalition would have at its disposal a much greater strength than that available to any individual member of the League.

The failure of the League of Nations has been explained in several ways. It has been said that the obligations imposed on the members to come to the defense of the victim were not binding enough, especially as regards military sanctions; the universal veto and other characteristics of the Covenant have also been mentioned. But the failure could also be explained more realistically. When an alliance (the Axis) was formed strong enough to balance the forces of the democratic countries which defended the status quo, the essential assumption of every collective security system disappeared, that is, the necessary fragmentation of political and military forces. The automatic reaction, concerted and universal, in defense of the victims of aggression (Ethiopia, Austria, and Czechoslovakia) became an empty abstraction within a dual, or at least, scarcely fragmented society.

Our epoch does not offer suitable conditions for the establishment of a universal, and therefore effective, collective security system, according to the classic pattern. At present, neither of the two specified assumptions is fulfilled. The postwar world is divided into two blocs of states moved by opposing ideologies and disposing of like military power. As long as there is no synthesis to furnish the homogeneity necessary for an international society or as long as no bloc definitely dominates the other, it will be impossible to have a minority of states voluntarily submit matters vital to their national security to majority decisions which probably reflect sentiments and interests dissimilar to their own. On the other hand, the bipolar distribution of forces does not permit the accumulation of enough strength to defeat the aggressor decisively. If a state belonging to one of the two blocs is attacked by the other, the former, at best, would only have available the resources of his own side for repelling the aggressor.

The Korean war clearly demonstrated the magnitude of the obstacles in our epoch working against the efficient functioning of collective security. Collective action, in view of the real power of the minority, did not result either in the submission of the aggressor or in a permanent political settlement of the problem, but at most, in a temporary and precarious military armistice reflecting the balance of forces between the two great world coalitions.

In the absence of the two assumptions mentioned, it is impossible to base world security on the presumption that all states, because it would naturally be to their interest, would come to the aid of the victim, whether or not the obligations of the members were reinforced or the voting rules changed. The problem is not one of application but of initial conception. While the world continues divided into two antagonistic coalitions which retain almost the whole of world power, world security and peace depend on the efforts made by the two blocs to rise above their opposing interests and arrive at voluntary agreements. In the absence of those agreements, only collective impotence remains. In practice, our world has been obliged to retrogress to a period prior to the League, when the only security was the possibility of defense with one's own resources and those of one's allies, that is, the period of balanced alliances. The system of inter-American security (Rio de Janeiro Treaty), the North Atlantic Treaty Organization, and the system of alliances among the members of the Soviet bloc are only crude expressions of collective security in our epoch. Collective self-defense, established in Article 51 of the Charter as an exceptional escape clause, has become the basis of collective security.

This unfortunate situation, which certainly was foreseeable when the Charter was signed in 1945, gives rise to doubt whether it would not have been preferable at that time, instead of seeking the impossible universalization of collective security, to recognize openly the force of these new realities and to build the world security system on the recognition of limited interstate communities. Scarcely a few years after the creation of the United Nations, collective security has been fundamentally reduced to just that. Perhaps it would have been preferable to depart radically from the League of Nations pattern, to think in terms of partial communities, to try to organize them on natural bases, that is, authentically regional—this was President Roosevelt's original conception of the United Nations—to attempt to coordinate to some extent their respective functions within the universal organization, avoiding anarchical actions outside the Organization, and, above all, to come to an understanding among the great powers from the start on their respective spheres of influence, as the Soviet Union initially proposed. Naturally, it is practically impossible to know what would have happened if collective security had been organized on such bases. It is merely desirable to recall that it was one of the possible alternatives at that time.

Outside of that possibility, which basically did not inspire the San Francisco Charter, only a last retreat was left to collective security: voluntary agreement between the two great coalitions in all questions relative to maintaining peace. This is the guiding principle of the San Francisco Charter. If an agreement were reached, it would be possible to preserve peace; if not, and if the matter were sufficiently serious, war would be brought on. The authors of the Charter frankly recognized this.[3] At present, no political or juridical instrument is conceivable which could evade the agree-

[3] The Secretary of State of the United States, Mr. Stettinius, speaking before the Committee on Foreign Relations of the United States Senate which was debating the approval of the United Nations Charter, said the following: "I submit that these five nations [the five permanent members of the Security Council], possessing most of the world's power to break or preserve peace, must agree and act together if peace is to be maintained . . . What would happen if one of the five permanent members used the unanimity rule to veto enforcement action against itself? The answer is plain. If one of these nations ever embarked upon a course of aggression, a major war would result, no matter what the membership and voting provisions of the Security Council might be." U.S. Senate, *Hearings Before the Ctte. on Foreign Relations on the Charter of the United Nations . . .* , 79th Cong., 1st Sess., 9-13 July 1945 (Washington: U.S. Govt. Printing Office, 1945), p. 250.

h

ment of the two great blocs. In peacetime, there is no substitute for unanimity of the great powers.

POSTULATES OF THE UNITED NATIONS SYSTEM

What is the basic postulate of the collective security system of the Charter?

It has been repeated, almost as an axiom, that agreement among the great powers is the postulate of collective security. According to the majority of authors, the entire system for preserving peace rests on this conception or reasoning which the authors of the Charter used as a basis: unanimous agreement among the great powers, which was created and maintained during the whole war and even for the drawing up of the Charter, would likewise endure in the future for the preservation of peace. The five great powers would be equally interested in harmonizing their occasional differences, in view of the danger to peace represented by a fundamental disagreement among them. Starting from that fact, from the agreement which existed at that time, the entire collective security system was to be constructed. In accordance with the most widespread opinion, the rule of unanimity of the five permanent members of the Security Council (veto rule) was inserted in the Charter precisely because a systematic disagreement among them was not foreseen. If, at that time, it had been thought that the veto would paralyze the action of the United Nations, it is logical that a different basis would have been sought for world security. Often cited in support of this theory are the assurances given by the great powers that they would not abuse the veto[4] and the optimistic and soothing declarations of many statesmen on the united peace aims of the former war allies. In other words, unanimous agreement among the

---

[4] See "Statement by the Delegations of the Four Sponsoring Governments on Voting Procedure in the Security Council," made on 7 June 1945 at the San Francisco Conference. France associated itself with this statement. *Documents of the United Nations Conference on International Organization, San Francisco*, 1945 (New York: United Nations Information Organization, 1945), Vol. XI, pp. 711-14. Hereinafter referred to as *UNCIO Documents*.

great powers was thought of as a postulate of collective security, that is, as a self-evident proposition. Starting from a fact, the agreement existing at that time, collective security was based on the belief that such an agreement would be maintained.

Accepting the above premises, it is easy to reach the conclusion, especially in terms of what has happened since 1945, that the system of the Charter rests on an incredibly utopian and unrealistic conception. The agreement that existed among the great powers did not endure as was hoped, and the collective security system of the Charter has become practically unworkable. It is said especially that the Charter did not provide adequate mechanisms for solving conflicts among the great powers, and, contrary to the expectations at San Francisco, it is precisely these conflicts that are menacing universal peace.

Practically all authors agree that the conception and the system of the Charter are unrealistic. Kelsen, for example, refers to the hope of maintaining the agreement as an "illusion," stating that, "we know now that the principle of unanimity of the five great powers was the most unrealistic approach to the problem of maintaining peace. The basic idea on which the Charter was founded has proved a failure."[5] The number of times that the veto has been used not only proves the existence of disagreement, but, more important, proves how that disagreement has prevented the functioning of collective security and the smooth running of the Organization. The forebodings of the small powers that opposed the veto in San Francisco have been realized. And for great sectors of public opinion that see the failure of the Organization symbolized in the veto, the only way to solve the problem is to eliminate agreement among the five great powers as a basis for sustaining world security and to permit the United Nations to act without obstacles, through majority decisions of its members.

On examining more closely the predominant theory on the pos-

---

[5] Hans Kelsen, "Recent Trends in the Law of the United Nations," *Social Research*, Vol. 18, No. 2 (June 1951), pp. 140-41.

tulate of collective security in the United Nations, a suspicion immediately arises: it seems difficult to accept the fact that the authors of the San Francisco Charter would have sought to found world peace on so fragile a basis as the belief that the United States and the Soviet Union would maintain unity of purposes and action in peace-time. Certainly, the horrors of the last war were very recent and risks of a permanent disagreement loomed very large, but even this does not explain such an error of judgment on the probability of the approaching struggle. Conceding a moderate and reasonable foresight to the statesmen at San Francisco, it would be difficult not to entertain a different interpretation of the way the postulate of collective security was conceived. Perhaps unanimous agreement among the five great powers was not actually thought of as a *foreseeable* or *probable* fact, but rather as a *necessary working hypothesis*, as the necessary condition for preserving peace.[6] But in the last

---

[6] Many of the official statements of that time on maintaining agreement among the great powers might also be interpreted mostly in that sense, or as an expression of a *desideratum*. One of the phrases most frequently used to prove the utopian character of the Charter is the following: "It was taken as axiomatic at Dumbarton Oaks, and continued to be the view of the Sponsoring Powers at San Francisco, that the cornerstone of world security is the unity of those nations which formed the core of the grand alliance against the Axis." This sentence may mean that in the author's opinion, world security is assured since there is and will continue to be unity. But another meaning may be given it which is perhaps closer to his intention: world security will be guaranteed *as long as* unity exists among the nations which defeated the Axis. In any event, some official statements of the great powers themselves clearly reveal that the unanimity of the permanent members was considered uncertain and that the peace and the fate of the Organization depended on such unanimity. In the report of the Secretary of State to the President of the United States, it is declared that the provisions for the Security Council recognize and take into account "the fact that the maintenance of their unity [of the permanent members] is the crucial political problem of our time." That is, the voting rules in the Council (including the veto) are not based on the assumption that unanimity will be maintained among the permanent members, but precisely on the fact that the preservation of that unity is a problem, i.e., that it is not certain. In another part of the same report it is said that "the prestige of the Security Council, its influence in world affairs generally, and its success in the maintenance of peace and security will depend upon the degree to which unity is achieved among the great powers." U.S. Dept. of State, *Report to the President on the Results of the San Francisco Conference by the Chairman of the United States Delegation, the Secretary of State*, Publication 2349, Conference Series 11 (Washington: U.S. Govt. Printing Office, 1945), pp. 67-68.

analysis, the essential question is not whether unanimity among the great powers was conceived of subjectively by the authors of the Charter as a *postulate*, as a fact sufficiently probable to sustain collective security, or whether it was thought of as a necessary *condition* to preserve peace. In either case, unanimity of the great powers is the basis for the maintenance of peace. In one case, it might be said that collective security does not operate because the agreement which was thought probable was not maintained; and in the second case, the conclusion would be the same, although the explanation given would be that the condition necessary for the functioning of collective security, that is, the maintenance of agreement, has not been fulfilled. What is important to know is whether the conditions of the postwar world permitted any other alternative, that is, whether it was possible to build a universal system of collective security on a basis different from that of universal agreement among the great powers.

As has been previously pointed out, at present the two requirements are not fulfilled which are necessary for basing collective security on an automatic, solidary, and universal reaction against aggression, outside of the voluntary agreement of the two greatest powers of the world. Assuming that, when the Charter was drawn up, these powers had clearly foreseen the fundamental disagreement which would divide them and had shared the fears of the small countries in San Francisco, would it have been possible to start from a different conception and work out a system which would have avoided the unanimity of the great powers as a guiding principle of the Organization? The answer is obviously in the negative since none of the great powers was willing to follow the only other possible alternative: to renounce its sovereignty to the extent necessary to permit decisions to be taken without its consent which would vitally affect its security. In those circumstances, the real dilemma at that time was to choose between the system of collective security of the Charter—accepting the fact that it rested on a precarious foundation, since it would be difficult to keep harmony between the great powers—and the absence of all universal organization.

If this hypothesis is accepted as valid, the conclusion must follow that the true postulate of collective security is not exactly the unanimous agreement of the great powers, but the *need for the existence* of that agreement, or to put it better, the need for *promoting* that agreement. In reality, the conception and the structure of the Charter reflect the expectation that there would be disagreements and not (as is often suggested) the expectation that an improbable unanimity would be maintained among the permanent members of the Security Council. In the last analysis, what would be the function of the requirement of unanimity if it was believed that the great powers would fundamentally maintain an agreement in principle? In that case, they would surely have been willing to submit to the majority rule. The veto has another function. If from a certain point of view the veto reflects division, its function is to encourage union. Above all, it acts as a brake which prevents the adoption of serious measures against a great power, measures which would probably lead to a Third World War, and every effort must be made to avoid this. But the brake which prevents the adoption of such measures has a second function: it tends to force the permanent members of the Council to search for another solution, a solution other than one that could bring about a world conflict.

The true postulate of collective security is that the great powers, when confronted with a problem affecting peace, should endeavor to reach an agreement, and if they do not succeed they should try again, and if at worst they do not arrive at an understanding, at least a group of powers would not be able to impose their will on others by means of force, which would mean a new world conflict. The veto prevents a majority of states from trying forcibly to impose their will on a minority which may not command as many votes, but which has a real power no less than that of the majority. That is, a juridical instrument was given to a minority to effect legally what would happen anyway in practice. The consequence of legalizing that *de facto* situation is to oblige the minority opponents to compromise, to look for new formulas acceptable to all, or to resign themselves to the collapse of the Organization and the rupture of peace. The requirement of unanimity is basically a pressure to encourage collaboration or at least peaceful coexistence between the two principal and different parts of the world. As R. de Lacharrière so well maintains in his previously mentioned work, agreement between the five permanent members is not a postulate but an *end* of the Organization.[7] The provisions relative to the Security Council and the whole collective security structure are only mechanisms meant to achieve that end.

Of course, it may be said that the entire system tends to place the minority in an advantageous situation and to pay a "premium" to intransigence, since it gives an isolated state the legal means to block a decision which seems desirable to the majority. Nonetheless, it must likewise be borne in mind that the "minority" in the Council is more apparent than real, that basically there is no correlation between the number of votes it commands and its political and real military force. The purpose of the veto is precisely to act as a counterweight, as an equalizer, and the whole system of collective security reflects, and at the same time maintains, a political balance between the majority of capitalist countries and the minority of communist countries. The only way to maintain this balance, that actually is peace, was to concede to the numerical minority a legal instrument of decision commensurate with its real force. In matters which relate to the preservation of peace, the power to contribute to a decision must be proportionate to the power to apply or resist the decision.

It has also been asserted that this ultra-realistic and stark conception of collective security may leave the victim of an aggression completely at the mercy of a great power, since the latter can veto any effective action of the Organization in defense of the victim; that for a state threatened with destruction, self-preservation is the

---

[7] De Lacharrière, *op. cit.*, pp. 316 ff.

overriding consideration. It is certainly true that the veto of a great power can prevent the operation of the universal system of collective security, but in accordance with the principles that will be specified further on, it cannot paralyze the individual or even the collective defense of the victim. In the last analysis, the victim may employ the same resources with the same practical result as collective security which, by its nature in this epoch, does not operate universally.

In any event, the situation is discouraging. The United Nations cannot legally act against a great aggressor power or against its allies. But this involves more than a defect in the Charter itself which could be remedied by a better juridical solution. It involves a real impossibility that originates in the historical conditions in which we live. If the Charter has any merit, it is its adjustment to reality. As long as the political circumstances which support it do not change, a juridical system closer to the ideal of automatic and universal reaction against aggression would not be feasible. This is no surprise nor has it been discovered ten years after the Charter was drafted. The Secretary of State of the United States himself, Mr. John Foster Dulles, declared that even at San Francisco the United States delegation realized that the United Nations was not likely to be an instrument for "enforcing peace."[8] World peace does not depend on the United Nations. The existence of the United Nations depends on peace among the great world powers.

Nonetheless, the limited scope of the system established by the Charter does not mean that it lacks value, nor that it cannot render worthy service to the maintenance or the restoration of peace. In spite of its limitations, the collective security of the Charter can operate marginally on certain frontiers of the "cold war." The Security Council has acted with some effectiveness in the cases of Palestine, Indonesia, and Kashmir by halting hostilities in difficult circumstances.

---

[8] John Foster Dulles, *War or Peace* (New York: The Macmillan Co., 1950), p. 38.

Furthermore, it must also be remembered that collective security does not only include enforcement measures, that is, what in the days of the League were called sanctions, which require a substantial area of agreement among the great powers. The mission of preserving peace is an organic whole including various related and complementary tasks which in practice should be carried on at the same time. The effectiveness of collective security would be increased if, instead of exaggerating the emphasis on enforcement measures, all possibilities of pacific action available to the Organization were vigorously explored and utilized. This action, by its nature, would encounter fewer difficulties in finding an area of understanding among the great powers than would the application of sanctions.

DIVISION OF FUNCTIONS BETWEEN THE SECURITY COUNCIL AND THE GENERAL ASSEMBLY

Unlike the League of Nations Covenant, which assigned practically identical functions to the Assembly and the Council, the United Nations Charter established a criterion of distinction which governed the division of jurisdiction between the General Assembly and the Security Council. The General Assembly, due to its membership and functions, is a debating body; the Security Council is an executive organ. The Assembly can discuss, consider, examine, and make recommendations on almost any matter (Article 10: "... any questions or any matters within the scope of the present Charter ..."), but it cannot *act* to maintain or restore peace. The Security Council, on the other hand, acts, that is, it can take *decisions binding* the members (Article 25), including the use of armed force. The principle guiding the division of jurisdiction is not so much the difference in *subject matters* (although there are certain qualifications which will be discussed later) as the difference in function.

In addition to the general prohibition placed on the Assembly by the principle of the reserved domain of states on matters which are "essentially within the domestic jurisdiction" (Article 2, paragraph 7), the Charter established two specific limitations on the power of the Assembly: (1) Any question relative to the maintenance of international peace and security "on which action is necessary, shall be referred to the Security Council by the General Assembly either before or after discussion" (Article 11, paragraph 2); and (2) The General Assembly shall not make any recommendations with regard to a dispute or situation while the Security Council is exercising the functions assigned to it by the Charter, unless the Security Council so requests (Article 12, paragraph 1).

The powers given to the Assembly by the Charter are broader than those originally provided in the Dumbarton Oaks Proposals. At the request of the small states, supported by the United States against the opposition of the Soviet Union, the San Francisco Conference definitely decided to grant the Assembly extremely free action in discussing and making recommendations on any question, just as is stated in Articles 10 and 14, although with the already mentioned limitations. Nevertheless, the San Francisco formula was far from satisfying the wishes of many small countries. Mexico, among others, had a completely different conception of what should be the powers of the Assembly. In the "Opinion of the Department of Foreign Relations Concerning the Dumbarton Oaks Proposals," Mexico proposed that the Assembly and the Council have joint powers, even as regards the power to take enforcement measures for maintaining or restoring peace, and, in a way, subordinating the Security Council to the authority of the Assembly, which would be the supreme organ and primarily responsible for maintaining peace.[9] The essential objection of the "Opinion . . ." to the limita-

---

[9] The principal provisions of the Mexican proposal in this regard were the following:

"21. The Assembly as well as the Council shall have authority to resolve all problems which affect or may affect the political independence and territorial integrity of all Nations, the collective security and general well-being of the Members of the P.U.N. [Permanent Union of Nations].

"22. At the request of any member of the P.U.N., the Council shall examine the questions referred to in Article 21, and its decision shall be binding an all Members of the P.U.N., with the exception referred to in the following article.

tions imposed on the powers of the Assembly by the Dumbarton Oaks Proposals was that "such limitation is not in accord with the principle of the sovereign equality of all peace-loving States."[10] The Mexican amendments, like the many others presented to the same effect, were all rejected by the Conference, even including those which only referred to the possibility of having the Assembly approve or disapprove of the annual reports of the Security Council. It was said that this would amount to changing the Council into a subordinate body, thus altering the balance of functions established between the principal organs.[11]

The question of the division of powers between the Assembly and the Council needs to be studied in the light of the conclusions previously arrived at. The problem is to determine which of the two organs is better fitted to carry out the purposes of collective security, in view of the postulates, assumptions, and present limitations of the latter. To determine this, the membership and voting procedures of the two organs must first be taken into account. Furthermore, it will be necessary to examine the problem, on the one hand, in relation to each of the several functions designed to carry out collective security; and, on the other hand, in terms of the practice of the Organization in recent years, studying each type of function to ascertain where the interests of the small powers lie and what has been Mexico's point of view.

The political functions of the General Assembly may be divided into two broad categories: (1) the formulation of general principles which have no direct bearing on any situation or dispute; and (2) the exercise of pacific action on specific political cases.

"23. Article 22 notwithstanding, on the request of a simple majority of the Members of the P.U.N., the Assembly shall examine any resolution approved by the Council, which resolution shall definitely have binding force if the three-quarters of the Delegations present in the Assembly shall approve it, if within these three-quarters are included the votes of all the Members of the Council." *UNCIO Documents*, Vol. III, pp. 112-13.

[10] *Ibid.*, p. 105.

[11] *UNCIO Documents*, Vol. IX, pp. 433 ff.

The first category of questions presents no difficulties as to a possible confusion of jurisdictions with the Security Council. This function, which is to formulate the long range political and juridical objectives of the international community, clearly belongs to the General Assembly. The Charter describes it in the following way: The General Assembly may "consider the general principles of co-operation in the maintenance of international peace and security, including the principles governing disarmament and the regulation of armaments . . ." (Article 11) and shall initiate studies and make recommendations for the purpose of "promoting international co-operation in the political field and encouraging the progressive development of international law and its codification" (Article 13).

General Principles of International Co-operation in the Political and Juridical Fields: These are general questions which are of as much interest to the large states as to the small. Since they are not directly and immediately linked to the maintenance of peace in particular situations, the reasons previously applied to the necessity of an agreement among the great powers have no bearing here. Moreover, the eventual validity of all the Assembly's recommendations depends a good deal on the extent to which they are adopted by public opinion and on their voluntary acceptance by governments. By its nature, the task of formulating broad principles of political co-operation and of international law belongs to all the states and not to a few, and, therefore, it should be performed within the General Assembly.[12]

---

[12] The functions of the General Assembly and the Security Council in this whole question overlap in the case of disarmament. Since disarmament especially affects the security of the great powers and necessarily requires the agreement of the countries of greatest military capacity, the Charter has charged the Security Council with "formulating . . . plans" for the regulation of armaments (Article 26). The Assembly may consider "the principles governing disarmament and the regulation of armaments . . ." (Article 11, paragraph 1). The association of functions has been beneficial. On more than one occasion the great powers have reached an impasse in the Council in this matter and they have renewed their efforts to arrive at an understanding thanks to the urgings and new directives formulated by the Assembly.

This is a fertile field for the action of the small states. Their voices can carry great weight in the search for and expression of certain bases of action common to all international society. The fair and intelligent solution may as easily originate with a small country as with a large one. Nevertheless, unfortunately, the small countries have not made full use of the Assembly to present constructive solutions in this field. The small countries have not contributed notably to the development of the broad general principles of political co-operation, partly because of the extreme and intransigent positions often adopted by the great powers, which make the conciliating function of the small countries extremely difficult; partly because, except for rare exceptions, the small countries have not been represented by truly eminent statesmen; and partly, also, because international tension has been inevitably reflected in these undertakings of the United Nations. Practically none of the relevant resolutions adopted by the General Assembly—"Measures to be taken against propaganda and the inciters of a new war," 1947; "Essentials of peace," 1949; "Uniting for peace," 1950; "Peace through deeds," 1950; "Methods which might be used to maintain and strengthen international peace and security in accordance with the Purposes and Principles of the Charter," (collective measures), 1952;[13] are due to the initiative of the small states,[14] although sometimes, for the political convenience of the group to which they belong, some of them appear as co-sponsors of resolutions drafted by a great power and inspired by its special interests.

As regards the codification and progressive development of international law, the contribution of the small countries has been more important both in the International Law Commission and in the General Assembly, although there is no doubt that their contribu-

[13] General Assembly Resolutions 110(II), 3 Nov. 1947; 290(IV), 1 Dec. 1949; 377(V), 3 Nov. 1950; 380(V), 17 Nov. 1950; and 503(VI), 12 Jan. 1952.

[14] An important exception to this was the resolution proposed by Mexico in 1948 entitled "Appeal to the great Powers to renew their efforts and to compose their differences and establish a lasting peace," which was unanimously adopted. See General Assembly Resolution 190(II), 3 Nov. 1948.

tion would improve if their most outstanding jurists would participate in the labors of the Assembly.

Creation of a New Political and Legal Order: Besides promoting studies to encourage co-operation in the political field and in addition to its power to intervene in the pacific settlement of specific situations or disputes, a power which will be studied further on, the Assembly has carried out another important activity; what Goodrich calls the "development of [a] new legal and political order."[15] It pertains to specific political questions and not to the formulation of general principles. But it involves questions in which peace is not exactly at stake and which call for the participation of the whole international community in the formulation of a new political and legal order to replace in a certain region another order which for some reason is no longer acceptable. The problems of the Italian colonies, the first phase of the Korean question, and some aspects of the Palestine question are examples of this function of the Assembly. In the first of these, the peace treaty with Italy provided that if the great powers did not reach an agreement by 15 September 1948 on the fate of the Italian colonies, the matter would be referred to the General Assembly for a final solution that the powers agreed in advance to accept. That is, an instrument, distinct from the constitutional charter, granted the General Assembly a power that it normally does not have. As Mr. Dulles says, the Assembly could in this instance solve adequately an extremely complicated problem and at the same time satisfy the indigenous populations' desires for independence, since this principle finds a greater and more sympathetic acceptance among the small powers that form a majority in the Assembly than among the councils of the great powers.[16] In the other cases mentioned, the Assembly could only act through non-binding recommendations, so that its action was not so fruitful. Nevertheless, due to the importance of

---

[15] Leland M. Goodrich, "Development of the General Assembly," *International Conciliation*, No. 471 (May 1951), pp. 262 ff.

[16] Dulles, *op. cit.*, pp. 64-65.

the moral pressure of the community of nations in the solution of this type of problem, the Assembly is a suitable place in which to present them, at least as long as peace is not immediately jeopardized.

Thus, in the case of Palestine—which Goodrich considers a good example of a suitable division of functions between the General Assembly and the Security Council—the Assembly initially established the bases of a new legal and political order in that region to replace the former League mandate when Great Britain withdrew from Palestine.[17] When hostilities broke out between the Arabs and the Jews, the Security Council assumed the responsibility of restoring peace.

When the United States originally submitted the Korean question to the Assembly (1947), under Article 14 of the Charter, it was also a matter of settling a situation left pending by the war and of creating the bases for uniting and politically organizing that country in a permanent form. Later, when the armed invasion of South Korea took place, the Security Council recommended the initial measures for restoring peace, although the General Assembly afterwards took over functions in this respect which are normally reserved to the Security Council, with implications and results to be studied further on in this volume.[18]

The cases of Tunisia and Morocco are significant in relation to the function of the Assembly under study. Although the Arab and Asian states did not put the case to the Assembly precisely in these terms, appealing instead to the pacific settlement function of the Assembly as regards disputes as such, a new political and juridical order (complete independence or a greater degree of domestic autonomy) was actually being advocated, to take the place of the protectorate rule established in favor of France by the former Fez and Bardo Treaties which no longer satisfied the new realities.

The creation of a new order and the examination of the broad principles of political co-operation should always be the task of the

---

[17] Goodrich, *op. cit.*, p. 264.
[18] See below, pp. 130-39.

Assembly; by its nature, it is the most suitable place for a wide discussion of fundamental principles.

The Pacific Settlement of Disputes: The functions of the Security Council and the General Assembly are most easily confused in the field of the pacific settlement of disputes. Articles 10, 11 (paragraph 2), and 14 of the Charter, which determine the jurisdiction of the Assembly in this regard, do not establish an exclusive "subject matter" for that organ different from that set forth by the Charter itself as within the jurisdiction of the Security Council. Article 35 even permits any member to bring any dispute or any situation which might lead to international friction or give rise to a dispute to the attention of either the Security Council or the General Assembly, as the member chooses.

It seems that the authors of the Charter did foresee different functions for the Assembly and the Council in the pacific settlement of disputes. According to the explanations of Dr. Leo Pasvolsky, one of the principal experts of the United States delegation in San Francisco, before the Committee on Foreign Relations of the United States Senate,[19] the Assembly could make recommendations, under Article 14, on any situation which could impair the general welfare or friendly relations among nations, but if such a situation might threaten international peace and security, then the Assembly would refer the question to the Security Council, instead of acting itself. That is, in principle, *only* the Council should make decisions on those grave situations which constituted a *serious* danger to the peace.

This criterion has not been followed in practice. On the contrary, the General Assembly has increasingly tended to broaden its field of action to deal with serious disputes. There are several reasons for this: first, the terms of the Charter are not sufficiently clear in this respect; second, the "seriousness" of a matter, as a criterion, turns out to be highly elastic and lends itself easily to broad inter-

---

[19] *Hearings Before the Ctte. on Foreign Relations on the Charter of the United Nations, op. cit.*, p. 250.

pretations; third, at least in the first years of the United Nations' existence, the Soviet Union repeatedly abused the use of the veto in this matter, sometimes preventing the Organization from acting effectively; and, last, fundamentally, since in general the solution of this type of dispute can hardly be enforced (the Security Council itself acts in these cases, under Chapter VI of the Charter, *only through recommendations*), states have prefered to have recourse to the Assembly where it is easier to marshal world public opinion in their favor. As is natural, this last reason has acquired more importance as the "cold war" has become intensified.

So long as the situations and disputes under study have not degenerated into a *breach* of the peace (a matter within the exclusive jurisdiction of the Security Council under Chapter VII of the Charter), the new broader functions of the General Assembly do not essentially change the structure of the Charter. However, this new development is to be regretted. The Assembly can be effective when disputes are not dangerous; in other words, when they can be solved through the moral pressure of a recommendation supported by a large number of votes. But when a dispute or a situation notably affects the interests of the great powers so that its actual settlement requires agreement among them, the Security Council is the organ best fitted by its membership and by its procedure to encourage and eventually force this agreement. The Assembly, on the other hand, due to its constitutional inability to adopt compulsory decisions and to its broad membership, which stamp the participation of states therein with special characteristics, frequently falls into the deceptively easy way of adopting resolutions which are known beforehand to be impracticable and which represent a moral sanction against a minority more than a formula for an effective settlement. Until now, the work of the General Assembly has been ineffectual in the search for settlement formulas to solve permanently this type of problem submitted to it.

In the field of pacific settlement of disputes, there is clearly a need to revise the division of jurisdiction between the Security Council

i

and the General Assembly. The present ambiguity of the Charter, which permits this type of case to be presented either to one or the other organ, in practice has not had the best results. The experience of these years shows, on the one hand, that the Security Council has been sometimes paralyzed by the rule of unanimity when the vital interests of a great power were not at stake, and on the other hand, that the General Assembly, by its nature, is highly prone to disregard the interests and the real force of the minorities and to adopt resolutions *mort-nées* which not only do not lead to a healthy settlement, but sometimes further heighten the tension and impede the settlement of the case. Specific disputes, of some seriousness, have not been adequately resolved by the Assembly. Their solution requires a small, compact body like the Security Council, presenting favorable conditions for negotiation and agreement among the great powers.

The basic problem is to give the Security Council greater facility in acting in the pacific settlement of disputes, that is, to eliminate the veto in this matter. The Council's inability to act in such cases, as happened in the initial phase of the Greek question, has had a serious consequence, as a by-product: the assumption by the Assembly of responsibility regarding matters which, by its nature and membership, it was hardly suited to resolve, with the result that once the tendency was initiated, the Assembly broadened its jurisdiction *de facto* to include a field (Chapter VII of the Charter: action with respect to threats to the peace, breaches of the peace, and acts of aggression), which was not only expressly prohibited it, but which signifies a complete change in the balance of the Charter.

From all viewpoints, it seems advisable that the function of settling specific, *serious* disputes (constituting direct and immediate threats to the peace) be clearly and exclusively assigned to the Security Council. But to accomplish that, it would be necessary to eliminate the veto in this field. It is even not improbable that the Soviet Union would accede to this, if it is borne in mind that on the occasions it has made use of a veto in this regard, it has not been able to prevent the matter from passing to the Assembly where resolutions have been adopted against its policy. Since it is to be expected that this tendency will continue as long as the Council is not given greater freedom of action, perhaps its enlightened self-interest would lead it to accept the condition needed to return these matters to the appropriate organ for resolving them, that is, to the Council: the condition being the elimination of the veto. On the other hand, in none of the cases up to this time in which the United Nations has intervened for the pacific settlement of disputes—as opposed to cases of breaches of the peace—has a great power been sufficiently affected in its interests to resist the intervention by force. The argument of the great powers in San Francisco for maintaining the veto in the pacific solution of disputes, to the effect that decisions of the Council "may even initiate a chain of events which might . . . require the Council . . . to invoke measures of enforcement"[20] (which should indeed be a matter for veto), does not seem any more convincing in the light of the experience of the years since. The considerations previously mentioned concerning the assumptions of collective security carry too little weight in the field of pacific settlement of disputes to justify the presence of the veto, that is, the necessary legal instrument to restrain the Organization when the action contemplated might touch off a world war.

At the same time that the veto is eliminated in the pacific settlement of specific, dangerous disputes, it would be indispensable to make clear that the Assembly has no joint jurisdiction in this field. The settlement of any grave dispute should fall exclusively to the Security Council. It would then be essential to change the terms of Articles 10, 11, 14, 39, and several other provisions of Chapter IV in order to do away with all doubt as to the Assembly's lack of authority to make recommendations when a dispute or a situation constitutes a direct and immediate threat to the peace. In this way,

---

[20] *UNCIO Documents*, Vol. XI, p. 712.

the original intention of the authors of the Charter, which was frustrated by ambiguous wording together with the abuse of the veto, will be recovered. To state it differently, Article 39 of the Charter (included in Chapter VII, which refers to the "action" that only the Security Council can take) will come to comprise the entire field of action which should belong to it: not only the Council's determination of the existence of breaches of the peace and acts of aggression, but also "of any threat to the peace." It must be clearly understood that "threat," as used in Article 39, is *a real and imminent danger*, unlike the other less serious situations or disputes of Chapter VI which should come under the joint jurisdiction of the Assembly and the Council.

CHAPTER VII OF THE CHARTER: THE VETO

The enforcement action of the Organization to maintain or restore peace is at the heart of collective security. Here, unanimity among the great powers is necessary, if the action taken in defense of peace is not to set off, in turn, a new world war. The Charter clearly established, without there having been any serious opposition in San Francisco in this respect, that the "action" of the Organization in case of serious threats to the peace, breaches of the peace, or acts of aggression should be reserved to the Security Council, where the rule of unanimity would operate. Article 39 refers *only* to the Security Council as the authorized organ—the maxim "*Expressio unius, exclusio alterius*" should be recalled—to "determine" the existence of these cases and then to take action: Article 11, paragraph 2, which grants the Assembly a broad field of discussion on "any questions relating to the maintenance of international peace and security," nevertheless obliges it to refer any question which requires "action" to the Council. Article 24 confers on the Security Council the "primary responsibility" for the maintenance of peace and security. The ruling of the Charter in this respect is, then, perfectly clear.

The reasons mentioned earlier which made no other Charter system possible at San Francisco are equally valid today. The experience of recent years offers no new convincing reasons for believing that a *universal* system of collective security could now be organized, without the agreement of the great powers. This is due to the balance of forces between the great coalitions, which embraces almost the whole of world power. If there has been any change in the last years, it has been to accentuate the division of the world and to make the known forces still more evenly matched. As long as the world constellation of political and military forces does not change, it is impossible to avoid the need for encouraging agreement among the great powers as a prerequisite of collective security.

The Veto in the Practice of the Security Council: However, the basis for the most frequent and forceful criticisms that have been leveled against the usefulness of the Organization is the difficulty of attaining unanimity among the great powers, precisely in those serious cases which should be effectively acted upon in defense of peace. In this regard, it is said that the Soviet Union has used the veto X number of times, implying that, since the veto paralyzes the action of the Organization, the latter has been prevented from acting on every one of these occasions. This conception, promoted and elaborated by a biased propaganda made necessary by the "cold war," has won broad acceptance in public opinion. Nonetheless, as almost always happens when complex questions are too simplified and an attempt is made to reduce them to numbers, it is easy to become unrealistic.

In the first place, one must agree with Leland Goodrich,[21] one of the most eminent American authors on this question, that on certain occasions the United States itself, undoubtedly considering an increase in the number of vetoes of the Soviet Union a propaganda victory, has deliberately forced the latter to use them.

Secondly, a high proportion of the Soviet vetoes have been applied to one issue, the admission of new members, which is not related

---

[21] *Op. cit.*, p. 278.

to the maintenance of peace. Actually, the Western bloc proceeded as much as the Soviet Union against the spirit of the Charter when it rejected applicants which satisfied the admission requirements, only because the countries concerned belonged to the opposing bloc. The only way to solve the problem was to agree to the simultaneous admission of all the applicants, which would have avoided any veto on this question. This solution, initially proposed by the United States, was for several years rejected by the latter and sponsored by the Soviet Union.[22] Therefore, the responsibility for the vetoes on the admission of new members cannot be solely attributed to the country that used them; particularly if it is considered that nine candidates were vetoed, but that in a deplorable "cold war" maneuver their applications were more than once put to vote in full knowledge that they would be vetoed, instead of seriously negotiating for an agreement. In any case, this problem could be resolved in the future by modifying the Charter in order to affirm clearly the universality of the Organization.

Other vetoes were not designed to prevent the action of the Organization, but to the contrary. The Soviet Union was fundamentally in agreement with certain proposals under study (for example, in the case of Spain and in the case of the French and British troops in Lebanon and Syria) and it did not seek to prevent the Council from taking action, but it considered that the proposals supported by the majority were too weak and voted against them for that reason, hoping thus to open the way to more forceful action by the Organization. In these cases the purpose of the veto was to strengthen and not to paralyze the action of the United Nations, that is, the opposite purpose to what public opinion generally supposes.[23]

Several other vetoes also should not appear in a numerical list as instances in which the action of the Organization was prevented,

---

[22] See Chapter 4.

[23] John MacLaurin, *The United Nations and Power Politics* (New York: Harper & Bros., 1951), p. 199.

since they were applied to the preliminary decision as to whether a matter should be considered as substantive or as procedural (double veto).[24]

The veto used on the Berlin blockade question eventually forced the two most interested parties to find a mutually acceptable solution. Here, the veto achieved its specific aim. It did not prevent a solution; on the contrary, it compelled negotiation and finally permitted the adoption of the only feasible solution, that is, one derived from agreement among the great powers.

Other interesting questions that reveal the true significance of the veto were the case of mines laid in the Corfu Channel (1947), and the appointment of a new Secretary-General. In the first case, the Soviet Union vetoed a British resolution placing responsibility on and condemning Albania in a matter which had important juridical implications. The use of the veto here also fulfilled its specific purpose: it resulted in eventual agreement, even if incomplete, on a solution of the matter. The rejection of the British resolution by the Soviet veto opened the way to unanimous approval later of another formula: to send the matter to the International Court of Justice. In view of the juridical implications of the matter, this was undoubtedly a more appropriate method of handling the case than the one vetoed.

The second case is still more revealing. It is obvious that the Secretary-General should have the confidence of all the great powers so that the exercise of his responsibilities will contribute to international collaboration. For that reason, the Charter expressly requires the unanimous vote of the five great powers for his election. Shortly after the beginning of the Korean war, the Soviet Union vetoed the reelection of the former Secretary-General, Mr. Trygve Lie, and proposed many other candidates who would normally have been acceptable to the Western countries, but on this occasion, because of the political significance of the election of anyone other

---

[24] For a list of cases of double veto, see Pierre-F. Brugière, *Droit de Veto* (Paris: Editions A. Pedone, 1952), pp. 154 ff.

than Mr. Lie, they were objected to by the United States and the other Western countries in the Council, without the candidates ever actually being voted upon.

Despite the Soviet veto of the Council's resolution to reelect Mr. Lie, and despite the clear intention of the Charter, the majority of the Assembly extended the term of office of Mr. Lie for three more years, as if this were not equivalent to a reelection requiring the unanimity of the great powers. To abuse the minority in this type of issue is not effective in the long run, in spite of the number of votes. Mr. Lie finally had to realize—after a two-year delay, incidentally—that his person was an obstacle to the lessening of international tension since a great power placed no confidence in him and did not recognize the legality of his position. He explicitly acknowledged this when he resigned the post of Secretary-General before finishing his term. At that time, the five permanent members of the Council were obliged to negotiate seriously and, relatively easily, they found a candidate acceptable to all. If the "reality" reflected in the veto in this case had been respected, the solution of a problem which upset the smooth running of the Organization would have been arrived at two years before. Here, too, the veto achieved its true purpose: it forced negotiation, agreement, and solution.

Several other vetoes of the Soviet Union were used to prevent approval of reports of the Atomic Energy Commission and of the Disarmament Commission, and of several proposals for studies on the regulation of armaments. These questions did not *directly* affect peace; moreover, since the carrying out of such plans necessarily depends on the subsequent voluntary acceptance of the powers with greatest military capacity, the vetoes, as such, did not alter the actual situation at that time and served the purpose of continuing the negotiations toward formulas acceptable to all.

Apart from the significant question of Korea, which will later be referred to separately, of the impressive total of vetoes used, the peace-making action of the Organization has actually been paralyzed or delayed by the veto only in the case of Greece and possibly in the case of Thailand's request in 1954 that a peace observation commission be sent to that country because of the danger of an extension of the war in Indo-China. In the Greek question, some of the vetoes were used in connection with the pacific settlement of the dispute—a function where the elimination of the veto would be desirable, as already pointed out—while other vetoes were used regarding measures properly falling under Chapter VII. The Assembly, which finally studied the matter, could not proceed with much more efficacy. The definitive settlement of the Greek question has probably been due more to the military aid of the United States to Greece and also, in part, to Tito's break with the Soviet bloc, than to the non-binding recommendations of the Assembly. This fact in itself can serve as a guide in the solution of the veto problem. The question is not just whether it is improbable that an organ subject to the veto can solve the problems, but whether there is any real possibility that the other organ, the Assembly, can solve them effectively.

Finally, a veto used in 1954 is highly significant for the understanding of the several functions of this institution and has special importance for the Latin American countries. In that year Guatemala brought before the Security Council the problem of the invasion of its territory by armed bands, organized and equipped in neighboring countries. The two Latin American members of the Council, Brazil and Colombia, presented a draft resolution to refer the whole matter to the Organization of American States. France introduced an amendment, accepted by the authors of the resolution, which recommended a cease-fire. The Soviet Union vetoed the entire resolution and France later presented its amendment as an independent proposal, which was approved unanimously. In this case, the purpose and effect of the veto were not to paralyze the Organization, but quite the contrary. The draft resolution favored by the majority referred the case to the Organization of American States, thereby preventing the United Nations from taking further action in the future. The rejection of this resolution, by means of the veto, opened the way for further Security Council action to restore peace. In the end, the Council's action was not effective because its first cease-fire recommendation was not heeded, and the Council decided not to place on the agenda a second Guatemalan complaint. This decision, being of a procedural nature, was not subject to the veto.[25]

---

[25] The precedent set by the Security Council in the case of Guatemala (not because of the joint draft resolution of Colombia and Brazil to refer the matter to the regional organization, since this resolution was vetoed, but because of the later decision of the Council not to place a second Guatemalan complaint on the agenda) has serious implications for the countries of the American continent. The precedent means that when a serious situation occurs among the American states, even if it is, as in the case of Guatemala, a breach of the peace, the Council may decline to consider the matter and send it to the regional organization, even when the plaintiff itself does not desire the intervention of the latter. In other words, the existence of a regional agreement like the Rio de Janeiro Treaty would make the United Nations not competent, or in any event would disqualify the United Nations in practice from dealing with any matter, even to restore the peace, if the case occurs among members of that regional organization. It could easily happen, because of the peculiar grouping of political forces in the American continent, that in a situation between two American states, one party might be less assured than the other of obtaining justice in the regional organization, and might not want the latter's intervention. If action is blocked in the world organization, where the majority of the members would have no direct interest and would probably proceed with greater impartiality, the state in question would find itself in a really difficult situation. The Latin American states should seriously consider the implications of the precedent established: membership in the regional organization would actually mean the loss of the rights and privileges of members of the United Nations in everything relative to political situations which might occur among the parties to the Rio Treaty. In the ninth session of the General Assembly, the delegations of Uruguay, Ecuador, and Argentina severely criticized the refusal of the Security Council to intervene in the case of Guatemala. The representative of Argentina rightly maintained that the recognition of the exclusive jurisdiction of the regional agency (vis-à-vis the world organization) would "lead to the absurd position that a State Member of the United Nations which was a party to a regional arrangement would be at a disadvantage as compared with other States which for some reason were not members of regional agencies." See, respectively, General Assembly, Official Records (G.A.O.R.): 9th Sess., 481st, 485th, and 488th Plenary Mtgs.; 28 Sept., 1 and 4 Oct. 1954; pp. 98, 148, and 174.

The Secretary-General of the United Nations himself, in his 1954 report to the Assembly, said the following: "A policy giving full scope to the proper role of regional agencies can and should at the same time fully preserve the right of a Member nation to a hearing under the Charter." See G.A.O.R., 9th Sess., Supple. No. 1, p. xi.

In brief, first, the membership of the Council does not reflect the real forces represented there, which partly explains the vetoes of the Soviet Union. The veto is a "compensating" instrument which benefits a numerical minority whose real power is greater than the number of votes at its disposal. Second, the vetoes have been due in large part to the uncompromising position taken by the "cold war" groups in their desire to gain propaganda victories, which are only illusory and which certainly do nothing toward lessening international tension, and, above all, to the slight desire to use the Security Council seriously as an instrument for *negotiating*, that is, for finding *mutually* acceptable formulas. But, even apart from these considerations, it is certain that the long list of vetoes does not truly reflect the situation. The rule of unanimity has in very few cases stood in the way of the action of the United Nations to preserve peace. It is true that some of the cases, those which involved the pacific settlement of disputes, cannot be justified on substantive grounds. In such cases, it would be preferable to eliminate the veto. When there has been a breach of the peace, the veto has been, rather than a cause of the impotence of the Organization, a symptom of an underlying situation which appears practically insurmountable within contemporary political reality. The true basic solution cannot be found in the present-day constitutional charter of an international organization. There are no technical-juridical procedures which can overcome this fundamental obstacle.

Significance of the Geneva Conference on Indo-China: Since the end of 1950, the Security Council has been practically in recess. The most serious matters for world security (such as the wars of Korea and Indo-China) have been dealt with either by the Assembly or by the directly interested parties, but without the intervention of the organ which was specifically created for their solution. It is now feasible, therefore, to form a judgment on the usefulness of the Security Council and on the way in which collective security can operate outside the initial conception of the Charter.

What happened in the war of Indo-China might suggest interest-

ing conclusions in this respect. The problem was not presented to
the Organization, but when it became necessary to begin negotiations to end hostilities, a conference was called which included
precisely the representatives of the five permanent members of the
Security Council, besides the parties in dispute. The sound and
permanent settlement of the problem depended on an agreement
reached through negotiations among practically all the great powers,
that is, this was a conference in which the rule of unanimity operated.
To put it plainly, it might be said without being too far from the
truth that the Security Council met in Geneva to resolve the war
in Indo-China.[26] Unfortunately, the meeting was not sponsored by
the Organization, and the non-permanent members, who might have
helped reconcile opposite viewpoints, were not present. But, in any
case, this situation shows that when a serious breach of the peace
exists, the only way to put an end to it is to have negotiations among
the great powers and that those negotiations must necessarily be
based on the principle of unanimity, even though they are not
carried on within the formal procedures of the Security Council.
When the intervention of the Council is dispensed with, the substitute found to resolve disputes effectively is only a replica of the
Security Council itself, and it also operates on the basis of the veto,
but outside the Organization and without the participation of the
small powers.

THE "UNITING FOR PEACE" RESOLUTION:
THE CASE OF KOREA

The "Uniting for Peace" resolution,[27] which was adopted in 1950
as a consequence of the Korean war, represents the most serious

[26] If the comparison were to be carried further, the fact that the United States
did not sign the "Final Act" of the Conference, but at the same time signified
that it would not oppose the arrangements adopted, was the equivalent of a
vote of "abstention" in the Security Council, which in accordance with the
precedents established would not have prevented the approval of a resolution
identical to the Geneva agreements.

[27] General Assembly Resolution 377(V), 3 Nov. 1950.

effort that has been made to evade the principle of unanimity of the five permanent members of the Security Council in dealing with situations which represent a serious threat to the peace, a breach of the peace, or an act of aggression. The two most important parts of this resolution are the following:

> *The General Assembly* . . .

> *Resolves* that if the Security Council, because of lack of unanimity of the permanent members, fails to exercise its primary responsibility for the maintenance of international peace and security in any case where there appears to be a threat to the peace, breach of the peace, or act of aggression, the General Assembly shall consider the matter immediately with a view to making appropriate recommendations to Members for collective measures, including in the case of a breach of the peace or act of aggression the use of armed force when necessary, to maintain or restore international peace and security. . . .

> *Recommends* to the States Members of the United Nations that each Member maintain within its national armed forces elements so trained, organized and equipped that they could promptly be made available, in accordance with its constitutional processes, for service as a United Nations unit or units, upon recommendation by the Security Council or the General Assembly, without prejudice to the use of such elements in exercise of the right of individual or collective self-defence recognized in Article 51 of the Charter. . . .

The "Uniting for Peace" resolution has been as much criticized from a juridical as from a political standpoint.

First, it has been said that the possibility of recommending the use of force to the members in case of a breach of the peace or an act of aggression requires previously and necessarily the competence, that is, the juridical capacity, to "determine" if either of these cases has occurred. Now, Article 39 of the Charter expressly confers that power on the Security Council, and no other provision grants a like power to the Assembly. In the second place, as has been pointed out before, Article 11, paragraph 2 of the Charter obliges the Assembly to refer any question "on which action is necessary" to the Security Council either before or after discussion. That is, the Assembly cannot take any action in this respect. And a question whose settlement requires the use of armed force is *par excellence* a question "on which action is necessary." According to Kelsen,

> In order to avoid absurd consequences, the term ['action' according to the Charter] must be interpreted in a restrictive way, which may mean: enforcement action, i. e., any use of force, especially any use of armed force. If the General Assembly is of the opinion that in a question under its consideration the use of armed force is necessary, it must refer this question to the Security Council without making a recommendation on that question. This was probably the intention of the framers of the Charter.[28]

From a political standpoint, the new power of the Assembly to recommend the use of armed force reveals the fundamental defect which has already been fully discussed: in this matter, the formal elimination of the principle of unanimity among the great powers does not suffice to do away with the reality on which it is based. That agreement is indispensable to prevent the employment of collective measures from creating, in turn, greater dangers for universal peace than those very ones that it seeks to avoid. Furthermore, the armed intervention of the United Nations—that is, its official "belligerence"—effected without agreement among the great powers, particularly the superpowers, makes extremely difficult the mediating and pacifying function of the Organization, perhaps jeopardizing the best possibility of restoring peace.

The action of the United Nations in Korea, which is generally presented as a triumph of the "new" collective security envisaged in the "Uniting for Peace" resolution, may serve to illustrate the above defects.

---

[28] See Hans Kelsen, "Is the Acheson Plan Constitutional?", *The Western Political Quarterly*, Vol. III, No. 4 (Dec. 1950), p. 516.

The initial resolutions of the Security Council authorizing collective action against the invasion of South Korea were taken in the absence of the Soviet delegate, who would certainly have vetoed them if he had been present. Shortly afterwards, the delegate of the United States, Mr. John Foster Dulles, when presenting the "Uniting for Peace" draft resolution to the fifth session of the Assembly, justified the necessity of the new measures proposed by maintaining that only the absence of the Soviet representative, together with other accidental circumstances, permitted the Security Council to act in the case of Korea; and that, since it was unlikely that those circumstances would be presented again, it was indispensable to adopt other legal provisions for the future (the recommendation of the General Assembly not subject to veto) in case the Security Council should be unable to take measures to resist aggression.[29]

This justification of the "Uniting for Peace" resolution overlooks one important fact: within the Charter system, it is always legally possible, even without prior authorization of the Security Council, to come collectively to the aid of the victim to resist aggression. Article 51 of the Charter permits "collective self-defense," even without prior authorization of the Security Council. That is, under Article 51 of the Charter, the United States and its allies could have helped South Korea in exactly the same way to resist the aggression.[30] Apart from the very debatable question of whether the Security Council could legally adopt a valid decision in the absence of one

---

[29] G.A.O.R., 5th Sess., 1st Ctte., 354th Mtg., 9 Oct. 1950, pp. 63-65.

[30] It might be said that the aid to the victim by its allies requires the *prior* existence of an "agreement" (treaty) for mutual defense in case of an attack on one of the parties (e. g., Rio Treaty or North Atlantic Treaty), which in this instance did not exist between the United States and the Korean Republic. In fact, the state being attacked is almost always rendered aid in accordance with a prior treaty. But neither Article 51 of the Charter nor any norm of international law makes the *right* to aid the victim dependent on that requirement. The effect of such treaties is not to create the right to render aid, but to convert that prior right into an *obligation*. Thus, those wishing to aid the Korean Republic voluntarily would have found no legal obstacle to doing so within the limits, naturally, of Article 51 of the Charter.

of its permanent members (since Article 27 expressly refers to the "concurring votes of [*all*] the permanent members"), to go into it more deeply, it is certain that the resolutions initially adopted by the Security Council in the matter of Korea were fundamentally valid, since they did not impose upon the members a greater obligation or, for that matter, grant them a greater right than the "inherent right" of collective self-defense which they enjoyed even without the authorization of the Security Council.

Certainly, Article 51 limits the right of self-defense "until the Security Council has taken measures necessary to maintain international peace and security." That is, it is a provisional authorization for a case of emergency. But, as will be seen later,[31] the failure of the Council to adopt a positive resolution—because of the veto or because of an insufficient majority—confirming the legitimacy of the measures initially taken in self-defense cannot have the legal effect of necessarily terminating them. Thus, it is not true that the veto can prevent the victim and its allies from resisting aggression. Thence, the assumption used to support this aspect of the "Uniting for Peace" resolution does not exist. What the veto can prevent is that the defense be carried on officially in the name of the United Nations and that the members who do not wish to participate in the collective action be legally bound to do so. It is interesting to remember what happened in this respect in the action in Korea.

Action Taken by the Assembly in the Case of Korea: Once the North Korean attack was driven back to its point of origin (38th parallel), there arose the possibility that the forces of the United Nations would undertake military occupation of North Korea. Since the original object of the resolution of the Council on 27 June 1950 was "to repel the armed attack and to restore international peace and security in the area," a new decision of the Council was indispensable, but this seemed no longer possible in view of the return of the Soviet representative to the Council. The Assembly then

---

[31] See Chapter 6, pp. 158-59.

provided the necessary authority to invade North Korea by a definition implying that "the area" signified the entire Korean peninsula.[32]

Of all the decisions taken by the two sides in the Korean war, surely the most serious in its consequences (with the exception, naturally, of the initial attack on South Korea) was the decision to invade North Korea. In spite of the clear warnings of the Indian representative, whose government was in close contact with Peiping, the forces of the United Nations, under the Assembly's authorization, moved toward the Manchurian border, thus setting off the Chinese military intervention which prolonged the war more than two years. In spite of the dangers of such a decision, the Assembly did not study, at that time, other alternatives nor did it make honest efforts to negotiate. Incomprehensibly—for those who thought that the Assembly's function was to restore the peace and not to continue the war—it reached the extreme of rejecting an Indian draft resolution (by 32 votes to 24, with 3 abstentions) which only proposed to establish a sub-committee of the Assembly to study all the draft resolutions presented on the Korean problem, including those of the Western and Soviet (obviously representing the viewpoints of Communist China and North Korea) groups, and to recommend "a draft resolution on the subject commanding the largest measure of agreement."[33] In other words, the Assembly rejected even the proposal to study the possibility of arriving at a formula acceptable to all which might restore peace to Korea. As a negotiation center, this organ could hardly have failed more miserably. The Assembly could certainly work efficiently, unimpeded by the veto, but in view of the decision which it took and of the subsequent events, it may be asked if this was for the good of international peace.

---

[32] See General Assembly Resolution 376(V), 7 Oct. 1950, in which the Assembly recommended that "all appropriate steps be taken to ensure conditions of stability throughout Korea; . . . ."

[33] See United Nations Doc. A/C.1/572, 4 Oct. 1950. Mexico voted in favor of this draft resolution.

k

Some two and a half months later (December 1950) the new negotiations sponsored by the Assembly when Chinese military intervention compelled the forces of the United Nations to withdraw from North Korea[34] came up against the obstacle that the Communist group did not recognize the moral authority of the Organization as mediator, since it had become a belligerent. The Assembly, by a majority decision which had not been accepted by the great power representing the interests of Communist China, had become a party in a military conflict while at the same time it sought to assume the impartiality of the mediator. If the collective action in Korea had been effected on the basis of legitimate collective self-defense and not in the name of the United Nations, the latter could have sponsored the peace negotiations with much more efficacy and moral authority.

Nevertheless, in January 1951 another fine opportunity to restore peace in Korea was presented when the group made up of the President of the Assembly, the representative of India, and the Canadian Secretary of State for External Affairs drew up the famous five-point program—the first of which was an immediate cease-fire—to solve the whole problem.[35] The dramatic events which

---

[34] The Chinese were not satisfied with the evacuation of North Korea, and they recrossed the 38th parallel toward the south, making the settlement even more difficult, in spite of the admonitions and warnings of the Asian-African bloc.

[35] The five-point program was as follows:

"1. In order to prevent needless destruction of life and property, and while other steps are being taken to restore peace, a cease-fire should be immediately arranged. Such an arrangement should contain adequate safeguards for ensuring that it will not be used as a screen for mounting a new offensive.

"2. If and when a cease-fire occurs in Korea, either as a result of a formal arrangement or, indeed, as a result of a lull in hostilities pending some such arrangement, advantage should be taken of it to pursue consideration of further steps to be taken for the restoration of peace.

"3. To permit the carrying out of General Assembly resolution [376(V)] that Korea should be a unified, independent, democratic, sovereign State with a constitution and a government based on free popular elections, all non-Korean armed forces will be withdrawn, by appropriate stages, from Korea, and appropriate arrangements, in accordance with United Nations principles, will be made for the Korean people to express their own free will in respect of their future government.

followed have made it difficult to remember this effort which, had it been sincerely followed through, would probably have re-established peace in Korea two years earlier. From the time they were presented, the five points met with serious opposition from those maintaining the most extreme positions in the Assembly.

As often happens, the initial reaction of the Soviet group revealed a complete lack of political vision; by the turn subsequent events took, it is to be assumed that the Soviet Union regretted its initial opposition. At the other extreme, the opposition to the five principles was reflected in an unprecedented series of procedural maneuvers (especially on the part of Nationalist China and El Salvador), one of which was no less than to substitute Nationalist China for Communist China in an eventual four-power conference (the United States, the Soviet Union, Great Britain, and Communist China) which would negotiate precisely those problems which concerned Communist China, including its representation in the United Nations. To top it off, the struggle between Israel and the Arab countries, although it had no more than a circumstantial character in this case, further complicated the situation. It was only thanks to the unexpected and skillful action of the Mexican delegate, Sr. Padilla Nervo, that it was possible to save the five principles and put them to a vote as an organic whole.[36]

The first reaction of Communist China was not favorable to the five principles, but the Indian representative, Sir Benegal Rau,

"4. Pending the completion of the steps referred to in the preceding paragraph, appropriate interim arrangements, in accordance with United Nations principles, will be made for the administration of Korea and the maintenance of peace and security there.

"5. As soon as agreement has been reached on a cease-fire, the General Assembly shall set up an appropriate body which shall include representatives of the Governments of the United Kingdom, the United States of America, the Union of Soviet Socialist Republics and the People's Republic of China, with a view to the achievement of a settlement, in conformity with existing international obligations and the provisions of the United Nations Charter, of Far Eastern problems, including, among others, those of Formosa (Taiwan) and of the representation of China in the United Nations."
G.A.O.R., 5th Sess., Annexes: Agenda item 76, p. 13.

[36] See *ibid.*, 1st Ctte., 425th Mtg., 13 Jan. 1951, pp. 495-96.

advised that the reply of Peiping should be considered as a partial acceptance and a partial rejection, partly a request for explanations and partly a group of counter-proposals which should be considered. There appeared to be solid grounds for an authentic negotiation, above all in view of the later explanations of its initial reply by the government of Peiping[37] (explanations which, it was subsequently learned, were requested by Canada and Great Britain through the government of India). Twelve Asian countries incorporated the bases of the five principles, modified in accordance with some counter-proposals of Communist China, in a draft resolution[38] and the Indian delegate stated that his government had received information to the effect that the draft resolution was regarded in Peiping as "providing a genuine basis for a peaceful settlement."[39] In spite of these explanations and the additional warning of the Indian representative that if Communist China were condemned all possibility of a negotiated settlement would disappear, the Assembly resolved to ignore the peace formula that had been worked out (the draft of the twelve countries was rejected) and thereby all likelihood of negotiations, and, on the other hand, to declare Communist China an aggressor and apply enforcement measures.[40]

---

[37] See *ibid.*, 428th and 429th Mtgs., 20 and 22 Jan. 1951, pp. 523-29.

[38] *Ibid.*, Annexes: Agenda item 76, pp. 5-6.

[39] *Ibid.*, 1st Ctte., 437th Mtg., 30 Jan. 1951, p. 590.

[40] A later incident which throws some light on the frustrated peace negotiations, as regards the five principles, is the following:

Secretary of State Dean Acheson was called as a witness before the United States Senate in the investigation of the administration's policy relative to the removal of General MacArthur. Senator Knowland began his questioning of Secretary Acheson by quoting a *New York Times* dispatch of 12 Jan. 1951 to the effect that the United States government had expected the Chinese Communists to reject the plan (the five principles of the Assembly) and implying that the United States government had supported the plan in view of this expectation. Continuing, Senator Knowland asked the following question: "Did we support the resolution having in mind that they would reject it?", to which Secretary Acheson replied, "I have stated we expected they would reject it, and we did support the resolution." U.S. Senate, *Hearings Before the Ctte. on Armed Services and Ctte. on Foreign Relations, Military Situation in the Far East*, 82nd Cong., 1st Sess., Part 3, 1-13 June 1951, p. 2052.

The action taken by the Assembly practically eliminated any settlement at that time. The armistice which was finally signed more than two years later turned out to be basically the same, militarily speaking, as that which could have been signed at the beginning of 1951, except that the formula then provided, in addition, machinery and established grounds for a permanent solution of the political problems of the Far East at a moment when their settlement was more likely. Now, the permanent solution of the political problem seems much more difficult.

Apart from the historical responsibility which must be assigned to the several governments in connection with the frustrated peace negotiations, those facts serve as a guide in judging the effectiveness of the Assembly as an organ entrusted with maintaining and restoring peace. In the first place, as has already been said, it cannot be accepted that the existence of the veto in the Security Council makes it "indispensable" that the Assembly intervene to come to the aid of the victim of an aggression, since collective self-defense is sufficient. Secondly, the Assembly is the least suitable place for *negotiating*, that is, for *taking into account the viewpoint of the two parties and coming to a mutually acceptable agreement*. The membership of the Assembly predisposes the majority to retreat from conciliatory efforts and to adopt decisions that do not sufficiently take into account the interests of the minorities. This would be justifiable if the majority had the strength necessary to enforce its decisions, but not when the only real and permanent solution of the problem requires mutual agreement. The way in which the Korean war was finally ended, by an armistice without victors or vanquished, arrived at through mutual compromises and with neither of the parties being able to impose its will on the other, proves that the activity of the United Nations should have been directed toward negotiations from the beginning.[41] The decisions of the Assembly to au-

---

[41] Nor can it be said that while the negotiations are taking place, the victim would be exposed to destruction by the aggressor, for meanwhile it can continue exercising collective self-defense.

thorize the invasion of North Korea and to declare Communist China an aggressor, ignoring the encouraging prospects that existed for a negotiated settlement, clearly not only did not hasten the end of the war but probably delayed it and consequently increased the number of casualties. All of this in order to culminate in an armistice, no better from a Western standpoint than that which could have been attained in 1951. The Security Council, where the veto was the best guarantee of the necessary "realism," was the appropriate place to carry on, or at least to sponsor, the peace negotiations. The anxiety to avoid the veto in the Council carried the solution of the problem of ending the Korean war to the tent of Panmunjom where the decisions were also subject to a veto, although without the aid of the mediation which might have been attempted by the other members of the Council.

It might be said that the moral support of the community of nations expressed through a majority vote of the Assembly is useful for defeating the aggressor. Without going into the evident truth of this idea and, in addition, recognizing that an important task of the United Nations is also to fix the juridical and moral responsibility for aggression, it is equally obvious that this function should be subordinate to the essential aim of maintaining and restoring peace. Therefore, it should be exercised with the prudence necessary not to embitter uselessly the feelings of the minority. In the case of Communist China, this became an additional obstacle to the success of the negotiations.

Aside from this, as de Lacharrière points out, the two groups which confronted each other in Korea gained nothing in the way of real resources from the decision that was adopted; world opinion "did not let itself be led one way or the other by the formality of a vote in the General Assembly: the American attitude would have had more or less the same supporters and the same opponents in the world if it had simply been presented as the exercise of collective self-defense." The intervention of the Assembly, in exchange for an illusory advantage, endangered the pacific and universal vocation of the Organization. There are different collectivities for each task. The agreements for collective self-defense (like the Rio de Janeiro Treaty or NATO), "respond to the necessity of partial formations to resist aggression; while the United Nations are called upon to perform the irreplaceable mission of pacifically regrouping the different elements of the world."[42] The new, broadened functions of the Assembly, far from being a unifying influence on the different groups within the United Nations and contributing to universal collaboration, tend to widen still more the division among the members.

POSITION OF THE SMALL AND MEDIUM-SIZED POWERS

Mexico's point of view on this problem is not based on special motives. Its interests are not different from those of the majority of the small and medium-sized countries. Although sometimes its position does not coincide with the official position adopted by many small countries, it is fundamentally interested in maintaining the functional equilibrium which the Charter establishes between the General Assembly and the Security Council. The elimination of the veto in cases of serious threats to the peace or breaches of the peace or acts of aggression would not benefit the small and medium-sized powers. The veto serves as a check against dragging small countries, often against their will, into undertakings which fundamentally serve the interest of the great powers. Paradoxically, the veto is more a defense of the small than of the great countries. The fact that the small countries dispose of a large number of votes in the United Nations, with which theoretically they could prevent the adoption of dangerous decisions which they do not want, does not signify a "real" defense for them. The close political dependence of all the small countries on some great powers and the fear of reprisals has obliged the former more frequently than is generally believed to support positions contrary to their best interests, or, in

---

[42] De Lacharrière, *op. cit.*, p. 332. Author's translation.

any case, they have been led to act irresponsibly, voting for the application of measures that they are not willing to fulfil or that they are not capable of effectively sustaining.

A good example of this phenomenon was the reaction of the Latin American countries to the request for troops to be sent to Korea. Despite their having appeared to be the most enthusiastic supporters of collective action in Korea and despite their close political and economic connection with the United States, only one country (Colombia) of the twenty sent troops to Korea. The true reason for this paradoxical situation was not the total impossibility of sending them—since, for this purpose, a tiny symbolic force like that of Luxembourg would have been enough—but probably the authorities' fear of an unfavorable reaction of public opinion. At any rate, the recommendation to give military support to the collective action in Korea was a sufficiently unpopular measure in Latin America to go practically unheeded. This fact cannot lead logically to any other conclusion than that such a recommendation represented a burdensome and difficult political commitment which was actually not desired in Latin America nor did it serve Latin American interest. A Soviet veto which would have prevented its adoption—although leaving those who voluntarily wished to aid the victim through the exercise of collective self-defense free to do so—would not necessarily have been detrimental to Latin America.

Even though the small countries—Mexico among them—in San Francisco were supporters in principle of broadening as much as possible the functions of the Assembly, where they have a majority, the experience of these last years should make them see the dangers of the Assembly being able to take enforcement action, urged on by political pressures difficult to resist and free of legal checks, in cases of serious threats to the peace, breaches of the peace, and acts of aggression. The small and medium-sized powers would be benefited by the strict application of those fundamental provisions of the Charter which establish the basic division of functions between the General Assembly and the Security Council.

DESIRABLE CHANGES IN THE STRUCTURE
AND FUNCTIONING OF THE SECURITY COUNCIL
AND THE GENERAL ASSEMBLY

Security Council: The most necessary change in the Security Council is of functional character. It is to restore fully its original functions and, to a certain extent, its original hierarchy. The indispensable constitutional reforms have already been set forth in full: on the one hand, the elimination of the veto in the pacific settlement of disputes (Chapter VI), and on the other hand, the necessary changes in some articles which determine the jurisdiction of the organs of the United Nations (especially Articles 14, 34, 35, and 39 of the Charter), in order to establish clearly, as was the original intention of the authors of the Charter, that all those situations or disputes which constitute a real or imminent threat to the peace, as well as all those cases of breaches of the peace and acts of aggression, are under the sole jurisdiction of the Security Council.

A revision of the membership of the Council might also be considered. The total number of members, the proportion of permanent members to non-permanent members, and the norms specified by Article 23 for the election of the latter (contribution to the maintenance of international peace and security and to the other purposes of the Organization, and also an equitable geographical distribution) are adequate and do not require any change.[43] But, in practice, an evident disparity has been created in favor of the Atlantic Alliance

---

[43] Lately, the suggestion is often heard that India be granted a permanent place in the Security Council. In support of this idea, it might be recalled that India is a country which understands and consummately performs the role of mediator in the United Nations. In view of the obvious need to strengthen this important function at the present time, and considering that that country has never shunned the difficult role of negotiator in all the serious crises, especially those which have occurred in Asia, it may be thought that its permanent participation in the labors of the Security Council would contribute to the cause of international peace. It must be borne in mind, moreover, that India not only has the will but also the real power to play an important role in world affairs, in its capacity as mediator as well as in other capacities. At present, it is a great Asian power and it will probably become a great world power.

to the detriment of the rest of the members. For example, during 1952, of the 11 members of NATO which were also members of the United Nations, 6 were represented in the 11-member Security Council. That is, NATO represented 54% of the Council in spite of only making up 18% of the total membership of the United Nations (60), with the legal majority in the Council 7 votes. This excessive representation signifies a large number of votes in favor of the Western bloc (although its practical effectiveness is very relative because of the use of the veto). It is also a situation which is not conducive to the Council's functioning as negotiator, which under present conditions offers the best possibilities for maintaining peace.

But beyond these issues and independently of the fact that the so-called "gentlemen's agreement" of San Francisco, which recognized two seats on the Council for the Soviet group, has not been in force for some years, there have been certain difficulties in practice in determining whether a country belongs to a specific group for the purposes of its election. There might also be considered the desirability of formulating in the eventual conference for reviewing the Charter a joint "declaration" or some other suitable instrument in order to establish clearly the membership of the different groups, as well as the number of seats which should be allocated to each of them.

The General Assembly: the Question of Weighted Voting.[44] There is frequent discussion of another fundamental modification in the structure of the Assembly, which if accepted would necessarily affect the functions of this organ in a very important way. The change would be to assign, according to a prior criterion, an unequal number of votes to the different states. It is said that the Assembly cannot be a truly representative organ, to which important decision-making or executive functions can be entrusted, so long as countries which have a population of less than a million inhabitants have

---

[44] The principal changes in the jurisdiction and functions of the General Assembly have already been fully discussed earlier in this chapter.

one vote, that is, a power of decision equal to that of others that have more than four hundred million inhabitants; that it is necessary to adjust the "weight" of a country in the Assembly to its real capacity to contribute to the solution of world problems.

This idea seems to have, as is natural, more acceptance with the great powers than with the small.[45] In Great Britain it has been supported by Sir Hartley Shawcross and in the United States, among the public officials, by the present Secretary of State, John Foster Dulles.

This type of measure, by its very nature, should be judged objectively, keeping in view the benefits or disadvantages it may signify for the entire Organization. Ultimately, if this measure tended to increase the effectiveness and authority of the United Nations, it might bring greater benefit to the small states than a power of decision disproportionate to their importance, their responsibility, and their present ability to use their power with sufficient independence. But, on the other hand, it must be agreed that it is very difficult to prove the validity of this proposition. Furthermore, there are also excellent reasons for maintaining the present system of a vote to a state, and in any event, the opposition of the majority of the small powers makes it highly improbable that the principle of the unequal vote in the Assembly will be adopted. In those circumstances, it seems preferable to study this question only as a simple possibility and not as a specific suggestion.

The main criticism that can be brought against this system of voting is that it is not democratic, that there should be no inequality among the states, just as there should be none among the different citizens within a state. In this connection, it must be observed, first

---

[45] When dealing with the problem in one of the four last volumes recently published of his monumental work, Arnold J. Toynbee says the following: "The U.N.O. [is not] capable of becoming the embryo of a world government, [among other reasons, because] the realities of the distribution of power in the World that had emerged from the Second World War were not adequately reflected in the clumsiness of a constitution that had embodied the unrealistic principle of 'one state one vote.'" *A Study of History* (London: Oxford University Press, 1954), Vol. IX, pp. 543-44.

of all, that the concept "democracy" has a particular sphere of application which is within the state, and that if it is used outside of its special sphere, it loses a great deal of its meaning and becomes almost a metaphorical expression. Secondly, even accepting the "democratic" criterion, it is certain that within some countries the various political entities which make up the state have a representation proportional to their population in some of the representative organs of the whole, that is, of the state political body. It is difficult to grasp clearly the reason why this same situation should not exist on an international scale, where the inequality of the population of the entities represented is even more emphasized (Iceland has three thousand times fewer inhabitants than China) and where such an inequality is necessarily reflected in a different ability to influence the affairs of the world community. Certainly, at present, it would be impossible to speak properly of a world "community" of peoples, since there is at most a society of states; for this reason, a direct representation of the peoples in a world organization is not possible. The state continues to be the axis of the political organization of our time and the indispensable link between the individual and the world organization. But, on the other hand, neither must it be forgotten that each day there is a greater tendency to consider the individual as the direct object of many international norms. With reason it is frequently emphasized that the very Charter of the United Nations refers to "We the Peoples of the United Nations," unlike the League Covenant which referred to "The High Contracting Parties," that is, to the governments, Surely, in our time, the element "people" might already be directly reflected, even in a partial way, in the structure of the world organization.

If an intermediate point of balance were sought between what has been accomplished toward creating a true "community" of nations and what remains to be accomplished, between the sovereign equality of states and the obvious inequality in their ability to contribute to the management of world affairs, perhaps it might be thought that representation in international organizations should continue to correspond *to the states as such,* but adjusting that representation to the variable factor of population through the granting of an unequal number of votes. In other words, each state would be entitled to a single "representation." There would be as many representatives as there would be states. The delegates would not directly represent a certain number of people, so that no state would have more than one "voice"; but each state would have a voting strength in proportion to its population.

The interesting proposals of Clark and Sohn for revision of the Charter in this respect[46] are based on a different conception. According to these authors, each five million inhabitants of a nation would be *directly* represented by a representative. The Assembly would thus include about four hundred representatives, each of whom would have the right to one vote, by instruction of his electors, which could be used freely, independently of the other representatives of the same country. That is, each delegate in the General Assembly would directly represent population groups rather than states. Apart from the contradiction between this direct representation of the world population in the Assembly and the designation of states as "members" of the United Nations though they would lack their own representation,[47] it is certain that this system of representation fits a much more advanced conception—it actually signifies world government—than is permitted by the present level of political development. For now, perhaps the most that could be hoped for would be a more realistic representation of states, but not actually to

---

[46] Grenville Clark and Louis B. Sohn, *Peace through Disarmament and Charter Revision* (Preliminary Print, July 1953), pp. 17-24.

[47] If the state as such is not "represented," it would be difficult to continue considering the Organization as interstate and the states as true members. Clark and Sohn refer to the "nations" instead of the states, as members (Article 3 of their proposals) but the use of this term does not do away with the contradiction, since it can only refer to the national entities which are politically and juridically organized, that is, to the states, although they do not designate them with that name. Furthermore, in Article 4 they propose that "any doubt in a particular case as to the existence of any nation as an independent state shall be determined by the General Assembly." *Ibid.*, p. 13.

eliminate state representation. The United Nations will continue to be an interstate organization for a long time to come.

Although these authors begin with a different initial conception, the method which they propose for the election of representatives and the sound reasons they give to support it are perfectly applicable, *mutatis mutandis*, to the determination of the number of votes that should be given to each state. It seems especially fitting to adopt population as sole criterion, independently of other factors,[48] and to assign one vote to every five million inhabitants, to fix a maximum of thirty votes to a state, and to require a minimum population of one hundred thousand for the granting of a vote.

Since it is unlikely that in the near future the principle of unequal voting in the Assembly will be accepted, it would be pointless to study further the functional changes which might be proposed for this organ in the event of its being ultimately adopted. Of course, the existence of a more representative Assembly might be reflected in a larger number of functions and in a greater power of decision. Above all, the adoption of such a system would permit the quasi-legislative function of the Assembly to become extraordinarily strengthened. Moreover, as Mr. Dulles proposed, a series of questions of organization, such as the election of the Secretary-General and the admission of new members, which are at present handled partly by the Security Council, could be reserved exclusively to the General Assembly.[49] The executive functions of the Organization for the maintenance or the restoration of peace should continue to be, on the other hand, specific matters for the Security Council,

---

[48] "The authors . . . . have considered various plans of weighted representation which would reflect such factors as economic and natural resources, productive capacity, national income, trade and literacy. They have, however, rejected such an approach upon grounds of principle. They believe that all such plans, which necessarily give weight to wealth and other economic factors that are largely the result of geography and history, involve an anachronistic discrimination. Such a discrimination would run counter to the inherent equality of all individuals, which in the modern world should not and cannot be denied." *Ibid.*, p. 21.

[49] Dulles, *op. cit.*, p. 193.

which has a different criterion for membership, namely the political and military ability to contribute to re-establishing the peace or to resist measures decreed to this effect, an ability which does not necessarily depend upon population.

The General Assembly: The Question of the Secret Vote: Another possible change, of a purely procedural nature, but which would have a considerable influence on the functioning of the Assembly, is related to the voting procedure of the latter. It is specifically proposed that the vote in the Assembly always be cast secretly. It is difficult to examine *in abstracto* the merits of this proposal. Theoretically, the member states act in the General Assembly with enough independence and responsibility to assume that they would vote the same way whether their vote were open or secret. Nevertheless, the situation is clearly different. Only those who are familiar with the workings of the Assembly know to what extent the constant pressure brought upon the small powers influences the result of the voting in the Assembly. Often the basic criterion used by a small state for voting is the fear of antagonizing the great power to which it is linked. Frequently the proposals concerning important questions are voted on with regard to their origin and not to their intrinsic merits. This situation is well known and even admitted by the delegates of many small countries.

So long as numerous states in the Assembly lack the necessary independence to pronounce themselves on important problems in accordance with their real convictions, the organ's labors will be futile. Of the evils that afflict the United Nations, probably "satellitism" is one of those which has most delayed the political maturity of the Organization and contributed to damaging the moral authority of its decisions.

This situation could be partly corrected if the great powers were to lose the instrument at their disposal to control the conduct of the small countries. The secret vote in the Assembly would permit the free expression of the will of the states and would thus contribute to lessening the satellitism in the United Nations. Undoubtedly, the great powers would not approve of the adoption of such a measure. But, actually, there is not a single legitimate reason of importance for opposing the acceptance of a system which would permit the small countries to express their convictions sincerely through the vote. If the great powers have faith in the worth of their proposals, they should not oppose having their lesser allies show their adherence without pressure.

The adoption of this system of voting does not require any constitutional change. The Charter makes no reference to the system of voting in the Assembly, so that simple reform in the rules of procedure of this organ would suffice. The objection that the secret vote is slow and cumbersome is without any value. Surely it is not outside the capability of present technology to devise a simple system so that delegates can cast their votes secretly from their seats, even simultaneously, and have the results automatically and instantaneously computed by the President.

chapter six

Collective Self-Defense
and Regional Arrangements

In previous chapters the fundamental principles and the limitations of the system of collective security established by the United Nations Charter were examined. It was emphasized that the system of the Charter reflects the reality of a world divided into two great political and military coalitions, headed by their respective great powers; that the primary objective of the Organization, to which the other aims are subordinated, is to prevent an armed clash between the great powers, even if this implies, at times, the sacrifice of justice or the legitimate interests of the small states when they do not coincide at a given moment with the need for maintaining universal peace. Therefore, if a dispute should endanger peace, the Organization would have as tasks: first, independently of the responsibility which might be ascribed to each party, to "freeze" the dispute, so as to avoid, above all, setting off or extending an armed struggle; and, second, to resort to the procedures for pacific settle-

1

ment of the substance of the dispute. For better or for worse, in San Francisco it was felt that this "ultra-realistic" conception of collective security represented the best guarantee for avoiding an armed conflict between the two great coalitions, or to put it another way, for maintaining universal peace in a deeply divided world. In any case, it seemed to be the only conception possible, since the division of forces which came out of the war did not permit the great powers to abandon their national security further in favor of a more democratic, but heterogeneous, organization which might be swayed by its majority to one or the other side, according to the political sympathies of the states.

Such a conception rests on a delicate balance, difficult to maintain over a long period of time. There has already been a discussion[1] of the effort made to break the balance of the Charter in favor of one of the two great coalitions, through the "Uniting For Peace" resolution which seeks to annul the inhibiting and moderating function of the veto and subjects the use of armed force to the play of majorities in the General Assembly. The system created by this resolution represents an "internal" modification of the United Nations. It basically alters the sphere of competence of the two most important organs. But, in addition, in recent years, a system has been formed which substitutes for or complements the system of collective security of the Charter and which to a certain extent operates "outside" the United Nations: this is the creation of permanent organizations for the preparation and exercise of collective self-defense.

Since San Francisco, it has been recognized that the rigid system of collective security of the Charter must be tempered. The small states, especially, could hardly be blind to the fact that, due to the absolute necessity of avoiding an armed clash between the great powers, their very existence might be sacrificed, without the Charter system even providing legal measures to avoid it, in case of disagreement among the permanent members of the Security Council.

---

[1] See above, pp. 157 ff.

That is, if the veto was accepted, at least the "inherent" right of the state to self-defense against armed attack should be recognized, not only individually—which, at times, might be insufficient—but even collectively, that is, with the aid that other states might lend it. This situation was recognized by the Charter itself, which, in Article 51, established the right of individual or collective self-defense. It was only later that the right of collective self-defense recognized by the Charter was used as a basis for creating permanent organizations, thus complementing and, to a certain extent, substituting for the collective security system of the United Nations.

ANTECEDENTS OF ARTICLE 51 OF THE CHARTER

The final text of Article 51 was the result of a compromise in San Francisco. The Latin American countries were not satisfied with the provisions of the Dumbarton Oaks Proposals on regional arrangements, which, although permitting the continuance and future creation of such arrangements, required that all the regional enforcement measures for the maintenance of peace and security be subject to the prior authority of the Security Council. These provisions had the effect of preventing the inter-American regional agency from taking measures to forestall or repress the aggression of one American country against another without the authorization of the Security Council, that is, without the necessity of an agreement among the five great powers, of which four completely lacked regional bonds with the American hemisphere. On the other hand, since the great powers, and especially the Soviet Union, did not seem willing to grant a greater autonomy to the regional agencies or arrangements so that they could take political action outside the world organization, the formula of Article 51 of the Charter was worked out as a compromise. The right of individual or collective self-defense without intervention by the Security Council was recognized—at least in the initial phase of defensive action—but only in case of *armed attack.* On the other hand, the *enforcement* action in the regional arrangement or agencies, as such, would remain under the complete control and subject to the prior authorization of the Security Council (Articles 52, 53, and 54 of the Charter).

The two situations are basically different. In the first case, under Article 51, several states, which may or may not belong to the same geographical region, can agree in a collective defense arrangement that if one of them suffers an armed attack the others will come to its aid under specific conditions. Collective defense is exercised without prior authorization of the Security Council, even though it must be immediately reported to this organ. In the second case (Articles 52, 53, and 54), several states may sign a "regional arrangement" or set up a regional agency to pursue manifold common aims (political, economic, social, cultural co-operation, etc.), including the performance of such functions relating to the maintenance of peace as are appropriate for regional action. The last-mentioned functions of regional arrangements and agencies can be of two orders. First, the regional organization may promote the pacific settlement of local disputes, that is, among the members of the arrangement or agency; the exercise of this function, under Article 52, does not require authorization of the Security Council. Second, it may happen that the Security Council determines to apply enforcement measures against some state and that it considers it appropriate, for a given circumstance, to utilize a regional arrangement or agency for that purpose; the exercise of this function of collective security is realized only with the authorization and under the control of the Security Council (Article 53).

The American republics put into force the right established in Article 51 of the Charter by means of the Inter-American Treaty of Reciprocal Assistance signed in Rio de Janeiro on 2 September 1947. Since then, other collective defense treaties have been ratified: one being signed in Brussels on 17 March 1948, by Great Britain, France, and the three Benelux countries; and the North Atlantic Treaty signed in Washington on 4 April 1949 by the United States,

Canada, and ten European states, later joined by Greece and Turkey.[2]

CONSISTENCY OF COLLECTIVE DEFENSE TREATIES AND REGIONAL ARRANGEMENTS WITH THE CHARTER

The creation of *permanent agencies* of collective defense represents quite a deviation from the system established by the Charter. Self-defense under Article 51 of the Charter was thought of as a real exception to the essential principle for an orderly coexistence—just as valid at the domestic as at the international level—that only the juridically organized collectivity can make use of armed force. There fore, its scope was limited to a simple *initial* and *provisional* action against armed attack legitimate only during the short lapse of time before the Organization would assume control of the situation. Collective defense was never conceived of as a substitute for the collective security system of the United Nations, nor was it thought that a right granted to the states for emergency cases would become a duty through treaties. The regional arrangements do not have that function either. Neither the Dumbarton Oaks Proposals nor the Latin American countries in San Francisco considered them to be military alliances or autonomous instruments of collective security. It was originally thought that the pacific settlement of local disputes could be better effected through the intervention of regional groups made up of similar states. As to the application of enforcement meas-

---

[2] In practice, it is difficult to distinguish between regional arrangements and collective self-defense treaties. As will be seen later on, the Rio de Janeiro Treaty shares this dual character. The authors of the North Atlantic Treaty deny that it constitutes "a regional arrangement under Chapter VIII of the Charter" (see statement by Mr. Bevin before the House of Commons, quoted in *Atlantic Alliance*, A Report by A Chatham House Study Group [London: Royal Institute of International Affairs, 1952]) undoubtedly to avoid the control of the Security Council imposed by Articles 52 and following of the Charter, especially that which refers to keeping the Security Council fully informed of the activities "in contemplation." Nevertheless, it presents all the characteristics of a regional arrangement. Hans Kelsen, for example, gives it such a character. See his article, "Recent Trends in the Law of the United Nations," *Social Research*, Vol. 18, No. 2 (June 1951), pp. 142-44.

ures by the regional arrangements or agencies, this function was granted as a *delegation* by the Security Council, so that, under Article 53 of the Charter, a prior decision of this organ is necessary in each specific case concerning the suitability of entrusting this function to the regional arrangements or agencies in order that they may take action.

It is of little interest to examine from a strictly legal viewpoint whether regional arrangements or collective self-defense agreements constitute a violation of the Charter. They represent a political reality of great importance in our time and, as Kelsen says regarding NATO, in any case, "there is no authority competent to annul it."[3] Although it may be possible, as has been argued, that the wording of the Charter authorizes the assumption of such functions by the agencies which have been created, there is no doubt that it is contrary to the manifest intention of the drafters of the Charter. Nonetheless, the essential question is not one of legal interpretation. The fact that should be analyzed is that the *direct* functions of collective security which regional arrangements and collective self-defense agreements seek to assume are obviously contrary to the principles and political assumptions on which the entire structure of collective security is based and that they alter the balance of the Charter.

THE "CENTRALIZATION" OF COLLECTIVE SECURITY IN INTERNATIONAL AGENCIES

The *ultima ratio* of the international organization, which gives meaning and justification to its existence, is the centralization of those powers relative to the maintenance of peace. The tendency toward centralization, as is natural, has become more accentuated as international solidarity has become firmer and it reaches its full significance in the creation of international agencies. Previously, the members of international society could take *final* decisions, legally

---

[3] *Ibid.*, p. 144.

valid, on the legitimacy of the motives or causes that they had for making war. In reality, at least at the level of positive law, the problem of the "legitimacy" of wars did not even arise nor did the related question of individual or collective self-defense, except, naturally, when a war violated a specific treaty as regards a certain country (for example, the violation of neutrality or of a non-aggression treaty). But, even in those cases, there was no higher authority to decide juridically, with compulsory binding effects, on the legitimacy of the action undertaken. The League Covenant and later the General Pact for the Renunciation of War (Kellogg-Briand Pact) reduced the sphere of decision of the states, thus centralizing, correlatively, the power of decision in the international agency. But the centralization was only partial. Under the League Covenant, states were free to wage war provided they observed the conditions and moratorium of three months established by the Covenant. In addition, the Covenant did not provide for the League's determination, in a final and legally binding form, of the existence of an act of aggression. This power was reserved to the individual members. Finally, the Council of the League could only make recommendations on the use of military sanctions and the individual members were empowered—not bound—to follow them.

The creation of the United Nations changed the picture fundamentally. In the words of Luis Padilla Nervo, speaking in his capacity as President of the sixth session of the General Assembly, its existence means "the juridical and political centralization of all the international factors of power in an Organization representing the whole world community."[4] Not only war, but even all use of force or the threat of the use of force are prohibited by the Charter. Only the Security Council can juridically determine, with binding effect on all the members, that an act of aggression has occurred. Finally, the use of any enforcement measure, whether or not it implies the use of force, is also centralized in the executive organ of the United

---

[4] General Assembly, Official Records: 6th Sess., 375th Plenary Mtg., 5 Feb. 1952, p. 528.

Nations, that is, in the Security Council. The Charter system, which represents the culmination of a long process of centralization, above all tends to remove from the individual state the power to decide juridically, by itself, on the legitimacy of its international acts, especially those which involve the use of force.

Certainly, the Charter system is neither complete nor perfect. The severe limitation on the power of judgment and decision on the part of states calls for an effective system to restrain aggression. The Charter system of collective security is not effective, nor can it do without the voluntary collaboration of the states. The Security Council lacks its *own* means to enforce its decisions. It can only rely on the resources and forces of the member states, which must make their armed forces and facilities available to the Council, under Article 43 of the Charter. But this is done in accordance with special prior agreements which the Council signs with the members, and the conditions and terms of these agreements cannot be forcibly imposed on the states. Therefore, the exercise of the enforcement power of the Organization depends to a great extent on the will of the states, and in that sense, the centralization of the power of the Organization is incomplete.

In consequence, the very nature of the situation made it apparent that states must partially retain—to the degree that the Organization is ineffective, to the degree that centralization is not complete —certain and limited rights to the use of force through the exercise of individual or collective self-defense. But this exceptional authorization in favor of the state can only be granted to the extent that the Organization needs to be supplemented because it lacks its own means of action, that is, only *in the use of force as such*. This same exceptional power could not be extended to that other aspect in which the centralization of the powers in the Organization is legally complete, in which it is qualified to act, that is, in the power to decide juridically and exclusively, on whether or not force should be used, on its magnitude, and on the conditions in which it is to be exercised.

The contrary solution would mean a retrogression to the use of methods left behind in history, the results of which we are still suffering. For the Organization to abandon its power of decision in this matter would in practice amount to legitimizing war. If the state were entitled to be the final judge in deciding when self-defense is justified, in practice it might happen that a war would be initiated and pursued in which both participants would simultaneously claim the right of self-defense. Moreover, as is well known, there has seldom been a case when an aggressor state has not used that claim in its favor.[5]

INTERPRETATION OF ARTICLE 51 OF THE CHARTER

The above consideration can serve as a guide for interpreting Article 51 of the Charter. Under this Article, self-defense lasts "until the Security Council has taken the measures necessary to maintain international peace and security. Now, who shall decide whether the measures taken by the Council have been those which are "necessary" to maintain peace? The Council itself or the besieged state? Who is supposed to decide if the state which claimed self-defense acted justifiably, that is, if it actually was subjected to an armed attack and if its reaction was not excessive?

According to what has previously been stated, it would be contrary to the very aims of the Organization, and to all that the United Nations stands for as an advance in international relations, to accept the proposition that the state should reserve to itself the power of decision on these questions. It would mean absolutely arbitrary rule and would again amount to legitimizing war. In this matter, it is particularly indispensable that the principle of the authority of the United Nations be maintained.

[5] Germany sought to justify the invasion of Belgium in 1914 by claiming self-defense against the imminent invasion by France, England, and Russia. Japan tried to justify in the same way its military operation in Manchuria in 1931, even by alleging that "the right of self-defense may extend beyond the territory of the power which exercises that right." (Statement by Count Yasuya Uchida, Minister of Foreign Affairs, 25 Aug. 1932. See *The New York Times* of that date.)

Nevertheless, it would also be difficult to agree that the state attacked should remain defenseless before the possible inaction of the Security Council. If the words "measures necessary" used by the Charter have any meaning, they certainly cannot be interpreted as synonymous with "no measures." It may actually happen that the Council cannot reach a decision on the measures that may be "necessary" and may not adopt any. But other hypotheses may also present themselves. In reality, it is impossible to set a uniform rule for solving the dilemma, since it may in practice take on many aspects. Therefore, it is advisable to analyze the situation with reference to the following cases that may be presented:

(1) The Security Council determines that an armed attack has occurred and justifies the defensive action taken, whether individual or collective. The Council can then do one of two things: (a) Recommend to the state or states which claimed self-defense that they go on defending themselves, under the supervision of the Council, and continue the measures initially taken to restore peace (in that case, there would be no problem); (b) Decide to take measures different from those employed in the initial defense action, in which case the state or states which claimed self-defense will cease action.

(2) The Security Council determines that an armed attack did not take place and the self-defense claimed is not justified or is excessive. Under this hypothesis the action of the state which claimed self-defense will cease, or if need be, it will comply with the decision of the Council on the manner of restoring peace.

(3) The Security Council does not reach a decision on the existence of an armed attack, or on the legitimacy or character of the defense, either because of a veto or because no resolution to that effect received the required majority of seven votes. In that case, the state attacked will be able to continue exercising the right of self-defense. As Kelsen says, "the fact that the Security Council does not take a decision is not equivalent to the condition under which the exercise of the right of self-defence must cease, namely that the 'Security Council has taken the necessary measure to maintain international

peace and security.'"[6] For the exercise of self-defense to cease, a *positive* decision of the Security Council is needed to the effect that the right invoked is unjustifiable, which is very different from the failure of the Council to reach a decision confirming the initial action undertaken. In other words, there is a presumption *juris tantum* in favor of the legitimacy of defensive action which exists as long as the authority for its exercise is not *expressly* withdrawn. But even should the Council adopt no decision, the juridical basis for continuing self-defense does not lie in the state's authority to decide this question for itself or to judge whether the action of the Council is adequate, but, as has been said, it lies in the non-fulfilment of the condition for cessation of the exercise of self-defense.[7]

THE INTER-AMERICAN TREATY OF RECIPROCAL ASSISTANCE

The Inter-American Treaty of Reciprocal Assistance fundamentally establishes the following: any dispute which arises among American states will be resolved by the procedures of pacific settlement in force in the inter-American system, before referring it to

---

[6] Hans Kelsen, *The Law of the United Nations* (New York: Frederick A. Praeger, 1950), p. 803.

[7] In his excellent analysis of the Inter-American Treaty of Reciprocal Assistance, the former Secretary General of the Organization of American States, Alberto Lleras Camargo, seems to reach a contrary conclusion. Without expressly confirming the power of the state to make a decision in this matter, he uses certain expressions that imply that he may have adopted that premise: "Certainly it is not verbal action that would paralyze collective self-defense, nor is it a question of automatic procedure such as that which deprives the Assembly of the United Nations of jurisdiction. Article 51 speaks of measures, that is, positive steps in defense of the victim taken by the Council, and qualifies them by saying they are *necessary* to maintain peace and security — not half-way measures or those incapable of restoring either." (Inter-American Conference for the Maintenance of Continental Peace and Security, Rio de Janeiro, August 15 — September 2, 1947. *Report on the Results of the Conference Submitted to the Governing Board of the Pan American Union by the Director General* [Washington: Pan American Union, 1947], pp. 38-39.) Nevertheless, it is to be supposed that he had in mind, particularly, the third hypothesis that is here established, that is, failure of the Council to act, as a consequence of the veto or the absence of the necessary majority, but not cases in which the Council *decided* that the defense was untimely, excessive, or inadequate to establish peace.

the United Nations (Article 2); an armed attack by any state against an American state will be considered as an attack against all the American states, and therefore all the parties to the Treaty are obliged to aid against the attack (Article 3); in case of aggression that is not an armed attack, of a conflict within or without the continent, or of any other incident which may endanger the peace of America, the Organ of Consultation will meet (in principle, the meeting of the Ministers of Foreign Affairs of the American republics) to agree on measures to be taken (Article 6), which will be binding upon the parties to the Treaty, with the sole exception that no state will be required to use armed force without its agreement (Article 20); finally, Article 8 of the Treaty specifies the various measures that the Organ of Consultation can decide upon: breaking of diplomatic and consular relations, interruption of economic relations or communications and, even, the use of armed force.

The Treaty of Rio de Janeiro has a dual character. On the one hand, it is an agreement to organize and legitimize collective self-defense in accordance with Article 51 of the United Nations Charter. On the other hand, the text of the Treaty itself reveals that it is also a regional arrangement as such, in accordance with Chapter VIII (Articles 52, 53, and 54) of the United Nations Charter, since it requires all parties to inform the Security Council—in accordance with Article 54 of the Charter, which is expressly invoked in the Rio Treaty and which refers exclusively to regional arrangements and agencies—not only about activities "undertaken" to maintain peace and security but also about activities "contemplated" for the same purpose. The obligation to inform the Council of activities "undertaken" might not in itself be different from that arising when the right of self-defense is exercised under Article 51, but the obligation to inform the Council of activities "contemplated" specifically concerns the parties to regional arrangements and agencies.[8]

---

[8] L. Oppenheim, *International Law: A Treatise* ([7th Rev. Ed., by H. Lauterpacht] London: Longmans, Green, and Co., 1952), Vol. II, p. 158.

The Rio Treaty operates as a collective self-defense agreement only under the hypothesis of an "armed attack" against some American state. Article 51 of the Charter, which is the basis for and establishes the scope of the Treaty (insofar as it is a self-defense agreement) is explicit regarding this: *only* "armed attack" justifies the exercise of the right of self-defense. Therefore, all the other hypotheses provided for in the Rio Treaty (aggression that is not armed attack, other incidents that can endanger the peace of America, etc.) and all the measures which might be adopted as a result of those hypotheses which are different from armed attack, are excluded from the authorization and provisions of Article 51 of the Charter and necessarily come under the provisions of the Charter which relate to the second aspect of the Rio Treaty, that is, to regional arrangements. In other words, if one of the possibilities foreseen in Article 6 should be realized, the Rio Treaty operates as a regional arrangement, the action taken under the Treaty being limited by the provisions of Articles 52, 53, and 54 of the Charter of the United Nations.[9]

Now, Article 8 of the Rio Treaty establishes that "for the purposes of this Treaty, the measures on which the Organ of Consultation may agree will comprise one or more of the following:" and there follows a list of the enforcement measures already mentioned which are substantially the same as the corresponding measures which are set forth in Articles 41 and 42 of the United Nations Charter. No provision of the Treaty makes a distinction between the application of the measures of Article 8 when the Treaty operates as an instrument of collective self-defense and their application when the Treaty constitutes a regional arrangement subject to Article 53 of the United Nations Charter. As the authorization to take action which is granted by the Charter is different according to the hy-

---

[9] Isidro Fabela, "La Conferencia de Caracas y la actitud anticomunista de México," *Cuadernos Americanos*, Vol. LXXV, No. 3 (mayo-junio de 1954), pp. 36-39.

pothesis that occurs (armed attack or other incidents) and, therefore, according to the manner in which the Rio Treaty operates
(agreement for collective self-defense or regional arrangement), it is
necessary to analyze separately the bases and consequences of the
possible application of the measures provided for in Article 8 in
each of the two situations:

(1) In case of an armed attack against any American state, when
the parties act in self-defense, it is obvious that the Organ of Consultation can decide, at its discretion, on any collective measure including armed force, with the sole requirement that it be "immediately reported" to the Security Council (Article 51 of the Charter).
Actually in this case there is no problem. The different situations
that can later arise, once the Council "has taken the measures necessary to maintain international peace and security" (approval of
the measures adopted, withdrawal of authorization, or absence of a
positive decision by the Security Council) have already been studied,
indicating courses of action for each one of the situations.

(2) On the other hand, if what arises is not an armed attack against
an American state, but one of the incidents anticipated in Article
6 of the Rio Treaty (aggression which is not an armed attack, conflict within or without the hemisphere, or any other incident that
endangers the peace of America), the Organ of Consultation provided for in the Rio Treaty shall comply with the obligations that
Article 53 of the Charter imposes on the regional arrangements for
the application of enforcement measures, since in this case the Rio
Treaty operates in that way. Now, under Article 53 of the Charter,
"no enforcement action shall be taken *under regional arrangements*
or by regional agencies without the authorization of the Security
Council" (author's italics), except against an "enemy state" (any
state which during the Second World War was an enemy of any
signatory of the Charter of the United Nations). Therefore, if there
is no fulfilment of the hypothesis of armed attack against an American state under the conditions anticipated in the Rio Treaty, the
Organ of Consultation shall always obtain the authorization of the

Security Council in order to apply any of the enforcement measures of Article 8, unless they are decreed against an enemy state.

This interpretation is not directly derived from the wording of the Rio Treaty itself. No provision of the Treaty requires the prior authorization of the Security Council for the application of enforcement measures in the cases foreseen in Article 6. However, juridically there can be no other interpretation. The Rio Treaty can have no other juridical basis than the provisions of the United Nations Charter. All the signatories of the Treaty are at the same time members of the United Nations and are bound to observe the provisions of the Charter. If, in spite of this, the Organ of Consultation were to decide on enforcement measures without observing the above requirement, the parties would not be obliged to apply them, in spite of the fact that the decisions of the Organ are, in principle, binding. In fact, Article 10 itself of the Treaty establishes that, "None of the provisions of this Treaty shall be construed as impairing the rights and obligations of the High Contracting Parties under the Charter of the United Nations."

In such a case, each party would judge for itself whether the activities contemplated or undertaken under the Rio Treaty were inconsistent with their rights and obligations as members of the United Nations. This is justified by Article 103 of the United Nations Charter, according to which, "In the event of a conflict between the obligations of the Members of the United Nations under the present Charter and their obligations under any other international agreement, their obligations under the present Charter shall prevail."

The situation under examination has special importance for the Latin American countries as a result of the declaration adopted at the Tenth Inter-American Conference which met in Caracas in March 1954. According to this declaration, which was not approved by Mexico,

> the domination or control of the political institutions of any American State by the international communist movement, extending to this Hemisphere the political system of an extra-

continental power, would constitute a threat to the sovereignty and political independence of the American States, endangering the peace of America, and would call for a meeting of Consultation to consider the adoption of appropriate action in accordance with existing treaties.[10]

The hypothesis which is referred to in this paragraph is not an armed attack, but one of those anticipated in Article 6 of the Rio Treaty and the "measures" which it mentions are precisely those established in Article 8 of the same Treaty. If this hypothesis should occur, the Treaty would operate as a regional arrangement and not as an agreement for self-defense. Therefore, if the Organ of Consultation should decide to take enforcement action under Article 8 against an American state, without the prior authorization of the Security Council, those states which felt such a decision to be illegal could claim its inconsistency with the Charter of the United Nations and refuse to apply it.

---

[10] Tenth Inter-American Conference, Caracas, Venezuela, 1-28 March 1954, Final Act (Washington: Pan American Union, 1954), pp. 94-95.

chapter seven

Regional Agencies: Pan Americanism

The existence of regional units rests on two assumptions contrary to one another: first, the recognition that world unity, based on a common way of life and common values, is still very distant; and second, the increasingly evident conviction that, in our time, the great majority of national states are political and economic units ill-equipped to develop fully and even survive on solely national bases. Politically, most states have lost ground in a world which has had its centers of power radically diminished in the course of a generation. Economically, they are units too small to develop fully their natural resources and overcome their poverty unless they work together. The modern world needs to create regional units as a bridge between the isolated national state and a sufficiently integrated world collectivity of the future.

Actually, it is impossible to speak of "creation" when dealing with regional agencies or units. Their possible existence depends on the prior existence of a certain number of "natural" factors, as much physical as spiritual. In some ways, the regional agencies have an existence which preceded their being internationally recognized as political units.

The San Francisco Charter authorized the existence of regional arrangements and agencies "for dealing with such matters relating to the maintenance of international peace and security as are appropriate for regional action." That is, it authorized the existence of regional associations of countries with fundamentally political ends. Even though the Charter does not prohibit the creation of regional economic units, it is surprising that none of its provisions referred to regional agreements of an economic nature.[1] The need to manage world affairs by areas in our time is due as much to economic necessity as to any other kind of factor. Outside of some countries with a large population and great richness and variety of natural resources, like the United States and the Soviet Union, countries which are regional units in themselves, the economic structure of the other regions of the world requires planning on supernational bases. In Western Europe, in Latin America, practically everywhere, it is indispensable to create commercial areas which include an entire economic region in order to take advantage of an incomparably greater market than can be offered by the majority of the present

---

[1] The British author, G. D. H. Cole, gives the following reasons for this: "The United States, while reserving its right to enter into any arrangements it may please with its neighbors on the American continent—or indeed elsewhere: witness the economic arrangements recently made with the Philippines—has been endeavoring to get the rest of the world to organize its economic affairs on the principle of 'no discrimination,' which means, in practice, mainly the right of free entry for American private enterprise into the markets of the world. The United States delegates were most unlikely, at the time when the drafting was done, to include in the United Nations Charter anything that might be interpreted as giving encouragement to regional arrangements. . . . Nor was the Soviet Union likely to wish to advertise in the United Nations Charter its far-reaching plans for replacing Nazi Germany as the controlling power in East European economic relations. As for Great Britain, its delegates knew very well that nothing suggestive of the maintenance of the 'sterling area' or of empire preference would find favor with the United States. Accordingly, when the U.N. Charter was being drafted, the entire problem was passed over in silence." *World in Transition* (New York: Oxford University Press, 1949), p. 580.

states. Production must be planned globally in order to attain specialization of national industries and to lower the cost of products so that the whole regional unit will benefit. Likewise, agriculture, industry, and transportation must be planned as complementary services within the economic region and not in terms of ruinous competition among the national economies. In brief, the raising of the living standards of backward countries and even the maintenance of present conditions by the other countries requires a high degree of international co-operation which is only possible in our time through the association of similar countries in larger economic units. The opposite solution—"non-discrimination" and the spontaneous international division of work on a world scale—can hardly be a satisfactory answer for the poor countries. From the Industrial Revolution to our time, its most tangible result has been to accentuate the differences between wealthy countries and poor countries and to contribute to the fact that four-fifths of humanity have not been able to develop enough economically to achieve a decent standard of living.

THE REGIONAL PROBLEM IN AMERICA

What is the regional "reality" of the American hemisphere? How favorable are conditions in this hemisphere for an authentic regional agency, both from a political and economic aspect?

Beforehand, a warning: the question posed here is not what has been under discussion for the last century and a half as to the essential unity of the New World, as to whether geography and history act to bring together or divide the American hemisphere. The answers which have been given and which can reasonably be given to these questions are innumerable. Along with André Siegfried and Luis Alberto Sánchez, among others, it might be maintained that geography tends to unite the two Americas in spite of the twofold culture of the hemisphere and that "it has been history, created by man, which has introduced dissension between South and North

America, and among the Indoamericans themselves."[2] On the contrary, it might be maintained with the well-known Colombian internationalist, J. M. Yepes,[3] that the historical factor, the similar origin of the Anglo-Saxon and Iberic parts of the hemisphere, to which with time has been added "the similarity of political regimes," has helped strengthen the bonds of solidarity between Latin America and the United States. It would not be pointless, however, to ask if "the similarity of political regimes" is not more apparent than real. Likewise, it would also be permissible to ask if the geographical factor—even accepting a relative similarity of the physical environment of the two Americas—at present operates as a political and economic tie among the countries of the hemisphere, when it is considered that North America is closer geographically to Western Europe than it is to the most distant regions of South America. Actually, even factors as objective as geography are very difficult to define in terms of relative importance and it is not easy to ascertain the role that it plays in the American hemisphere. The study of more subjective elements, such as the existence of a conscience common to the American man and others of this type, or in general, cultural factors, produce even more dissimilar replies.

A closer and more practical consideration of the problem leads us to study only the question whether at present it is to the interest of Latin America and particularly Mexico to have a regional agency, as conceived of by the United Nations Charter, which embraces not only the Latin American countries but the United States, or if the former should not try for a closer economic and political association among themselves, thus creating the basis for a more integrated Latin American community in the future. An examination of this problem would necessitate a study of whether the existence of cer-

---

[2] Luis Alberto Sánchez, *¿Existe América Latina?* (Mexico: Fondo de Cultura Económica, 1945), p. 31. See also André Siegfried, *Amérique Latine* (Paris: A. Colin, 1934).

[3] J. M. Yepes, *Philosophie du Panaméricanisme et Organisation de la Paix: Le Droit Panaméricain* (Neuchâtel, Switzerland: Editions de la Baconnière, 1945), pp. 77-78 and 82-85.

tain factors and circumstances peculiar to the postwar world—such as the new role of the United States in the world and the creation of the United Nations, among others—have not altered the importance and the cohesivecapacity of the centripetal forces of the Pan American system.

ECONOMIC CO-OPERATION AND PAN AMERICANISM

One of the reasons most frequently brought forth in favor of a regional entity which includes not only Latin America but also the United States is the economic factor. It is said that the economies of the Latin American countries and of the United States are complementary. The first-mentioned are producers of raw materials and importers of manufactured goods and of capital, while the second consumes raw materials produced by Latin America and exports the manufactured goods and capital needed there.

The complementary character of the economies justifies the advisability of an active trade between the two Americas, but it does not necessarily, in itself, establish the existence of a regional economic entity. Economic associations can just as well be created in terms of the *common*, rather than the *complementary*, interests of the associates. Undoubtedly, there does exist an economic interdependence between sellers and buyers or between producers and consumers, but this does not necessarily lead the first and the second to associate themselves permanently. Often it is the contrary that occurs: sellers, for instance, form organizations to defend their common interest, which is opposed to that of buyers.

The United States in itself is a real regional system. The abundance and variety of its natural resources, the extent of its domestic market, its industrial and agricultural capacity for over-production, the integration of its transportation system, and the small proportion represented by foreign trade in its economy make that country an economic unit comparable in size and importance to that which might be formed by all Western Europe if it ever became a regional economic entity.

Latin America, on the other hand, is not an economic unit nor is it probable that it will become one in the near future. But the Latin American countries have common economic problems, interests, and aspirations, at least fundamentally. On the other hand, the specific economic interests of the United States, although they may sometimes be complementary to those of Latin America, are basically in opposition. This opposition of interests has been reflected in a divergence of economic criteria and principles between the United States and Latin America practically since the beginning of modern Pan Americanism.

Since the first Pan American conference (Washington, 1889-90), the United States has proposed—and Latin America rejected—the creation of a customs union embracing the entire hemisphere, which would have ruined any future possibility of industrialization in Latin America and would have condemned it to the never-ending extraction of raw materials for industry in the United States. The differences in viewpoints have not lessened with time. At present, Latin America and the United States take opposing positions, the result of antagonistic interests, on practically all the important economic issues of our time: on the problem of trade parity, that is, on the very principle and on the methods to achieve a balance between the prices of raw materials and manufactured goods; on tariff policy; on methods of public and private financing for the economic development of underdeveloped countries; on the function and character of foreign investment in Latin America; even, at least to a certain extent in the case of Mexico and some other countries, on the mutual function and importance of private enterprise and public resources as instruments of economic progress in individual countries. This opposition of principles has been evident in all the sessions of the General Assembly and of the Economic and Social Council of the United Nations and in all the inter-American conferences since Chapultepec (1945).

The basic conclusion that might be gathered from this situation is that the existence of economic problems, interests, and aspirations common to the Latin American countries should be reflected in the adoption of a common economic policy of their own which would specifically serve Latin American interests: not an economic policy or philosophy common to the two Americas, but principles for use in Latin America which would give it greater cohesion and force in its economic relations with other countries or regions, among others precisely with Anglo-Saxon America. The wrong course, on the other hand—which Pan Americanism sometimes gives the impression of following—is to make an effort to find an economic decalog common to the United States and Latin America.

If Latin American countries seek to improve their position vis-à-vis other countries, including the United States, and if they wish to adopt practical measures for raising their standard of living, they should begin by setting forth principles and establishing bases which translate *their* community of economic interests. To some extent, those common principles exist and, if there had been a suitable place or occasion, perhaps they would have come to be defined. Latin America lacks political and juridical institutions which reflect and put into force that community of Latin American interests. Until now, their efforts have been fruitless, mostly because they have been carried on within a Pan American framework which unrealistically assumes the economic unity of America.

POLITICAL CO-OPERATION AND PAN AMERICANISM

From the first Pan American conference to the present time, inter-American coexistence has been moulded by a certain number of political-juridical principles which regulate the reciprocal relations among the countries of the hemisphere. These principles of political coexistence represent Pan Americanism's greatest achievement to date. Economic relations between Anglo-Saxon America and Latin America, by their nature, have to this time not been able to give rise to an authentic regional economic entity, or even to the establishment of certain common principles which might form the embryo of a Pan American economic unit in the near future. Nor has Pan Americanism made enough progress in the field of social co-operation to be credited with a positive and direct contribution to the raising of the social conditions of life in the American hemisphere. Perhaps some positive achievements can be mentioned, especially recently, in the field of cultural co-operation. But fundamentally, until now, Pan Americanism has consisted of the norms which regulate and restrict the political action of some states as regards others within the American hemisphere.

What are these norms of political coexistence and to what extent have they contributed to the integration of an American community of nations? The answer to these questions contains the whole problem of the "reality" of Pan Americanism. For the Organization of American States, like any interstate association, is in the last analysis only a web of political-juridical ties among states. Basically, the value of these ties and their impact on American international life will determine the answer to the fundamental question which all Latin American countries should ask themselves: Is Pan Americanism, that is, the permanent association of the United States and Latin America in a regional agency, the best possible solution to the necessity for a regional life in America? In order to answer this question, various principles of inter-American coexistence will be examined, analyzing in each case, first its distinctiveness, that is, if it is a matter of principles which are common only to the American countries, since if they were also common to other parts of the world, there would be no reason to build a special entity on them; and, second, the extent to which they have contributed to strengthening solidarity among the American countries and to giving cohesion to the system.

To estimate objectively the value of Pan Americanism, or in other words, to measure the importance of these political-juridical principles, it is necessary to reject in the first place, at least as a peculiarly Pan American tie, the existence of certain principles or norms which some enthusiastic supporters of Pan Americanism consider to be the heritage of this system. Thus, J. M. Yepes indicates as norms of the "Pan American *jus gentium*," the adoption of the principle *pacta sunt servanda* as a basis of international law; the principle of the self-determination of peoples; "the existence of a certain form of civilization based on respect for the individual, on spiritual freedom, on respect for treaties, and on an international morality both binding and objective"; and others of the same type.[4] If what is meant is that such principles are *desiderata*, postulates, or even norms juridically in force in America, it is undoubtedly a true affirmation. But, in that case, they could hardly be considered as special factors of union among the American republics, since such principles, either as postulates or even norms, likewise regulate the relations among other states foreign to the American hemisphere and also the relations among the countries of America and other states. If, on the other hand, what is meant is that these principles have been scrupulously and widely enforced and observed in America, to a degree that its situation in this respect might be contrasted fundamentally with that of other regions of the world, such an affirmation would be truly difficult to demonstrate.[5]

A more realistic and modest analysis of the situation would limit our considerations here to only those principles which, because they have arisen in America, because they have received a special interpretation, or because they have been invoked or applied with special

---

[4] *Ibid.*, pp. 86-87.

[5] Unfortunately, the immodest appropriation of universal *desiderata* or of the great principles of *jus gentium*—which frequently have no relation to the institutional reality of the Latin American peoples—is not limited to some zealous Pan Americanists. The Pan American Conferences themselves have often fallen into this tendency which certainly does not increase the universal prestige of Pan Americanism, but, on the contrary, has led many European authors to describe it as unreal, bombastic, and insincere. The following affirmation contained in the "Declaration of Mexico" approved by the Inter-American Conference on Problems of War and Peace (Chapultepec Conference, Mexico, 1945) might serve as an example of the tendency: "The American community accepts the following essential principles as governing the relations between the States composing it . . . . The American man cannot conceive of life without justice, just as he cannot live without freedom."

frequency in inter-American relations, may be thought of as principles which have outstanding importance in the American hemisphere.

These principles are, to our mind, the following: the pacific settlement of disputes; the non-recognition of the validity of territorial conquest; the various principles relating to the status of foreigners (equal treatment of foreigners and nationals, the Calvo Doctrine, the Drago Doctrine, and the principle of the non-responsibility of governments for damages suffered by foreigners in civil wars); non-intervention; the common aspiration of the American republics for representative democracy; and finally, the principle of joint defense against outside forces.

PACIFIC SETTLEMENT OF DISPUTES

The principle that all disputes should be settled pacifically has occupied the attention of the American governments since the first Pan American conference. The establishment and elaboration of this principle undoubtedly is one of the dominant topics of Pan Americanism. Nevertheless, it can hardly be considered as a principle peculiar to America nor can it be said that these countries had anticipated the recognition of this principle or that this principle has greater juridical force or has received a broader application in America. Proof of this is that the first productive consideration of this principle by the Pan American conferences (Mexico, 1901), resulted in the recognition, as norms of international American law, of those principles relative to arbitration which had previously been established on a world-wide scale by the three Conventions signed at the international conference at the Hague in 1899.[6] The Gondra

---

[6] Article 1 on the Protocol of Adherence to the Conventions of the Hague, which was approved by the Second Pan American Conference in Mexico, states: "The American Republics, represented at the International Conference of American States in Mexico, which have not subscribed to the three Conventions signed at the Hague on the 29th of July, 1899, hereby recognize as a part of Public International American Law the principles set forth therein."

Treaty, signed at the Fifth Conference of American States in 1923, and the General Convention of Inter-American Conciliation of 1929 signified an advance of Pan Americanism in this field, although as regards technical perfection and approximation to the ideal of compulsory arbitration, they are far behind the principles recognized during the same period in the General Act for the Pacific Settlement of International Disputes (Geneva, 1928), which sought to have universal force.

At the Bogotá Conference (1948), the American republics ratified the American Treaty of Pacific Settlement (Bogotá Pact) which represented a considerable advance over all that had been achieved up to then, in the world sphere as well as in the inter-American sphere, since the Pact established the principle of compulsory arbitration and set up adequate machinery to prevent the frustration of this aim, moreover establishing the compulsory jurisdiction of the International Court of Justice for disputes of a legal character. Unfortunately, the two reservations formulated by the United States involve these very two principles. In those disputes to which the United States is a party, the principles of compulsory arbitration and jurisdiction, wherein lies the value of the instrument, are practically ineffectual. If it may be surmised that some of the most important disputes to involve the Latin American countries will be precisely with the United States—history confirms this—the conclusion cannot be avoided that the above-mentioned Pact has a rather relative value for Latin America. Aside from this, its force is still limited. Seven states signed it with reservations, and nine years after its adoption only nine countries have ratified it, one having done so with reservations.

In conclusion, if indeed the importance of the principle of the pacific settlement of disputes cannot be underestimated as a postulate of Pan Americanism, neither should its value be exaggerated as a specific principle that has had or has considerable influence on the political integration of the hemisphere.

NON-RECOGNITION OF THE VALIDITY
OF TERRITORIAL CONQUEST

This principle has been recognized since the first Pan American conference, which declared that wars of conquest among American nations were "unjustifiable act[s] of violence and spoliation"; territorial concessions should be considered void if they were effected under threat of war or pressure or armed force. The same principle later received an important extra-continental application, due to the Manchukuo case (it was then given the name of Stimson Doctrine).[7] Later, several Pan American conferences restated the same principle and finally it was clearly and categorically established in the Charter of the Organization of the American States (Article 17).

As happens with various principles related to the rights and duties of states, this principle is not expressly established in the United Nations Charter, which lacks a chapter on that subject.[8] Nonetheless, it could not be doubted that at present it is a universally valid juridical norm. The International Law Commission of the United Nations itself included it in the Declaration on Rights and Duties of States which was drafted in 1949 (Articles 9 and 11). This principle could not then be considered as a norm pertaining only to so-called American international law, even though it must not be forgotten that its first recognition as positive law was within the sphere of Pan Americanism.

STATUS OF FOREIGNERS

This question includes various connected principles which sometimes are presented as different aspects of the same problem. As is

---

[7] The League of Nations established this principle in a resolution adopted by the League Assembly on 11 March 1932, in the following terms: "The Members of the League of Nations [shall not] recognise any situation, treaty or agreement which may be brought about by means contrary to the Covenant of the League of Nations or to the Pact of Paris." League of Nations, *Official Journal*, Special Supple. No. 10, Records of the Special Sess. of the Assembly on the Sino-Japanese Dispute (1932-33), Vol. I, 4th Plenary Mtg., p. 87.

[8] See above, Chapter 2.

well known, in this matter perhaps more than in any other, there has traditionally existed a conflict between the interests and the point of view of the United States and those of the Latin American countries. At the time of the first Pan American conferences, these principles were already beginning to be discussed. In the Conference of Mexico (1901) a convention was approved which established equality of civil rights for nationals and for foreigners, to which only the United States did not subscribe. In the same Conference, another convention was approved which established the norm that the state is not responsible for the damages caused to foreigners by civil wars or internal disturbances, a norm which was not only in force at that time between many Latin American countries, but between several of these and some European countries. The United States neither voted on nor signed this convention. The general North American position (which had been expressed in the previous conference at Washington by Mr. W. Trescott) was that only in the case of contracts that were not of a public character—and that, with serious reservations—can it be accepted that a foreigner has not the right to demand a greater protection than that given to a national.[9] The United States has never accepted the Calvo Doctrine, under which from the time the contract is concluded or the concession is granted, the foreigner subjects himself to local courts and renounces all claim to the diplomatic protection of his country. It has maintained that the right which is renounced actually belongs not to the individual, but to his country. The right of the state *ex jure gentium* cannot be modified or annulled *pactis privatorum*.[10] With the passing years, there has not been much progress made in this field, which might be considered as the cornerstone of American solidarity. Even at the present time, the United States does not accept this principle.

---

[9] Alberto Guani, "La Solidarité Internationale dans l'Amérique Latine," *Recueil des Cours*, Académie de Droit International, Vol. 8 (1925, III), pp. 259-62.

[10] Karl Strupp, "L'Intervention en Matière Financière," *Recueil des Cours*, Académie de Droit International, Vol. 8 (1925, III), p. 80.

The Latin American countries managed to insert into the recent Bogotá Pact the important Article VII, which provides the following:

> The High Contracting Parties bind themselves not to make diplomatic representations in order to protect their nationals, or to refer a controversy to a court of international jurisdiction for that purpose, when the said nationals have had available the means to place their case before competent domestic courts of the respective state.

The United States expressly rejected this principle through the introduction of a direct reservation against this article. Common juridical principles of international character can hardly be spoken of when the hemisphere continues to be divided on this question which is vital to the Latin American countries and which has given rise to so many serious disputes.

Neither did the Drago Doctrine[11] become in its time a Pan American principle, in spite of the great importance that its recognition would have had at that time for the Latin American countries. The United States did not accept it, declaring that:

> No independent nation in America need have the slightest fear of aggression from the United States. It behooves each one to maintain order within its own borders and to discharge its just obligations to foreigners. When this is done, they can rest assured that, be they strong or weak, they have nothing to dread from outside interference.[12]

As to the Porter counterproposal, presented in the name of the United States at the Hague Conference of 1907 on this same subject,

---

[11] According to this Doctrine, non-payment of the public debt cannot authorize the armed intervention and even less the occupation of the territory of American states.

[12] Note of the Secretary of State, Mr. Hay, quoting from a message of President Theodore Roosevelt on 2 December 1902. U.S. Dept. of State, *Papers Relating to the Foreign Relations of the United States, with the Annual Message of the President Transmitted to Congress December 2, 1902* (Washington: Govt. Printing Office, 1903), p. xxi.

it suffices to remember that it was subject to formal reservations by practically all the Latin American republics that attended that Conference.[13] In the opinion of Strupp, the convention which was approved at the Hague (based on the United States proposal) was practically valueless due to its not having been ratified by the majority of the states which had suffered interventions by creditor countries.[14]

At the present time, the Drago Doctrine is outdated. The prohibition of the use of force and the inviolability of territory have been recognized by Article 2, paragraph 4, of the United Nations Charter and by Articles 15, 16, 17, and 18 of the Charter of the Organization of American States.

Acceptance by the United States of the principles relative to the status of foreigners would have had a decisive importance in the strengthening of the bonds of friendship between the two Americas. The history of Latin American relations with the United States during the last hundred years is to a great extent the memory of the opposition of two interests and two positions which innumerable times conflicted in this matter. If there were an appropriate adjective for these principles, it would be "Latin American," but never "Pan American."

NON-INTERVENTION

The principle of non-intervention perhaps represents the greatest conquest of Pan Americanism. No other international principle has had such deep roots in the juridical conscience of the American states or had greater importance in the life of the hemisphere.

The principle certainly has a universal validity, but it has been

---

[13] The texts of the reservations are found in the previously cited work of A. Guani, pp. 290-91.

[14] Strupp, *op. cit.*, p. 111.

worked out in America with more preciseness and effectiveness than elsewhere. The fact that this principle has been perfected on American soil is undoubtedly a cause for pride; but that same circumstance also says much more about its causes and origins. This principle has acquired force precisely as a defensive reaction of the Latin American countries from their painful experience, from the innumerable interventions which have been suffered from European countries as well as from the United States. Paradoxically, the international norm of America which is most characteristic and important was not born of the union, but of the disunion of the hemisphere.

Non-intervention is a negative principle, a defensive principle. It represents the first step toward coexistence. It is barely a *modus vivendi*, a formula of tolerance which, especially in America, facilitates the coexistence of twenty Latin American republics on the one hand, and the United States on the other. But it is not, either by its origin or by its nature, a principle of positive co-operation; it is barely its prerequisite.

The "reality" and the value of a regional system cannot be measured in terms of a negative principle such as non-intervention. It must be measured in terms of the positive aspects of coexistence. But, while the international organizations continue to base themselves on respect for state sovereignty, non-intervention will continue to be a necessary prerequisite of all political and economic solidarity in a world made up of states which are unequal in strength and at different levels of development. When the states have common interests, when there exists a regional system of homogeneous composition in which the factors of integration dominate the divisive forces, the states can afford to be less jealous of their sovereignty. The barriers put up by a state against others that are members of the same international group become higher as the organization becomes more heterogeneous. Within the world organization those barriers must be very high; in the regional agency they might be minimal. Nevertheless, paradoxically, the principle of non-intervention is established in America with more exactitude and strictness than in the world Charter.[15]

If a demonstration were desired of the political and economic dualism of the hemisphere and the scanty integration of the Pan American system, the American formulation of the principle of nonintervention would be a good proof of this, notwithstanding that it is considered one of the mainstays of Pan Americanism. It actually is, but precisely to the extent that it represents the dual reality of the hemisphere, and that its strict provisions reflect the necessities of coexistence between the United States and Latin America.

Recently, a dangerous trend has come to the fore with regard to the principle of non-intervention in America. It is the idea that the principle of non-intervention should apply to the action of other states, but not to the collective action which a regional agency may adopt. That is, according to this position the measures decreed by the Organization of American States would not be considered intervention. In a previous chapter[16] it was, in effect, stated that the principle of non-intervention only concerns the action of other states and that this question should be distinguished from the other question of the existence of a reserved domain which is not subject to the action of the international organizations. Naturally, this reserved domain or domestic jurisdiction does not include the *international* activity of the state. The purpose of international organizations is precisely to limit, to "intervene" in order to regulate the international action of the states. But the idea is only acceptable up to this point.

It was also previously stated that, under Article 2, paragraph 7 of the United Nations Charter, those "matters which are essentially

---

[15] Article 15 of the Charter of the Organization of American States says: "No State or group of States has the right to intervene, directly or indirectly, for any reason whatever, in the internal or external affairs of any other State. The foregoing principle prohibits not only armed force but also any other form of interference or attempted threat against the personality of the State or against its political, economic and cultural elements."

[16] See above, p. 54.

n

within the domestic jurisdiction of any state" cannot be subject to intervention by the international organizations. That is, there is a jurisdiction which embraces the domestic life of the state and which is "reserved," which is exempt from all foreign action, even of the international organization, since no country would wish to be a member of the latter if its participation implied the renunciation of their domestic autonomy. Thus, that prohibitive norm should be considered an essential, characteristic element that is at the very foundation of any international organization made up of sovereign states, independently of the fact that it may be expressly established in the constitutional charter, as in the case of the United Nations, or it may not be specified, as in the case of the Organization of American States. Actually, it would not have been necessary formally to set forth the principle of domestic jurisdiction (as was recognized by the committee of the San Francisco Conference which drafted Article 2, paragraph 7 of the United Nations Charter) since by its very nature it is implicit in the structure of all international organization.

Nonetheless, some recent developments of Pan Americanism are obviously contrary to that structural principle of the Organization of American States. The Tenth Inter-American Conference held in Caracas in 1954 adopted a resolution entitled "Declaration of solidarity for the preservation of the political integrity of the American States against the intervention of international communism," which authorized collective action against the member states in the event of certain possibilities which undoubtedly relate to and belong to the domestic jurisdiction of the states, such as the domination or control of their institutions by communism. Mexico vainly presented many amendments aimed at specifying, at the very least, that the premise for collective action should be subversive action by foreign agents. That is, it sought at least to ascribe a clear international character to those factors which form the basis for the collective action of the inter-American organization, at the same time taking them out of the sphere of domestic jurisdiction. However, all the amendments offered by Mexico were rejected. Moreover, when drafting the resolution entitled "Declaration of Caracas," Mexico tried to include as one of the guiding principles of the system the following:

> The political system and economic and social organization of the peoples belong essentially to the domestic jurisdiction of the State and, therefore, cannot be subject to any intervention, direct or indirect, individual or collective, by one or more countries or by the Organization of American States.[17]

In spite of the fact that the Mexican draft only applied a principle already established by the United Nations Charter, it was rejected by the Conference, having gained 4 votes in favor (Bolivia, Mexico, Argentina, and Guatemala), 2 against (United States and Brazil) and 14 abstentions (according to the voting system of the Organization of American States, a resolution requires for its approval in plenary session the absolute majority of the states present in the Conference, in this case 11 votes).

The rejection of this principle signifies a frank retrogression of Pan Americanism. The states are insufficiently protected in that aspect of intervention which has become most dangerous and important in our time. The American hemisphere has left behind the phase of unilateral and arbitrary intervention, at least of a military character. The modern form of intervention is through collective action obtained by votes in international meetings.

REPRESENTATIVE DEMOCRACY AS A COMMON AIM OF THE AMERICAN REPUBLICS

The exercise of representative democracy is one of the postulates of Pan Americanism. In the famous Resolution XXXII adopted at the Bogotá Conference, the peoples of the New World reaffirmed the faith that they "have placed in the ideal and in the reality of democracy." The Organization of American States Charter itself (Article 5, paragraph d) states that "the solidarity of the American

---

[17] No official translation available.

States and the high aims which are sought through it require the political organization of those States on the basis of the effective exercise of representative democracy."

This is one of the Pan American principles which is most distant from reality. At present, more than half the member states do not fulfil the minimum requirements of a democratic system of government. What is worse, if the present situation is compared with that of some years ago, the democratic ideal of America seems to be increasingly remote.

Nonetheless, it is impossible to criticize the fact that the American republics pursue an ideal which they are not at present in a situation to put into practice. But it is interesting to observe that, if a conclusion is desired concerning the factors of solidarity which operate in the American hemisphere, the dual political composition of the hemisphere has not historically favored nor does it favor at present the practice of representative democracy in America. The existence of dictatorships in the hemisphere is due to a complex of causes and factors peculiar to the countries which are afflicted by them. But it could not be denied—and that is a truth which is repeated as an axiom in Latin America—that one of the most powerful reasons for the perpetuation of dictatorial regimes in America is the decided moral and material support which they have been historically furnished by the United States. Even North American writers who might also be considered almost as official apologists of Pan Americanism, like Whitaker, admit this fact.[18] What is most deplorable is that the postwar conditions have made the situation worse. The political and ideological struggle of the United States against communism has had the indirect consequence in America of strengthening dictatorships. The continental reality is not union in democracy, but disunion, the division between dictatorships and demo-

---

[18] Arthur P. Whitaker, *Las Américas y un Mundo en Crisis* ("Biblioteca Interamericana," Vol. XV [New York: Carnegie Endowment for International Peace, 1946]), p. 287.

cratic countries. The postulate of representative democracy has no value as a factor of solidarity and cohesion in America.

In America, some praiseworthy steps have been initiated which represent an effort to set these countries on the path to democracy. There might be cited, among others, the famous proposal of Rodríguez Larreta of Uruguay to take collective action in America in behalf of democracy and human rights;[19] the Guatemalan proposal on the recognition of non-democratic governments submitted to the Chapultepec Conference and the like proposals repeatedly presented by Uruguay (the last time at the Caracas Conference); and perhaps also the so-called Tobar Doctrine.[20] The acceptance of these ideas would undoubtedly represent a considerable advance in the political life of America. However, none of them has been accepted up to this time; in part, because of the opposition of the dictatorships; but also because some democratic governments have been compelled to reject them in view of the political conditions which prevail at present in the American hemisphere. Unfortunately, even the liberal element of America, which would hardly be able to find fault with them as such, has had to be reserved about these proposals, and, concretely, has had to oppose them.

The reason is not difficult to uncover. There is the fear that these proposals may be used as instruments of pressure and undue interference for politically aligning the American republics, either by refusing diplomatic recognition or by sponsoring collective action to intervene in domestic affairs. For this reason, Latin America has been hindered from carrying out formulas which would mean democratic progress and a higher level of coexistence in America. While this fear exists, while the present situation does not change, the cornerstone of the inter-American system, its guiding principle, will not be democracy, but intransigent non-intervention.

---

[19] See above, pp. 53-54.

[20] According to this Doctrine, no government should be recognized which is the result of a revolution or a *coup d'état*, so long as the people have not had an opportunity to organize the country constitutionally, by freely elected representatives.

Mexico has fully understood this situation. Although a considerable sector of the country's public opinion is openly antagonistic to Latin American dictatorships, the government has maintained a consistent anti-interventionist policy, even though it serves equally to cover up and protect the dictatorial regimes.[21] The least change of position would ultimately help not the progress of democracy, but probably the establishment of new dictatorships. As far as Mexico is specifically concerned, it would weaken a position of principle which will continue to be, perhaps for many years to come, the best safeguard of its political independence.

COLLECTIVE DEFENSE AGAINST OUTSIDE FORCES

The principle of collective defense represents a more advanced level of cohesion among the members of a regional system insofar as it reveals a common desire to set up a united front against outside forces. This principle might become one of the factors of solidarity which would best contribute to building up an integrated regional community. Nonetheless, the parties to the Rio Treaty, where this principle took shape, are beginning to lose sight of its purposes in two important aspects.

The first aspect is the tendency to use the enforcement measures provided for in the Treaty, not for their fundamental purpose— which is to repel armed aggression or to serve as an instrument of

---

[21] A Mexican diplomat and author, Luis Quintanilla, has worked out a "test" for democracy which would indicate all the faults which prevent a state from being considered democratic. See *Panamericanism and Democracy*, Inter-American Monographs, No. 1 (Boston: Boston University Press, 1952), pp. 35-38. In spite of the fact that the test, because of its intrinsic worth, might have been presented in the international centers and turned into an inter-American resolution, it has never been formally introduced as a proposal. In the first place, it is not certain that the present political setting in America would permit discussions on such a proposition to result finally in anything like what Quintanilla had in mind. Secondly, even though this author does not suggest international collective action to preserve democracy, the mere fact that it is defined internationally implies a divergence from the principle that the governmental regime and the economic system of the nations belong to their domestic jurisdiction and, therefore, are outside the orbit of international organizations.

collective security of the United Nations under the authority of the Security Council—but as a means of pressure to judge, condemn, and eventually to overthrow the internal regimes of the states, to the extent that they do not meet with the approval of the majority of the American republics. In discussing the non-intervention principle in America, reference has already been made to resolution XCIII adopted in the Tenth Inter-American Conference of Caracas, which clearly reflects this trend.[22] The Rio Treaty was conceived of and drawn up as an instrument which would protect the hemisphere in the international and not domestic aspects of common defense. Certainly, the extremely vague wording of Article 6 ("any other fact or situation that might endanger the peace of America") allows the Organ of Consultation a wide field of action. But the best proof that the authors of the Rio Treaty did not provide for or desire collective intervention in such domestic matters as are contemplated in the Caracas resolution is that when the Rio Treaty was drawn up, two proposals to that effect were presented and they were both rejected. Uruguay proposed that the Treaty be applied to the violation of the essential rights of man or to departure from the democratic system, and Guatemala to any act or situation which might endanger the democratic structure of the hemisphere. The specific rejection of these proposals largely strengthens the interpretation that the governmental regime of the American states is outside the scope of the collective action provided for in the Treaty.

Unfortunately, that is not the only aspect in which the purposes of the Rio Treaty may be vitiated. The very composition of the regional arrangement and the new role played by the United States in world politics are changing the arrangement into a military alliance which fundamentally serves to carry out the extracontinental objectives of the United States. That is, it is being transformed from a *regional* instrument of defense to an instrument of *world* policy. The triple participation of the United States in the Rio de Janeiro

---

[22] See above, pp. 163-64, 182-83.

Treaty, in the North Atlantic Treaty, and in the defense agreements of the Pacific creates political and military risks for the Latin American states which are very different from those which are normally understood as involved in hemisphere defense. The only *extracontinental* responsibilities which should be undertaken by Latin American countries are those which arise directly out of the United Nations Charter, with precisely all the guarantees which it carries. The meaning which the Rio Treaty has for the Latin American states is that it prevents aggression from approaching Latin American shores. To the extent that one of its members, which must be defended by all, has direct interests of its own in other areas of conflict—to that extent, the war draws nearer to the hemisphere. A defensive regional arrangement has meaning for the Latin American countries only if it compels joint defense of those countries which have no political and military interests beyond America which might bring about a war. In the past, perhaps until a few years before the last war, as long as the United States followed an isolationist policy, the advantages for the Latin American countries of a joint defense treaty with the United States would have outweighed the disadvantages. Today its benefits are not evident.

CONCLUSIONS

The preceding considerations do not lead to the conclusion that Pan Americanism is the best answer for Mexico to all the problems which require a regional solution.

In the economic aspect, Pan Americanism has not even succeeded in establishing those basic principles of inter-American co-operation which might contribute positively toward raising the standard of living of the Latin American peoples. The reason largely stems from the fact that the Pan American organs and instruments, by their very nature, do not reflect nor are they based on the real division of the hemisphere into two clearly differentiated economic zones, which have fundamentally opposing economic problems, interests, and aims, although their economies are complementary. If this was true when modern Pan Americanism began, it is more so now. What is interesting to observe is not merely the fact that Latin America and the United States maintain different viewpoints on those economic problems that most affect them. This is not to be wondered at in view of their different structures and the opposition of their economic interests. Furthermore, the division of the hemisphere into two distinct economic regions may signify a positive benefit to the Latin American countries. What is important is that the necessary and desirable proximity of the two different economies in the hemisphere, together with the impossibility that they will ever be brought together into a single entity, places on the Latin American countries the necessity of looking at problems from a Latin American viewpoint and creating a common policy of their own which satisfies the interests of the group and of its individual members. Perhaps it may be difficult to achieve this, but at present there is no other firm basis for building an authentic regional economic entity. In the contemporary world, the creation of larger economic units represents the best solution for wholly developing the human and natural resources of the underdeveloped countries.

The essential norms for political co-operation in America have been examined. Those principles which are most important in the hemisphere have not yet formed, because of their nature or because of other circumstances, bonds of solidarity sufficiently strong to create a political Pan American community. Some, such as the non-recognition of the validity of territorial conquest, the pacific settlement of disputes, or the postulate of representative democracy, are common to but not exclusive to the American peoples. That is, many of the institutions that are common to the United States and Latin America are also common to all the nations which inherited the political and juridical tradition of the West.

Other important principles, like that of non-intervention, have a negative character and their very nature, origin, and importance reveal the basic political antagonism that divides the two Americas.

The principles regulating the status of foreigners could have been the basis for a pacific and friendly coexistence between Latin America and the United States, but in reality they have not gained the adherence of the latter country. The principle of common defense against outside forces, which by its nature might contribute to the strengthening of American solidarity, has become a principle which today presents serious risks for Latin America due to the extra-continental political and military interests of its North American associate. Moreover, a principle that was fundamentally conceived of as a defense against foreign attack or contingencies tends to become transformed into an instrument of intervention in the domestic affairs of the Latin American states. Other principles, excellent in themselves, like the international protection of democracy and human rights and the non-recognition of dictatorships imposed by violence have not been established in America for fear that they might be used as instruments of intervention in the Latin American countries. Lastly, other less important institutions not discussed here, such as diplomatic asylum and the *uti possidetis* principle, are Latin American, but not Pan American. One of the few institutions of some importance which is common to Latin America and to the United States is the recognition of the territorial principle instead of the *jus sanguinis* as a basis of nationality.

The Pan American Spirit: The nature and function of the great Pan American principles in America demonstrate the meager political integration of the hemisphere. This phenomenon has been at the same time cause and effect of the absence of a true Pan American spirit. What has living reality in the conscience of peoples is the feeling and the bonds of Latin Americanism. Pan Americanism, on the other hand, has existed almost behind the back of public opinion both in the Latin American countries and the United States. Important sectors of American public opinion still are convinced that the permanent activity of Pan Americanism, centered in the Pan American Union and other principal bodies located in Washington, is closely tied up with the United States administration. The

Pan American conferences, because of their importance and public character, could have made a greater contribution to the formation of a Pan American spirit. Nevertheless, with the notable exception of the Conference of Buenos Aires (1936) and perhaps some others to a lesser extent, public opinion has found them more siginificant for the divergences between the viewpoints of the Latin American countries and the United States than for any constructive unity which has been manifested. Pan Americanism has existed for more than sixty years as a system and it still has not succeeded in penetrating the conscience of the Latin American peoples. Except for some isolated incidents during the "Good Neighbor" period, it would be difficult to find during this long period any powerful and spontaneous public manifestation which would have lent it force and reality. The personality of Latin America on the one hand and of the United States on the other are the only ones which are recognized by the Latin American and the North American as such. Outside of the official declarations of the governments, the common tasks or destiny of the American hemisphere are seldom referred to, at least as something specific not included in the patrimony of the West.

The new grouping of political forces in the world has helped accentuate the artificial character of Pan Americanism. The common element which during a century gave a certain cohesion to the two Americas and some appearance of reality to Pan Americanism was our common and conscious removal from world power politics or, at least, our desire to remove ourselves from it. From the moment that the United States became an extracontinental power, that element of solidarity lost all meaning. Pan Americanism has become one of many elements of world policy of the United States. To the extent that the Latin American peoples are compelled to pursue ends which are not their own but are foreign, they deny their own destiny and gradually lose their independence.

Pan Americanism and Pan Latin Americanism: The postwar period has not been an easy one for the Latin American peoples. Due to the economic and social structure of their countries, the artificial prosperity brought by the Second World War did not spread to the most numerous and needy segments of the population. On the other hand, the economic maladjustments of the postwar world had a serious impact on the economy of the Latin American countries, and their increasing dependence on the United States has weakened them politically.

Nevertheless, this period in itself at least presents favorable conditions for a radical review of their situation and for finding their own course. The war acted as a leavening agent, stirring up anxieties and awakening Latin American consciousness of the causes of backwardness and of the possibility of new solutions. Even though the obstacles arising out of the international situation are great, not the least of these being the new North American ideological and political predominance over the Latin American countries, the postwar era offers Latin America the possibility of a synthesis of the formulas and the broad trends of thought which sweep the world. In many sectors there is a clear consciousness of the need for remodeling Latin America's budding capitalism by enriching it with a deep social sense, and of the desirability of developing Latin America through the exploitation of its own riches.

The postwar period also offers Latin America the opportunity of participating actively in international life. The division of the world into two antagonistic camps limits Latin America's field of action a great deal. But to the extent that its alignment within the Western bloc is a responsible and independent one, the relative political balance established in the world offers a great opportunity for Latin America to make its voice heard and to increase its importance in world decisions. Certainly, Latin America does not have real force or the political maturity necessary for becoming a decisive factor in world affairs. But the example of many recently created Asian countries, which have less international experience than Latin America has, demonstrates that Latin America can and should have a very important voice if it decides to act with independence, even though it is fundamentally included in one of the two great world blocs. Latin America has its own mission in the international field. It might generally exercise a moderating and conciliatory influence of extraordinary importance. It might sometimes mediate in certain disputes among the great powers. It might present constructive solutions, in the interest of all humanity and not based on considerations of power politics, to questions such as disarmament, and also it might aid, perhaps decisively, in the liberation of colonial peoples. Its twenty votes, which represent a sizable proportion of the total membership of the United Nations, might always be at the service of just causes and of peace.

But the basic conditions for realizing the possibilities of Latin America are that it assert from the start its own personality, that it become conscious of its historic unity, of its calling and of its potentiality, and that it discover its capacity for acting as an independent community. Pan Americanism has been negative for Latin America especially because it has represented the greatest obstacle to the creation of that authentic international community which rests on real and natural factors, that is, the Latin American community. Pan Latin Americanism is the only hope of creating an organic community in the future.

The eventual creation of a regional Latin American organization would not mean that the Latin American countries should lose their important political and economic ties with the United States. The bonds established between Latin America as a whole and the United States might become stronger and more fruitful than at present. The countries of Western Europe seem to be on the way to integrating themselves politically and economically into larger units and, if this happens, a more active collaboration between the European community and the United States is to be anticipated. But that has not led to the creation of a regional organization encompassing both. It is to be wished that this will also happen in the American hemisphere.

Mexico's position: The position of Mexico in relation to the American regional problem is not a simple one. Even if Mexico were to become convinced that Pan Americanism does not represent the best regional solution in America, the possibilities of its changing the situation are limited. Institutional Pan Americanism has existed for more than sixty years. Although it does not rest at present on sufficiently solid real factors to perform profitably the functions of a regional organization, it certainly exists as an undeniable political reality in America. It has in its favor, if not a consensus of vigorous and conscious public opinion, at least inertia and the obvious difficulties of creating something better. Undoubtedly it will be difficult for some time to establish a Latin American political and economic community. It is not to be anticipated that the United States would favor its creation and the forces working against its being set up within Latin America itself are still very powerful. Under those circumstances, and in the absence of an instrument which better answers the interest of Mexico, the Organization of American States is a solution preferable to possible bilateral relations with the United States in those matters in which Mexico has interests in common with the rest of Latin America. At least on some occasions, a certain solidarity has been shown among the Latin American countries that has resulted in the adoption of viewpoints which could hardly have been maintained by an isolated country in direct and bilateral dealings with the United States.

In spite of this, the situation of Mexico has not been easy. Mexico is one of the countries which has shown greatest independence and which has most vigorously opposed the recent interventionist trend of Pan Americanism and the eagerness to project it on the world stage. In view of the political picture which now prevails in America, Mexico has most of the time been in a clear minority when these questions have been discussed, especially recently. The experiences of the last two Pan American meetings were especially significant in this regard.[23]

---

[23] The three most important resolutions approved in these last two conferences (the meeting of Ministers of Foreign Affairs at Washington, 1951, and the Tenth Inter-American Conference at Caracas, 1954) were considered quite un-

Since it is likely that those tendencies which Mexico considers
contrary to its interests and to those of Latin America will increase
in the near future, it must be asked if the moment has not arrived
when Mexico should proceed to review its Pan American policy,
taking into account a series of considerations: first, the possibility
that Mexico may have a decisive influence on the solution of serious
questions is becoming more and more remote, above all when there
is involved the adoption of directives or important general policies
for the pursuit of the extracontinental objectives of the United States.
Second, when Mexico has taken a position of principle and opposed
the adoption of measures that it feels are contrary to the basic purposes of the Organization, it has not been possible to avoid the
regrettable impression that there is a serious political antagonism
between Mexico and the United States, an impression that is usually
enhanced by the media of information and which has psychological
repercussions that certainly do not encourage good relations between the peoples of the two nations. And third, the participation
of Mexico in the Organization of American States has politically
led it to accept dangerous political commitments which it obviously
does not at bottom desire. In these circumstances, it would appear
advisable that Mexico withdraw somewhat and adopt a more reserved
attitude concerning the activities and commitments of the Pan American system. This attitude should be flexible and adjustable to the
circumstances, in each case weighing the seriousness of the eventual
commitment and the disadvantages for Mexico in not accepting it
or in disengaging itself. As a concrete example of what might be

---

desirable by Mexico as being representative of the above-mentioned trends, and
the Mexican delegates opposed their adoption, although in vain. The three
resolutions are the following: "Preparation of the Defense of the American
Republics and Support of the Action of the United Nations" (Washington, II);
"Strengthening of Internal Security" (Washington, VIII); and "Declaration of
solidarity for the preservation of the political integrity of the American States
against the intervention of international communism" (Caracas, XCIII). The
fact that Mexico did not vote against these resolutions (though it abstained on
the last one) does not necessarily mean that the Mexican government welcomed
their presentation and adoption.

the revised attitude of Mexico in relation to certain serious Pan American commitments, the following might be mentioned: If, as seems possible at present, the Inter-American Treaty of Reciprocal Assistance were to be used, contrary to its purposes, for intervention in the domestic affairs of the American states, Mexico should seriously consider the advisability of denouncing that Treaty, thereby disengaging itself from the commitments which it implies.

chapter eight

The Colonial Problem

The Second World War marked the beginning of a new stage in the history of movements for national freedom. In the period between the two wars, the colonial powers, by means of force, could easily put down the relatively ineffectual rebellions of the native populations of their colonies. But during the last war, new factors arose that strengthened the resistance of the colonial populations against European domination. In Eastern Asia the Japanese invasion produced domestic resistance movements which united and heightened the independence sentiments of the native population, sentiments which eventually took on an anti-European cast. In some of the zones relatively distant from the armed struggle, the war was reflected in an economic improvement for the native peoples, which, combined with the memory of the difficult economic situation and the insecurity associated with the prewar period, helped intensify the drive for liberty. In practically all the colonial areas, except

o

perhaps in the most primitive, some form of nationalist movement inspired and directed by native leaders has made an appearance.

When the San Francisco Conference was held, six hundred million human beings lacked self-government in varying degrees. Within ten years, India, the Philippines, Jordan, Pakistan, Burma, Ceylon, Israel, Indonesia, and Libya had gained their independence, forming as many free states. At present, the inhabitants of territories which still do not enjoy independence have been reduced to less than two hundred million. In some cases, freedom was achieved by armed combat. In other cases, the enlightened self-interest of some of the colonial powers, at times aided by the intervention of the United Nations, has been an important factor in the pacific evolution of the native populations toward independence.

Recently, the anti-colonial struggle has taken on an intensified rhythm and violence. Just a few years ago, in 1949, the British author G. D. H. Cole saw slight possibilities for the total independence of the Dutch East Indies and Indo-China.[1] The same ideological and political struggle which divides the world tends to aggravate and intensify the dilemma between armed rebellion and pacific change of the colonial status quo. Every day it seems more difficult to prevent independence movements from being carried out by force. Therefore, today, the energetic and enlightened action of the United Nations is more than ever imperative to channel peacefully the independence aspirations of the colonial peoples. Soon, it will be practically impossible to localize the anti-colonial struggles. Any violent independence movement can easily become a focus of world conflict.

It is useful to compare what has happened in Indo-China and in Indonesia in order to anticipate the character that may be assumed by the independence struggle of the colonial populations. At the end of the war, the conditions in the two regions were fundamentally

---

[1] See G. D. H. Cole, *World in Transition* (New York: Oxford University Press, 1949), p. 530.

alike. The character of the colonial exploitation of the native populations, the natural resources of the two countries, the degree of
political development and general progress of the people, and even
the international factors which during the war were forerunners of
the independence struggle were similar. However, in the case of
Indonesia, the armed struggle lasted only a short time and this
country achieved its independence, partly because the Netherlands
understood the situation and avoided a fruitless battle in which it
would have finally been defeated, and also, in part, because of the
timely intervention of the United Nations. On the other hand, France
refused to grant independence to the three kingdoms of Indo-China
and the struggle was prolonged more than eight years. The granting
of independence to Indonesia—and probably the same might be
said in the cases of India, Pakistan, Ceylon, and Burma—prevented
the situation from going beyond its local setting and becoming a
phase of the world conflict. In other words, such independence
movements were completely "national" and they could triumph
without the protection of any specific ideology of international
character and without the aid of foreign armed forces. On the other
hand, in Indo-China the prolonging of the struggle and the obstinacy
of France in not making an opportune concession of those liberties
which would have at least partially satisfied the native aspirations
(in the matter of finances, foreign affairs, justice, foreign trade, etc.),
strengthened the position of the most extreme anti-French sector,
that is, the communist faction, and allowed it to appear as almost
the only sponsor of the national liberation movement. Thus, the
struggle in Indo-China became a frontier of the world conflict.

The reaction of the colonial powers to the new independence
movement of their colonies consists fundamentally in the creation
of supranational agencies which embrace the mother country as well
as the colonies. In reality, at least in the case of France, the existence
of these associations of countries has been considered by the native
populations to be an instrument for perpetuating colonial domination. The French Union was not the adequate answer to Indo-China

and probably will not definitely solve the French colonial problem. Under the French Constitution, the French Union is said to be "composed of nations and peoples who wish to place in common or co-ordinate their resources and their efforts in order to develop their civilization, increase their well-being and ensure their security."[2] But basically the essential voluntary aspect of the Union is pure fiction. Independence is conceived of only within the union with the metropolitan country.

As an example of the way in which the wishes of the people have been respected, the case of the Cameroons, which since 1946 has formed an integral part of the French Union as an associated state, might be cited. As was stated recently by the representative of India in the Trusteeship Council of the United Nations,[3] not only is there no proof that the Cameroons population *wishes* to form part of the French Union but, on the contrary, the United Nations has at hand proof that points in the opposite direction.[4] Fundamentally, the incorporation of the Cameroons into the French Union was nothing but an act of annexation.

The British position postulates a greater degree of autonomy and independence between the components of the association and the metropolitan country. Great Britain hopes to create a free community of nations. The concept of trusteeship (or mandate) has been

---

[2] Official English translation, courtesy of the French Press and Information Service, New York.

[3] Trusteeship Council, Official Records (T.C.O.R.): 13th Sess., 494th Mtg., 11 Feb. 1954, p. 93.

[4] Furthermore, the incorporation of the Cameroons into the French Union not only violates the principle of the self-determination of peoples, but the provisions of the Charter itself on the trusteeship system and the agreement concluded between the United Nations and France for the establishment of that regime in the Cameroons. This territory is not a French colony, but a territory under the trusteeship system, that is, subject to an international status, which cannot be modified unilaterally. If one of the essential objectives of the trusteeship system is to prepare the native population for independence, how is it possible to reconcile the possibility of becoming independent with unwilling participation in a Union which does not provide for the right of secession?

replaced in the vocabulary of British colonial policy by the term "partnership."[5] Since the Second World War, British policy has been moving toward independence for the great Asian and African communities and their free and mutually profitable association with the other members of the community. If, as is to be presumed and desired, this recent trend continues, the problem of the remaining colonial possessions of Great Britain will be resolved.

Another factor which at present complicates the adequate and rapid solution of the colonial question is the new position of the United States regarding this problem. During the war, the United States maintained an anti-colonial position. President Roosevelt seemed determined not to identify his country with prewar European colonialism. For example, he thought that Indo-China should not be returned to France but that an international trusteeship should be established there. Nevertheless, recently, due to the exigencies of the "cold war," the United States has frequently found itself in equivocal and contradictory situations in everything relative to the colonial problem. The majority of the members of the North Atlantic Treaty Organization are colonial powers. The ANZUS Pact is also made up of powers that administer trust territories. The United States has been obliged to support its Western allies in their aim of maintaining their colonial domination, against its tradition and, also undoubtedly, against its best interests.

In the battle which it has undertaken against communism, the United States also requires, necessarily, the collaboration and good will of the new Asian and African states which are violently anti-colonial. These states suspect that the lukewarm position of the United States, and its repeated pronouncements in favor of the slow but sure pacific evolution of the native populations toward independence, actually signifies that the evolution must be carried out precisely at the rate and in the conditions which are agreeable to

---

[5] See Alison Smith, "Trusteeship and Partnership in British Africa," *The Year Book of World Affairs, 1953* (London: Stevens & Sons, 1953), pp. 170 ff.

the colonial powers.[6] The position of the United States is even more complicated by the fact that colonial problems tend to become factors in the struggle between communism and anti-communism, with the result that the United States is frequently put in an anti-independence position. What has happened in the countries of South Asia since the war ended should indicate that those conflicts in the long run take on an ideological cast and become the centers of the world conflict, precisely because the nationalist and independence aspirations of the native populations have been blocked instead of being abetted. One of the worst mistakes that might be made at present would be deliberately to confuse or identify the anti-colonial struggle with communism.

The position of the Soviet Union also places a considerable obstacle in the way of achieving the independence of the colonies more rapidly but pacifically. According to the Soviet viewpoint, complete liberation from the foreign yoke is inconceivable without a *revolutionary* national struggle of the colonial peoples against imperialism. The revolutionary struggle is the principal road to the solution of the national-colonial problem. The Soviets accept the trusteeship system though unenthusiastically—from their standpoint, it is only a reformist and unorthodox course which does not threaten the foundations of imperialism—because instead of substituting for the revolutionary struggle, it indirectly contributes to it. The revolutionary struggle will not succeed, nor can it even be conceived of, without the proletariat in the role of director, in the vanguard, carrying along the peasants and other social classes. They feel that it is possible to advance the anti-colonial struggle in combination

---

[6] A recent example of the new North American way of presenting the problem is the following declaration of John M. Cabot, a United States delegate to the Tenth Inter-American Conference, held in Caracas: "While our object is the progress toward self-government and later the independence of non-self-governing peoples, if they choose independence, we are at a moment in which the development of genuine independence constitutes an extremely difficult and delicate task and in which enthusiasm must be tempered with patience." (Tenth Inter-American Conference, Caracas, Venezuela, March 1-28, 1954. Official translation not available.)

with the democratic-bourgeois elements of the colonies only if the revolutionary proletariat has the opportunity, within the general movement, of pursuing its own objectives without weakening them in the common current. While the native bourgeoisie is incapable of struggling for an authentic independence and often compromises with foreign imperialism, the proletariat is a real revolutionary force which can unite the great masses of peasants in order to organize resistance not only against imperialism but also against feudalism and the native upper bourgeoisie. In other words, although the Soviet Union does not oppose—and even encourages—the independence of a colony even if the new government falls into the hands of the bourgeoisie, it feels that the *true* liberation of the colonial peoples is only achieved when, in addition to driving out the foreign master, the proletariat represented by the Communist party assumes control of the former colony.

The dangers of this thesis are evident. It makes it practically impossible to solve the colonial problem by pacific means, since it declares civil war inevitable, even in the case of a pacific transition from the colonial regime to independence. Since the most favorable setting for the triumph of the Communist parties is the violent revolutionary struggle against foreign domination, it is not just chance that the Communist parties seek to direct national independence movements by way of armed rebellion. From the Western standpoint, the conclusion is obvious: the best way to prevent the independence of the colonies from being achieved under communist leadership, with all the consequences that this implies, is to satisfy in time, instead of repressing, the independence aspirations of the colonial peoples.

The small countries, especially the Latin American and the Asian and the African, have until now played an important role in the solution of the colonial problem in the United Nations. Confronted by the new and grave dangers for international peace which arise from the opposing positions of the great powers on the colonial question, the small countries should redouble their efforts to encourage further the action of the United Nations, by strengthening its functions as tutor of the dependent populations, by helping to prevent the colonial problem from bursting into violence, and by utilizing in an independent and imaginative fashion all the resources of the Organization for speeding up the independence of the colonial peoples.

DECLARATION REGARDING NON-SELF-GOVERNING TERRITORIES

General Remarks: Chapter XI of the Charter contains international standards for the administration of "territories whose peoples have not yet attained a full measure of self-government." These territories range from colonies to protectorates, the latter being true subjects of international law, although with limited sovereignty.

The guiding principle in this matter, which represents a considerable advance over the past, is the international responsibility of the colonial powers for the administration of the non-self-governing territories. Chapter XI does not establish, as does Chapter XII which refers to trust territories, a system of international *supervision* to ensure the responsibility of the administering powers. But at least these powers recognize, in the words of Article 73 of the Charter, "the principle that the interests of these territories are paramount," and they accept "as a sacred *trust* [author's italics] the obligation to promote to the utmost . . . the well-being of the inhabitants of these territories . . ." In contrast, Article 23 of the League Covenant only obliged the members "to undertake to secure just treatment of the native inhabitants of territories under their control."

The first problem posed by this Chapter is to determine whether the obligations assigned to the colonial powers have a juridical or a purely moral character. The colonial powers have insisted on the difference between Chapter XI on the one hand and Chapters XII and XIII on the other, maintaining that the first is not mandatory in spite of the clear declaration of the obligations of Article 73.

Frequently, they have claimed in their defense the principle of domestic jurisdiction in this matter, asserting that the relations between the government of the metropolitan country and the colonial subjects are affairs which essentially belong to the domestic jurisdiction of states. But the United Nations has decided in the majority of the cases that the Assembly has the power to examine and even to make recommendations to the colonial powers concerning the matters covered in Chapter XI. The manifold resolutions approved by the General Assembly on these questions form an adequate framework for considering that the international responsibility of the colonial powers, set forth by Chapter XI of the Charter, has given rise to true juridical institutions and norms.

Meaning of the term "non-self-governing territories": Since its adoption, the term "non-self-governing territories" has engendered a series of difficulties arising from the absence of a juridical definition. The Charter refers to the inhabitants of these territories as "peoples who have not yet attained a full measure of self-government." In the League Covenant reference was made to territories "inhabited by peoples not yet able to stand by themselves under the strenuous conditions of the modern world." The League formula, which was reproduced in the proposal presented by the British government to the San Francisco Conference, was not accepted.

In the first session of the General Assembly the question of the definition of the "non-self-governing territories" was again raised. The United States had suggested that the term include those territories which do not enjoy self-government to the same extent as that of the administering country's metropolitan area. Unfortunately, it was finally decided not to accept any definition and it was agreed that the meaning of the term would be examined in relation to the circumstances of each case. The resolution adopted merely enumerated the territories regarding which information had been transmitted or promised by the administering powers.[7]

---

[7] General Assembly Resolution 66(I), 14 Dec. 1946.

Factors to Determine Whether a Territory is or is not self-governing:
In recent years, the solution of this important problem has taken
a new turn. Some powers which have the responsibility of administering non-self-governing territories have sought to stop transmitting the information referred to in Article 73(e) on the conditions
of the population. Since the only legal way not to submit such
information is to demonstrate that a territory "has ceased to be
non-self-governing," in view of the fact that the territories can only
be removed from the scope of Chapter XI when they have attained
full autonomy, there have arisen in the General Assembly not only
the question of defining full autonomy, but also discussions on
specific cases to determine if a territory really has attained self-
government or if it may be withdrawn from the supervision of the
General Assembly, no matter how weak this may be, under a false
or incomplete autonomy.

The General Assembly has been examining this problem since
1948. In 1952 an *Ad Hoc* Committee on Factors was set up to
study the factors to be taken into account in deciding whether a
non-self-governing territory really has attained a full measure of
self-government.[8] Since the Committee was composed equally of
administering and non-administering countries (thus reflecting not
the structure of the Assembly, where there is always an anti-colonial
majority, but that of the Trusteeship Council), it is not to be wondered
at that the Committee did not reach an agreement on a precise
definition of self-government. Nevertheless, the resolution approved
by the Assembly in its following session[9] represented an effort to
define the factors indicative of the attainment of a full measure
of self-government. There are three means recognized by which a
territory can achieve self-government: independence, other "separate" systems of self-government (such as, presumably, the British
Commonwealth), and free association with another country as an

---

[8] General Assembly Resolution 567(VI), 18 Jan. 1952.
[9] General Assembly Resolution 648(VII), 10 Dec. 1952.

integral part of that country. The lists set forth numerous factors—constitutional, legal, political, ethnic, cultural, and geographical—to determine the legitimacy of the association in the last two cases. But since the resolution does not include any definitive criteria and declares that each case should be judged on its own merits, it turns out that in reality the "factors" are not that at all, but are just a classification of considerations or reasonings that are used as a guide so that in each specific case, and with each country following its own judgment, the Assembly may decide the question before it by a majority vote.

The eighth session of the Assembly adopted Resolution 742(VIII) which represents considerable progress in this matter.[10] This resolution made clear the "competence of the General Assembly to consider the principles that should guide the United Nations and the Member States in the implementation of obligations arising from Chapter XI of the Charter and to make recommendations in connection with them," a competence which had been systematically denied it by the colonial powers. In the second place, the resolution recognized that the primary method by which the non-self-governing peoples can attain a "full measure of self-government" is by achieving independence (this important aspect of the resolution was due to the Mexican amendment). Thirdly, the resolution established that

---

[10] This resolution was adopted under difficult circumstances. Brazil had presented a draft resolution which did practically nothing but repeat the list of factors adopted in 1952. Eleven anti-colonial countries (including Mexico) presented twenty-four amendments to the proposed draft, of which ten referred to the text of the Brazilian resolution and fourteen to the annexed list of factors (United Nations Docs. A/C.4/L.273 and L.274, 6 Oct. 1953). Each one of the twenty-four amendments was approved by the Fourth Committee of the Assembly, although by slight majorities. The colonial powers hoped to defeat them in the plenary meeting, alleging that as "important questions" they would have to be adopted there, under the Charter, by a two-thirds majority of votes. The Mexican delegation presented a motion in the plenary meeting to the effect that any matter relating to the non-self-governing territories only required a simple majority and not a two-thirds majority. In an agitated plenary meeting the Assembly decided this point in favor of the Mexican motion and all the draft provisions on non-self-governing territories were adopted by simple majority. General Assembly, Official Records (G.A.O.R.): 8th Sess., 459th Plenary Mtg., 27 Nov. 1953, pp. 305 ff.

any association, be it in a community or as an integral part of another country, should be accomplished on the basis of two essential principles: self-determination and absolute equality.

Two cases of the application of the criteria specified in the 1952 resolution came up in 1953: Surinam and the Netherlands Antilles, on the one hand, and, on the other, Puerto Rico. In presenting its case the Netherlands did not claim that the territories in question had achieved a full measure of self-government but stressed that the new constitutional arrangements of the two territories made it impossible to continue reporting. The General Assembly subsequently adopted a resolution[11] requesting the Netherlands (1) to resume the transmission of information until the Assembly decided that it be discontinued and (2) to transmit to the Secretary-General information on the constitutional changes that the territories were undergoing. The Netherlands representative informed the Assembly that his government would be unable to comply with the request or resume reporting. Regarding the request for information on constitutional changes, the Netherlands informed the Committee on Information that the final constitutional instrument negotiated by the Netherlands with the two territories had been referred to the Parliaments of the three countries, i. e., the Netherlands, Surinam, and the Netherlands Antilles. When final action had been taken by these legislatures the requested information would be transmitted. The data requested was supplied in 1955, when the constitutional changes affecting these territories had been completed.

The United States, on the other hand, presented Puerto Rico as a case of the achievement of a full measure of self-government, declaring its intention to cease transmitting information under Article 73(e) of the Charter. The resolution presented in favor of the point of view of the United States was adopted by a majority of 22 votes for, 18 against and 19 abstentions in the Fourth Committee, and 26 votes for, 16 against and 18 abstentions in the plenary

---

[11] General Assembly Resolution 747(VIII), 27 Nov. 1953.

meeting. Mexico voted against this resolution on the ground that the self-government granted to Puerto Rico, although very advanced, did not constitute a "full measure of self-government" and did not give the island an equal position with the United States of America.[12]

Other Questions Related to Chapter XI of the Charter: Paragraph b of Article 73 of the Charter imposes on the colonial powers the obligation "to develop self-government, to take due account of the political aspirations of the peoples, and to assist them in the progressive development of their free political institutions, according to the particular circumstances of each territory and its peoples and their varying stages of advancement."

This paragraph contains the core of the whole colonial problem. When its wording was discussed in the San Francisco Conference, China proposed the introduction of the concept of "development toward independence" as one of the objectives of colonial administration. On the other hand, in the working draft which had the support of the colonial powers, the following objective was specified: "to develop self-government in forms appropriate to the varying circumstances of each territory." In support of the Chinese resolution it was stated that independence was the aspiration of many dependent peoples and that this objective could hardly fail to be established in the Charter. The League Covenant itself recognized such an aspiration, and several territories which had previously been subject to a League mandate had become independent states. Furthermore, the right of self-determination of peoples was recognized in Article 1 of the United Nations Charter itself.

The opposition of the colonial powers defeated the recognition of this aspiration. It was said that the concept of independence was vague, that the acceptance of the Chinese proposal would result in the formation of a large number of small states, while the requirements of the times made it desirable to emphasize the interdepend-

---

[12] See General Assembly Resolution 748(VIII), 27 Nov. 1953, and G.A.O.R., 8th Sess., 459th Plenary Mtg., 27 Nov. 1953, pp. 319-20. For statement by the Mexican delegate, see *ibid.*, 4th Ctte., 349th Mtg., 2 Nov. 1953, pp. 222-23.

ence of peoples, and, finally, that the concept "self-government" did not exclude the possibility of independence.[13] A compromise was reached with the acceptance of the obligation "to take due account of the political aspirations of the peoples, and to assist them in the progressive development of their free political institutions, according to the particular circumstances . . ." (Article 73, paragraph b).

The obligation set forth in paragraph e of Article 73 is what constitutes, in the final analysis, the greatest practical advance over previous international norms. Article 73 (e) provides that the members of the United Nations which have or assume the responsibility of administering non-self-governing territories are obliged "to transmit regularly to the Secretary-General for information purposes, subject to such limitation as security and constitutional considerations may require, statistical and other information of a technical nature relating to economic, social, and educational conditions in the territories for which they are respectively responsible."

This is the only provision of Chapter XI in which there is created, in some form, a procedure for establishing a relative supervision by the international community over the way in which the colonial powers fulfil their obligations. The information referred to in this paragraph, although it had in most cases been available through the reports rendered by the colonial administrations to their respective national legislative bodies, acquires by virtue of Article 73 (e) a new importance and a new meaning due to international diffusion.

The limitations of this provision are, nonetheless, considerable. In the first place, the most important aspect of the information which should be rendered by the administering powers is not compulsory: the information concerning the political progress of the native populations. Nor are the frequency and form of the presentation of the information specified. Finally, there is no indication of the way in which the information should be utilized by the Organization.

---

[13] See *United Nations Conference on International Organization Documents, San Francisco, 1945* (New York: United Nations Information Organization, 1945), Vol. X, pp. 453-54. Hereinafter referred to as *UNCIO Documents*.

The General Assembly has to a certain extent made up for the gaps in this important provision. Several significant resolutions were adopted on 3 November 1947. In the first place, although the Assembly did not approve—by a slight margin—a resolution recommending to the members the transmission of information concerning the political progress of the dependent peoples, this organ at least recognized that the voluntary transmission of such information should be encouraged.[14] The Assembly sought to give the information certain uniformity and to have it presented at regular intervals. A standard form was drawn up with an optional section for information concerning political progress and a compulsory part on economic, social, educational, and cultural questions.[15] This has since been revised and broadened in scope and detail. The Assembly also created a Special Committee on Information Transmitted Under Article 73(e) of the Charter, successor to the *Ad Hoc* Committee set up in 1946 and composed of an equal number of administering and elected non-administering powers, to study and classify the information furnished by the administering powers, thus aiding the Assembly in its consideration of the data.[16] The Special Committee, renewed in 1948 for one year and since 1949 extended for three-year periods (the word "Special" was dropped from its title in 1952), has gained great importance and influence with time.

INTERNATIONAL TRUSTEESHIP SYSTEM

Unlike the non-self-governing territories, the territories under the trusteeship system receive in the Charter a treatment which might very well, in spite of its limitations, effect the attainment of self-determination by the peoples concerned. Since its establishment, the

[14] G.A.O.R., 2nd Sess., 108th Plenary Mtg., 3 Nov. 1947, pp. 719-20 and 732, and General Assembly Resolution 144(II) of that date.

[15] General Assembly Resolution 146(II), 3 Nov. 1947.

[16] General Assembly Resolution 142(II), 3 Nov. 1947.

trusteeship system has been serving as a point of contact between the colonial powers and the currents of world public opinion.

Chapter XII of the Charter clearly establishes the principles of responsibility, administration, and international supervision over some dependent territories. The basic objectives of the entire system are contained in Article 76 of the Charter.

Independence as an Objective of the Trusteeship System: Article 76 of the Charter establishes as an objective of the system (unlike Article 73 which refers to non-self-governing territories), the progressive development of the native populations "towards self-government or independence." In this manner, self-government and independence are presented as two alternative objectives. Independence means, in contrast to self-government, the rupture of all political bonds with another state, or at least, the right to do so. The factors which may influence the selection of one of the two alternative objectives are, according to the same paragraph, "the particular circumstances of each territory," "the freely expressed wishes of the peoples concerned," and, lastly, what may be provided "by the terms of each trusteeship agreement."

The principal limitations of this article, as of the entire chapter on the trusteeship system, are that it does not concretely specify, even in an approximate way, how long each administering power should take to lead the population under its tutelage to independence or self-government, and does not establish what should be the various stages of "progressive development" toward these objectives.

All the special trusteeship agreements between the United Nations and the administering authorities refer to the question of how the objectives of self-government or independence are to be attained. Nevertheless, practically all the agreements merely emphasize an increasing (usually progressively) share in the administrative and other services of the territory by the indigenous inhabitants. In some cases participation in the legislative and advisory bodies and in the government of the territory is mentioned. In others, there is only a general statement of the vague obligation to take appropriate measures with a view to the political advancement of the inhabitants, in accordance with Article 76(b). The agreement for the administration of the Pacific Islands by the United States gives as a goal "self-government or independence."

When the draft trusteeship agreements submitted by the colonial powers were discussed in the General Assembly there were strongly expressed opinions that the colonial powers should commit themselves more specifically to the attainment of the objectives of the trusteeship system, that is, self-government or independence. It was proposed that means be provided for the inhabitants of the territories to express their opinion or at least that a time limit be placed on the agreements so that conditions might be reconsidered after a given period. Generally speaking, none of these proposals was accepted by the administering authorities. Under Article 79 of the Charter, the terms of the trusteeship agreement for each territory, and its alteration, require the consent of the administering authority.

Territories to Which the Trusteeship System is Applied: Article 77 defines the territories to which the trusteeship system is applicable: (a) territories formerly under League mandate; (b) territories which may be detached from enemy states as a result of the Second World War; and (c) territories voluntarily placed under the system by states responsible for their administration.

The Assembly has recognized that it is not obligatory to place under the trusteeship system all of the territories mentioned in the above three paragraphs. When the Union of South Africa refused to transfer the territory of South West Africa, which it held under a League mandate, to the trusteeship system, the United Nations Assembly, after extended debate, accepted the viewpoint that the establishment of the trusteeship system over a territory formerly under a mandate is desirable and contributes to the attainment of the general purposes of the Charter, but that it is not compulsory. The International Court of Justice held in an advisory opinion that the Charter did not impose on the Union of South Africa the legal obligation to place South West Africa under the trusteeship system.

P

The Assembly did not even accept the statement that "it is the clear intention of Chapter XII" to transfer all territories under mandate to the trusteeship system.[17]

To date, no territory has been voluntarily included in the trusteeship system by the administering authorities in accordance with paragraph (c) of Article 77. Actually, Article 77 is in some ways a step backwards from the corresponding provisions of the League of Nations Covenant. According to the interpretation of Goodrich and Hambro, Article 22 of the Covenant, although it did not juridically oblige League members to include specific territories under mandate, at least established the moral obligation to do so in view of the clear references contained in paragraphs 4, 5, and 6. The United Nations Charter places greater emphasis on voluntary "agreement." The drawing up of the agreements seems to carry less moral obligation than in the League Covenant.[18]

Trusteeship Agreements: Article 79 of the Charter states that "the terms of trusteeship for each territory to be placed under the trusteeship system, including any alteration or amendment, shall be agreed upon by the states directly concerned, including the mandatory power . . ." The phrase "states directly concerned" has given rise to controversies since the Charter was drawn up. It is not exactly known which are these states in addition to the administering authority itself. From the standpoint of the fundamental objectives of the whole trusteeship system, the principal objection to this article, besides the vagueness of the phrases mentioned, is that the agreement of the administering authority is always required in order to establish the conditions under which these territories should be administered. If it is recognized that the administration of dependent peoples is an international function which essentially belongs to the

---

[17] Such a statement was included, at the initiative of India, in a draft resolution adopted by the Fourth Committee, but it was withdrawn in plenary meeting because it obviously would not receive the necessary two-thirds majority. See G.A.O.R., 2nd Sess., 105th Plenary Mtg., 1 Nov. 1947, pp. 648-49.

[18] Leland Goodrich and Edvard Hambro, *Charter of the United Nations* (2nd rev. ed., Boston: World Peace Foundation, 1949), pp. 435-36.

international community and that the colonial powers have only the character of *trustees*, and that they therefore only enjoy a "delegated" authority of the international community, this situation cannot be justified. In practice the veto of the colonial powers makes it really impossible to change the provisions of the trusteeship agreements. Even in this question there seems to have been a step backwards as compared to the League of Nations. Article 22, paragraph 8, of the Covenant states that "the degree of authority, control or administration to be exercised by the Mandatory shall, if not previously agreed upon by the Members of the League, be explicitly defined in each case by the Council." It is true that, in reality, the mandate agreements were drafted by the colonial powers and later submitted to the approval of the Council, and that the League Council acted by unanimity, but at least the principle was established that the final authority for deciding the conditions of the administration of these territories belonged to the international organization.

Administrative Unions: Another of the questions which has given rise to serious disputes in the Trusteeship Council as well as in the General Assembly has been that of administrative unions. In several trusteeship agreements, the colonial powers were authorized to include the trust territory in a customs, fiscal, or administrative union or federation united with the adjacent territories under its rule and to establish common administrative services. This practice has been severely criticized in the United Nations. It has been said that under the pretext of administrative convenience, these unions have been progressively converted into real political entities in which the interests of the populations of the trust territories are being bound to, if not subordinated to, the interests of the non-trust areas and especially to those of the metropolitan country. In spite of the assurances offered by the colonial authorities to the effect that the political autonomy of the trust territories will be maintained, it becomes difficult to distinguish this situation from a pure and simple annexation.

Other provisions of the special trusteeship agreements which have stirred up criticism are those that give the administering authorities the right to treat the trust territory, for administrative purposes, as an integral part of the metropolitan territory. It has been said that this authorization fundamentally amounts to an annexation and that it is incompatible with the progressive development of the indigenous populations toward self-government or independence.

THE TRUSTEESHIP COUNCIL

The membership of the Trusteeship Council, in accordance with Article 86 of the Charter, consists of: (a) those states which administer trust territories; (b) those permanent members of the Security Council which do not administer trust territories; and (c) such other states as may be necessary to ensure that the total number of members of the Trusteeship Council be equally divided between administering and non-administering authorities. This means that the membership of the Council is variable according to the number of powers that administer trust territories.

After the presentation and approval of eight trusteeship agreements in the second part of the first session of the General Assembly, the Trusteeship Council was set up and included Mexico and Iraq as elected members of the Council. In July of 1947, when the United States became an administering authority by signing the trusteeship agreement for the Pacific Islands, which had been under Japanese mandate, the balance established between administering and non-administering states was altered and two new members, Costa Rica and the Philippines, were elected. The balance was altered again in 1955, when Italy became a member of the United Nations and, as administering authority for Somaliland, a member of the Trusteeship Council. Burma was elected as the new non-administering member. Prior to 1955, Italy had participated in the work of the Council without vote.

The membership of the Trusteeship Council, which was the result of a compromise, has given rise to many difficulties in practice. By the very nature of the matters dealt with in this organ of the United Nations, the constructive proposals designed to accelerate the political evolution of the native populations originate, as is natural, with the non-administering members. At the same time, it is equally understandable that some of the colonial countries, which were against the establishment of the trusteeship system over their dependencies and which only accepted it due to the pressure of world public opinion, must be opposed to the majority of the measures proposed by the non-administering members. As a result of the membership of the Trusteeship Council, this organ has often been reduced to inaction.

The principal functions and powers of the Trusteeship Council under Article 87 of the Charter are the following: (a) to consider reports submitted by the administering authority; (b) to accept petitions and examine them in consultation with the administering authority; and (c) to provide for periodic visits to the trust territories.

The procedure for examining reports submitted by the administering authority is: first, the representative of the administering authority introduces the annual report with an initial statement; following this, the representative is questioned by the Council members and analyses and criticisms are made which are often constructive and penetrating; and, finally, recommendations are drawn up and adopted which are included in the report of the Trusteeship Council to the General Assembly.

The Council's function of accepting and studying petitions of the inhabitants of the trust territories has brought about the formation of a Standing Committee on Petitions which initially screens and examines them, and then submits its recommendations to the Council. The petitions system is one of the most effective aspects of the entire trusteeship system. The inhabitants of the trust territories regard it as a true recourse for appeal against unjust decisions of the administering authority. Unfortunately, the Committee on Petitions suffers from the same partial inaction as the Council due to the operation of political forces. Nonetheless, by means of the petitions, as well as by personal contact with the members of the visiting missions, the indigenous inhabitants acquire a direct knowledge of the functioning of the trusteeship system as well as of the international responsibility of the administering authority which cannot fail ultimately to have a favorable influence on their political advancement.

An inevitable limitation on the system of international supervision is the frequent control which the administering authority exercises over the political parties of the trust territories. As the delegate from India, Mr. Krishna Menon, so well put it,

> In every oppressed country the population has two languages: one for each other and another for the conqueror. There will always be political parties who will offer evidence meeting with the approval of the administering authority. There will always be political parties who will come forward when a visiting mission arrives in the territory.[19]

These words undoubtedly reflect a real and regrettable situation. But there has not been a lack of persons or parties willing to tell of the just grievances of the aboriginal populations. Those who remember the moving pleas of the Rev. Michael Scott in the United Nations, and the impact which they had on public opinion, could hardly deny the usefulness of the international system of petitions.

CONCLUSIONS

The problem of suggestions which might properly be made concerning the colonial question may be examined from two different angles. On the one hand, certain changes might be proposed which, in view of the essential purposes of the United Nations and of certain moral considerations, would result in an ideal solution. On the

---

[19] Unofficial transcript of a speech summarized in T.C.O.R., 13th Sess., 494th Mtg., 11 Feb. 1954, p. 93.

other hand, the discussion might be confined to the real possibilities for reforming the Charter, taking into consideration the existing political obstacles in the way of approaching this ideal.

If the problem is examined from a moral standpoint and from the general aims of the United Nations, the entire colonial question should be ruled by the principle of self-determination of peoples. There is no way to justify morally a country's exploitation of another's territory and resources for its own benefit, nor its domination of other populations, without the latter's consent. The international community should provide for means by which all peoples can really be or become free and independent. When an international organization representative of the community of nations did not exist, the colonial action of the European countries might have been justified to the extent that they performed the function of tutor and brought civilization to the aboriginal populations. From the moment of the creation of international organizations which aspire to represent and protect the interests of all humanity, there was no longer any *raison d'être* for the unilateral and uncontrolled administration of the colonial powers over populations which have not attained a full measure of self-government. The exercise of the civilizing mission and the care of backward native populations should be the responsibility of the international community through the United Nations Organization.

The general conception and, in part, the machinery of the trusteeship system reflect the above considerations. But this is not true of the provisions of Chapter XI of the Charter. This Chapter permits the unilateral action of the colonial powers. Even though it provides "that the interests of the inhabitants of these territories are paramount" and that the colonial countries accept as a "sacred trust" the administration of the territories, the absence of adequate procedures and measures of international supervision and responsibility actually permits colonial action to be carried on solely for the benefit of the metropolis. In the final analysis, Chapter XI only legitimizes previous situations of privilege in favor of certain powers which exploit the native populations for their own profit. If this were not the case, it would be inexplicable that the Charter did not establish an international supervision identical to that which exists over the trust territories. Strictly speaking, there should only be one centralized system of responsibility and supervision for the administration of all the territories and peoples that are not at present prepared for self-government.

From a realistic point of view, and taking present factors into account, it would be pointless to propose reforms which cannot be carried out now due to the magnitude of the vested interests and of the power of the colonial countries. The Charter unquestionably reflects political realities which must be used as a starting point. Unfortunately, it will still be necessary for some time to maintain the division between the non-self-governing territories subject to the unilateral administration of the colonial powers and the administration of trust territories subject to an international supervision.

As has already been pointed out, many small and medium-sized countries have an interest in easing the situation of the dependent populations and in accelerating their evolution toward independence. In the face of the necessity of compromising between what would be the ideal for this purpose—that is, a single system of strict international supervision over the dependent populations—and the existence of political realities which cannot be ignored, the small countries should propose the most advanced reforms consistent with the maintenance of the dual system of the Charter. Aside from the question whether the proposed reforms might be adopted in view of Article 109 of the Charter, the voice of the small countries might represent the moral conscience of humanity in the entire colonial question, and might influence world public opinion to force, as far as possible, voluntary acceptance by the colonial powers.

In this respect, it has been maintained that the conditions of advancement of the populations without self-government basically depend on the spirit in which the provisions of the Charter are interpreted and on the will of the colonial powers; that the system established by the Charter is an adequate basis for the solution of colonial problems and that reforms of this system would be of less importance than the fulfilment in good faith of the existing obligations. This idea is only partly true. The good will of the colonial powers is essential in this matter but undoubtedly there exists a wide margin for constitutional reforms which would surely have the effect of a positive advancement in the condition of the dependent populations.

The reforms which in the author's judgment should be proposed or supported by Mexico and which are in the interests of Mexico and of the majority of the small states, would be the following:

1. The General Assembly should have the legal power to decide definitively when a non-self-governing territory should be placed under the trusteeship system, without the consent of the power responsible for administering it. This solution, which clearly stems from the objective of fulfilling the principle of self-determination of peoples, was proposed by Mexico and other countries in San Francisco.[20] During the second session of the General Assembly India presented a similar proposal, although of smaller scope, by which the members were "invited" to place those territories which were not prepared for self-government under the trusteeship system. This proposal, naturally, was limited by the framework of the provisions of the Charter then in force, by which the voluntary acceptance of the administering authority was provided for. For the purposes of Charter review, it would be desirable to propose the final and definitive decision of the matter by the Assembly.

2. Likewise, it would be desirable for the Assembly to determine legally when a territory under trusteeship is ready for full independ-

---

[20] In an alternate constitution for the international organization which Mexico submitted, there was a provision for a Council similar to the present Economic and Social Council, which was to have among its functions the *"protection of countries under mandate."* Mexico proposed that this Council "shall decide, as it may deem appropriate, which territories (colonies) shall be removed from the jurisdiction of a State in order to be entrusted to an international mandate." See *UNCIO Documents,* Vol. III, p. 172.

ence. A proposal to this effect was presented by Mexico[21] as well as by Egypt and other countries in the San Francisco Conference.

3. In connection with the two proposals above, it would be desirable to establish, even though in an approximate and provisional way, a time limit for the change of a territory without self-government to the status of a trust territory, and also for the transformation of a trust territory into an independent state. The fixing of time limits would psychologically prepare the administering authority as well as the indigenous population for assuming new responsibilities. This suggestion has been made at various times in the General Assembly and the Trusteeship Council.

4. The greatest possible similarity should be sought between the non-self-governing territories and the trust territories. As a start, Article 73(e) should be modified so as to oblige the administering authorities to present regular reports on the political advancement of the indigenous population.

5. It appears desirable to change the present membership of the Trusteeship Council, which in practice has not had the best results. The present equality between administrators and non-administrators has resulted in the frequent rejection of proposals which are reintroduced and later approved in the Assembly. The Council should reflect more truly the membership of the General Assembly, to which it is actually subordinate (although the Charter grants it the character of a principal organ of the United Nations).

6. As to the special agreements between the United Nations and the administering authorities, it would be desirable to have their terms approved definitively by the General Assembly, representing the community of nations, without requiring the consent of the administering authority. By changing Article 79 of the Charter in this way, the problem of the "states directly concerned" would

---

[21] "As soon as a country under mandate arrives, in the opinion of the Council, at the degree of progress necessary to govern its own destinies, the Council shall take the necessary steps to the end that this territory may become a sovereign State." See *ibid.*, pp. 172-73.

automatically disappear. If the conditions of trusteeship are established in favor of the indigenous population and not of a colonial power, the necessary compliance of the latter is not justified. In the final analysis, the colonial power has only the role of "administrator," that is, of "mandatory." In case an administering authority feels the terms of the agreement are too onerous, it always has the choice of declining the "sacred trust" of administering the territory for the benefit of its inhabitants and letting the Organization itself or some other country undertake to do so.

7. A model trusteeship agreement should be drawn up, taking the best of each of the different existing agreements, for the purpose of establishing certain minimum basic conditions for the administration. This model agreement would only contain such conditions as might be applied equally to all the territories. The Assembly would be at liberty later to include special modifications in the different agreements according to the particular circumstances of each case. For example, there is no reason why the excellent provisions of the Tanganyika agreement concerning education could not be equally applied to all the trust territories. It would be particularly important that the model agreement should establish the essential obligation of protecting the natives' ownership of arable lands, leaving a margin wide enough to permit special regulation of the matter in each territory.

8. It also seems of great importance that a system of progressive taxation be accepted which would permit an increase in the budgets of the trust territories without having the greater part covered by the indigenous inhabitants, whose incomes barely permit them a precarious existence. The budgets should be covered to a much greater extent by contributions from the metropolitan state, this permitting the economic, social, and educational advancement spoken of in the Charter and of which there has been little in the territories in question during these years. The metropolitan governments insist that the colonial reforms be paid for from the income of the colony itself. Any amount from the metropolitan budget for

the colony's benefit is considered a real burden. Nevertheless, the large sums that are taken from the colonies as investment returns, and as salaries and pensions for administrators, indirectly enter into the budget of the metropolitan powers through the tax payments. The native realizes that a substantial part of the national income of his country is withdrawn by the colonial power and he feels that those incomes should be reinvested for the benefit of the indigenous population.

9. Without excluding the possibility that the administering authority be, as heretofore, a specific country, the small countries should insist that, when it seems desirable, the Organization itself should act as administering authority under Article 81 of the Charter.[22]

10. The administering power should be prohibited, either in the Charter or in the model agreement, from establishing military, air, or naval bases, from quartering its national troops, or from constructing fortifications in the trust territories. In almost all the agreements concluded to date, the administering powers have reserved that right. This clearly represents a step backwards from the same situation in the League. The League Covenant expressly prohibited, at least for mandates B and C, the establishment of fortifications or bases and the military training of the natives for purposes other than the defense of their own territory or the formation of a police force. The only exception to this prohibition should be the strategic zones which include part or all of a trust territory, as authorized by Article 82 of the Charter. But, correlatively, the administering powers should no longer have the right unilaterally to consider the trust territories as strategic zones. This function should belong to the Organization. In general, outside the above case of the strategic zones, a kind of permanent neutrality status might be thought of for all the trust territories.

----

[22] When the fate of the Italian colonies was discussed at the September 1945 meeting of the Council of Foreign Ministers (of the four principal powers which were victors in the last war), the United States proposed that the Organization be the collective administering authority for those colonies. The USSR and India later made separate proposals along this line.

11. In order to maintain the truly international character and the special status established in the Charter for the trust territories, it would be necessary to prohibit positively any administrative union of these territories with adjacent colonies, in a way that might impair the political autonomy of the territories. Likewise, it would be desirable to prohibit the administering powers from considering the trust territory as an integral part of the metropolitan territory for administrative purposes.

chapter nine

Conclusions

In the course of this study, it has been stated time and again that the Charter of the United Nations represents the apex of the political balance established between the opposing interests and aspirations of the different groups of states which make up the international society of the post-World War II period. The Charter represented in 1945—and probably still fundamentally continues to represent—the broadest agreement possible among the different governments toward regulating the international relations of states. From this point of view and leaving aside numerous technical defects of the Charter which do not affect its substance and which were the result of the haste with which it was drafted, the Charter was the only document which could have been drawn up in the conditions prevailing in 1945, and, in that sense, it was the best possible Charter.

We believe that this consideration may serve as a basis for any judgment on the desirability of reviewing the Charter of the United

Nations. Now, as then, the same criterion continues to be valid. If the preservation of a universal organization is desired, the only feasible Charter is that which is agreed upon by all the important groups of states of contemporary international society. The necessity of having any change in the Charter approved by a minimum of two-thirds of the members, including the permanent members of the Security Council (Article 109), is not just a "juridical" obstacle which "derives" from the Charter of the United Nations, but it also is the result of a situation existing prior to and going deeper than the Charter, which the latter only recognized and established. Any fundamental change in the Charter, if not voluntarily agreed upon by the various groups of countries, may alter or even destroy the balance which this document seeks to maintain among the real factors of power existing at the present time, and, in consequence, may bring about the breakdown of the Organization which we know, or at least a notable reduction in the sphere of competence of the United Nations. Thus, the elimination of the veto or a fundamental alteration of the present colonial system—changes requested by many small countries—if imposed without the consent of the principal interested powers, might result in either the withdrawal of several important states from the Organization, or at least, indirectly, in a removal from the Organization of the functions of collective security still held by the United Nations and of the function of guardianship of the populations of dependent or trust territories.

The fundamental question is whether an early or a later date would offer better prospects for the principal interested powers to accept solutions more consistent with the wishes of a majority of the small countries, in such problems as the colonial system and the elimination of the veto. It might be stated that it seems unlikely that an agreement will be reached in the near future on amending the Charter in the matter of such important structural changes as those mentioned above.

Nevertheless, this does not mean that the Charter does not need reviewing in certain matters which might be solved in a way acceptable to all. When the problem of collective security was studied, it was emphasized that the elimination of the veto in the pacific solution of disputes might, under certain conditions, gain the assent of all the great powers. Likewise, it is possible that the colonial powers might be willing to make certain concessions which would permit the United Nations to give the dependent populations better and more effective protection. The problem of the admission of new members, though no longer as urgent as it was, might also be more easily dealt with in a conference for a general review of some of the basic assumptions of the Organization, such as universality. In other important questions, it also seems desirable and not entirely impossible to review the Charter. Thus, this study has suggested that the Charter should have an additional chapter on the rights and duties of states. Probably this idea, shared by several small countries, would not, in principle, encounter strong opposition. The many technical defects of the Charter which might be corrected without altering its substance are also mentioned—they are termed "minor amendments." Reference is also made to the desirability of bringing the Charter up to date, either by eliminating articles that are only of historical interest (such as Article 107 on enemy states and Articles 110 and 111 on the ratification and signature of the Charter) or by reviewing provisions that are a dead letter, such as the one which makes the contribution of the states to the maintenance of peace and security a criterion for election to the Security Council (Article 23).

The fact that certain reforms are desirable in matters which do not essentially affect the political balance reflected by the Charter is not in itself sufficient reason to advocate the holding of a general conference for the purpose of reviewing the Charter of the United Nations. Even in matters which theoretically might be agreed upon, it is not certain that this would happen, due to the probable political climate of the conference. At present, there is neither the urgency nor the absolute necessity for drawing up the Charter that there was in 1945 and which had a decisive influence on the acceptance of compromise solutions. It is not unlikely that in a future conference, states may take more rigid positions and that the discussions may serve more to emphasize differences than points of agreement.

On the other hand, certain rules arising from practical necessities have been created outside the Charter, and these serve to complement, replace, or interpret it. Many of these rules are challenged by the different groups of states, and in more than one case, their legality is debatable. But these rules are actually applied and they represent the will of the majority of the states. On the one hand, it is probable that any attempt to codify them would endanger their existence; on the other hand, it is just as uncertain that, for at least some of them, their codification, or in other words, their official incorporation into the "Law of the Charter," would be desirable.

In the matter of collective security a series of institutions have been created which are parallel to the Charter or simply outside it, and they would be difficult to codify. Even the common practice of considering that the vote of "abstention" by a permanent member of the Security Council does not prevent the adoption of substantive resolutions—a practice which is probably not authorized by the Charter but which has been useful and which is agreed upon by all the permanent members of the Council—might give rise to serious difficulties if a codification were to be undertaken. The statement by the four sponsoring governments in the San Francisco Conference on the interpretation of the Yalta veto system, although of doubtful juridical value, has certainly been useful as a guide for the Security Council. The attempt to codify this question would probably have no positive results.

The "Uniting for Peace" resolution represents the most serious effort so far to change the division of functions established by the Charter among the organs of the United Nations. The study of the problem of collective security sought to make clear the dangers involved in this resolution and the disadvantages of its application in the Korean War. Nevertheless, although its legality was challenged by the Soviet group, as long as it did not bring about a split in the

q

Organization and its application was tolerated, the "Uniting for Peace" resolution is a real factor in collective security as an expression of the desire of the majority of the members, and it may even help prevent future aggressions. But even assuming that the incorporation of its principles could be forced into the Charter, and that this would not bring about a split in the United Nations, still it cannot be concluded that this would be beneficial. Its codification would legalize and perpetuate a situation which at best can only be accepted as provisional and it would tend to aggravate the dangers and disadvantages pointed out in this connection. In the practice of collective security, the possibility of comparing the above resolution with the text of the Charter in each case may help maintain its application within careful limits and to moderate certain developments and corollaries to which it might lend itself. It is obvious that the existing ambiguous situation does not furnish a desirable juridical certainty, but it is not clear that juridical certainty is in this connection the supreme aim.

With regard to other matters which might seem indicated for review in the Charter and which might be agreed upon, it is also not positively known whether their consideration by a future general conference would be useful. Even as regards the purely technical amendments, it is likely that serious difficulties might arise from a lack of confidence which would not favor codification. Of course, in a document like the Charter, it is often not easy to determine where form ends and substance begins. The provisions which have not been effectively applied are also frequently mentioned as suitable for review. In the above-mentioned example (contribution to the maintenance of peace and security as a criterion for the election of non-permanent members to the Security Council), there is no convincing reason why a good provision should be eliminated because it has been forgotten. Although it has practically never been taken into account, that does not mean that it should cease to figure in the Charter as a *desideratum* or perhaps as a reproach to obviously unwise elections. A similar statement might be made about the provisions contained in Article 28(2) of the Charter which refer to periodic meetings of the Security Council in which the members may be represented by high ranking officials (Ministers of Foreign Affairs or other members of the governments).

As to matters which might be subjected to review, it is extremely difficult to measure *a priori* the possibilities of agreement. It might only be affirmed that it would be dangerous to hold a general conference for review of the Charter without previously being assured of some success. A failure would disillusion the peoples of the world; it would tend to make the situation of certain institutions even more confused and it would further alienate the different countries. But, on the other hand, if there were any likelihood of reconciling the various points of view of the states, at least on certain matters, the opportunity of reviewing the Charter should not be passed over.

The only way to predict the chances of success would be to carry out serious and extensive exploratory studies. An attempt could be made to ascertain before the conference under what conditions and to what extent the different groups of states would be willing to reconcile their various points of view. To that end, adequate machinery should be set up by the General Assembly.

In this study the proposals made for Charter reforms or for changes in the practice of the organs of the United Nations are based on different premises. The examination of each matter in itself suggested such changes as seemed most compatible with the interests of Mexico, without taking into account the probabilities or the desirability of holding a meeting in which they might be maintained. In other words, attention was given to the matters which to our mind should be defended by Mexico should it have suitable occasion to do so. Naturally, an attempt was made to approach this survey realistically, although at the same time trying in each case to weigh the proposed solutions against other factors, including, in some cases, the chances of their being acceptable to most of the governments. Nonetheless, the fact that particular reforms have been suggested, even assuming that they are considered relatively feasible, does not necessarily mean that it is thought desirable to propose them in certain circumstances, at a specific time and place.

The conclusions regarding each matter dealt with have been summed up at the end of the chapters. Sometimes, the conclusion has been fundamentally to suggest a specific course of action or position for the small countries in general or for Mexico in particular. Regarding other questions, reform of the Charter or changes in the practice of the organs of the United Nations have been proposed, although almost always limited to the general character and meaning of the proposed modifications, without specifying them in precise formulas. In view of the nature of the conclusions and of the disadvantages of presenting them apart from their backgrounds, it was not felt suitable to sum them up in a special chapter.

Index

United States (*Continued*)
  aid to Greece, 125
  and colonial questions, 62, 201, 202, 205, 208, 224n
  and communism, 201, 202
  and domestic jurisdiction, 42, 53, 55
  and election of Secretary-General, 123
  and General Assembly powers and voting, 110, 143
  and Indo-China, 128n
  and Korean conflict, 115, 131n, 135, 136n, 140
  and NATO, 152, 187-8
  and Pan Americanism, 168-71, 175-84 *passim*, 187-95 *passim*.
  and regional arrangements, 166n
  relations with Mexico, 5, 195
  relations with Soviet Union, 104
    see also Coexistence; "Cold war."
  and Tunisia and Morocco, 59, 60
  and trusteeship, 213, 216
  and veto, 121
"Uniting for Peace," resolution, 5, 113, 128-39, 150, 229-30
Universality of membership, 76-95, 228
  see also Admission of new members to UN.
Uruguay
  and admission of new members, 81, 82
  and democracy and human rights, 53-4, 185, 187
  and Guatemalan complaint, 126n
  and sovereignty, 42, 45
Uti possidetis principle, 190

V

Venezuela, 53n
Veto, 62, 70
  and admission of new members, 92, 121-2
  and Charter review, 227-8, 229
  and collective security, 101, 102
  double veto, 123
  and League of Nations, 99
  Mexico's attitude, 45, 120-8
  and pacific settlement of disputes, 118, 141, 228
  and procedural questions, 123, 126
  and self-defense, 151, 158
  and Soviet Union, 56, 57, 89, 90, 117, 118-9, 121-7 *passim*, 140
Vietnam, 89

W

War, threat of, or resort to, 25, 29-30
Washington Conference (1889-90), 170
Washington Conference (1951), 194
Whitaker, Arthur P., 184
Wilson, Woodrow, 40, 98
Withdrawal from membership in UN, 13, 81, 83
World War II, 15, 41, 57, 67, 82, 143n, 192, 197
World government, 13-4, 16

Y

Yalta Conference, 229
Yemen, 89
Yepes, J. M., 168, 173

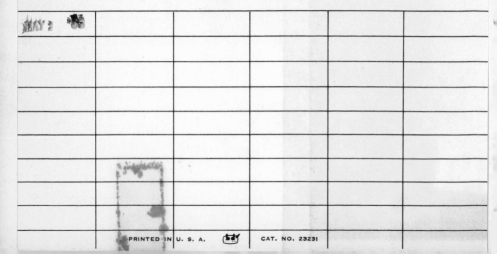

Date Due

MAY 7					

PRINTED IN U. S. A.   CAT. NO. 23231